Ethics
in End-of-Life Decisions in
Social Work Practice

Also Available from Lyceum Books, Inc.

Advisory Editor: Thomas M. Meenaghan, *New York University*

EVIDENCE-BASED PRACTICES FOR SOCIAL WORKERS: AN INTERDISCIPLINARY APPROACH, by Thomas O'Hare

MENTAL HEALTH IN LITERATURE, edited by Glenn Rohrer

USING EVIDENCE IN SOCIAL WORK PRACTICE: BEHAVIORAL PERSPECTIVES, by Harold E. Briggs and Tina L. Rzepnicki

MODERN SOCIAL WORK THEORY: A CRITICAL INTRODUCTION, 3E, by Malcolm Payne, foreword by Stephen C. Anderson

GENERALIST PRACTICE IN LARGER SETTINGS: KNOWLEDGE AND SKILL CONCEPTS, by Thomas M. Meenaghan, W. Eugene Gibbons, and John G. McNutt

CLINICAL ASSESSMENT FOR SOCIAL WORKERS: QUALITATIVE AND QUANTITATIVE METHODS, 2E, edited by Catheleen Jordan and Cynthia Franklin

A PRACTICAL GUIDE TO SOCIAL SERVICE EVALUATION, by Carl F. Brun

ENDINGS IN CLINICAL PRACTICE: EFFECTIVE CLOSURE IN DIVERSE SETTINGS, by Joseph Walsh

BEST PRACTICES IN MENTAL HEALTH: AN INTERNATIONAL JOURNAL, edited by Catherine Dulmus and Karen Sowers

Ethics

in End-of-Life Decisions in
Social Work Practice

Ellen L. Csikai
University of Alabama

Elizabeth Chaitin
University of Pittsburgh Medical Center
Shadyside Hospital

LYCEUM
BOOKS, INC.
CHICAGO, ILLINOIS

© Lyceum Books, Inc., 2006

Published by

Lyceum Books, Inc.
5758 S. Blackstone Ave.
Chicago, Illinois 60637
773+643-1903 (Fax)
773+643-1902 (Phone)
lyceum@lyceumbooks.com
http://www.lyceumbooks.com

10 9 8 7 6 5 4 3 2 1

ISBN 0-925065-52-8

Library of Congress Cataloging-in-Publication Data

Csikai, Ellen L.
    Ethics in end-of-life decisions in social work practice / Ellen L. Csikai,
Elizabeth Chaitin.
        p. cm.
    Includes bibliographical references.
    ISBN 0-925065-52-8
    1. Euthanasia—Moral and ethical aspects. 2. Palliative treatment—
Decision making—Moral and ethical aspects. 3. Terminal care—
Decision making—Moral and ethical aspects. 4. Assisted suicide—
Moral and ethical aspects. 5. Right to die—Moral and ethical aspects.
6. Death—Social aspects. 7. Medical ethics. 8. Social work. I. Chaitin,
Elizabeth. II. Title.
R726.C83   2005
179.7—dc22
                                                            2005009032

CONTENTS

ABOUT THE AUTHORS

Ellen L. Csikai, MSW, MPH, PhD, is an associate professor in the School of Social Work at The University of Alabama. Her medical social work practice experience in a trauma intensive care unit and in hospice services in Pittsburgh sparked her interest in end-of-life care and bioethics. She has pursued issues involving social work practice in hospital and hospice ethics committees, euthanasia and assisted suicide, and other ethical issues in end-of-life care in her research. She focuses on these areas in both her teaching and research. In 2001, Dr. Csikai was a recipient of a Social Work Leadership Development Award from the Open Society Institute, Project on Death in America. Teamed with Mary Raymer, ACSW, she has developed The Social Work End-of-Life Educational Project, an end-of-life care continuing education curriculum for social workers. The future plan for the project is to further develop and institutionalize the curriculum/project so that all social workers may access it. To date, the project has gained the support of many healthcare social work professional organizations and the National Association of Social Workers and the National Hospice and Palliative Care Organization.

Elizabeth Chaitin, MA, MSW, DHCE, serves as the director of the Medical Ethics and Palliative Care Services Department of UPMC—Shadyside Hospital. She is an assistant professor of medicine through the Department of General Internal Medicine within the Section of Palliative Care and Medical Ethics at the University of Pittsburgh, and also serves on the faculty of the Consortium Ethics Program of the University of Pittsburgh. Dr. Chaitin is a clinical instructor in medical ethics and palliative care for the Family Practice and Internal Medicine Residency Services of UPMC—Shadyside Hospital and is a clinical instructor for students in the MA in Ethics Program of the University of Pittsburgh. She has been the co-chairperson of the Biomedical Ethics Committee for UPMC—Shadyside Hospital for the past nine years and serves as an ethics consultant for the Ethics Consultation Service at the Center for Bioethics and Health Law of the University of Pittsburgh. In 2003, Dr. Chaitin was a recipient of a Social Work Leadership Development Award from the Open Society Institute, Project on Death in America. She used this grant to train other hospitals in the development of Palliative Care Services Departments. She is a co-director of the University of Pittsburgh's Institute for the Enhancement of Palliative Care.

PREFACE

Perhaps the most significant opportunity for social workers to expand their influence in healthcare settings is in the emerging and fast-changing fields of bioethics and end-of-life care. To take advantage, social workers will need firm grounding in the theory, issues, and language of these fields, as the training of most healthcare professionals with whom social workers will interact usually includes bioethics content.

In recognition of the growing numbers of social workers working in this new arena and the need for guidance, the National Association of Social Workers (NASW) in 2005 set forth *NASW Standards for Social Work Practice in Palliative and End of Life Care* (Appendix B). A steering committee composed of social workers with expertise in these areas from a range of practice arenas across the lifespan participated in the creation of the document. The organization's membership then had an opportunity for open comment after which the document was revised into the current form.

Standard one in this new set of practice standards, "Ethics and Values," suggests that traditional social work values, ethics, and standards should guide practice in palliative and end-of-life care, along with those of contemporary bioethics. A minimal knowledge of basic ethical principles is recommended, as well as awareness of those issues with potential to demand complex bioethical and legal considerations, such as the right to refuse treatment, surrogate decision making, withdrawal of life-sustaining treatments, including nutrition and hydration, and assisted suicide.

The other practice standards address the following: knowledge; assessment; intervention/treatment planning; attitudes/self-awareness; empowerment and advocacy; documentation; interdisciplinary teamwork; cultural competence; continuing education; and supervision, leadership, and training. Other NASW resources include policy statements on "Health Care" and "Client Self-Determination in End-of-Life Decisions." The latter was slated for revision in August 2005 by the NASW Delegate Assembly into a policy that will have a more global focus on end-of-life care, but will still include guidance on understanding end-of-life options and the appropriate social work role in decision making. *Ethics and End-of-Life Decisions in Social Work Practice* goes over foundation bioethics material recommended by NASW (although not directly linked to NASW) that we have found invaluable to know in our experiences working in our own social work practice in healthcare settings.

Our profession's long-standing values have been assets in examining the profound effects of new technologies on quality of life, but new moral dilemmas have come to the fore as we endeavor to assist patients and families in end-of-life choices. These choices speak to the very meaning of life, its beginning, the quality of its continuation, and its end (Howell & Sale, 1995, p. 1). An understanding of the theory and practice of bioethics in end-of-life care combined with the communication skills integral to social work training and practice will lead to more effective social work practice in health settings and help to enhance the quality of patients' and families' lives.

Bioethics has been defined as the application of moral reasoning to issues that arise in applying medical treatments, new technologies, and new knowledge of life sciences (Howell & Sale, 1995, p.1). It is a multidisciplinary field where health care, academia, and the law come together. In examining bioethical concerns, moral values and principles are applied to potential courses of action. Areas of interest in bioethics span the life course, however, the focus here is on end-of-life issues for adults. These individuals may be facing a variety of medical conditions, either as a result of trauma or chronic illness, but each may require decisions about care at the end stages of the condition.

As a basis to understanding bioethics, chapter 1 introduces foundation philosophies that were important in the formation of the field. The core principles of bioethics are autonomy, nonmaleficence, beneficence, and justice. Decision making in ethically complex situations in health care is based on these principles, which closely parallel values highly regarded in the social work profession, such as self-determination and the promotion of social justice. Along with the biomedical principles, ethical theory offers a foundation for how to think about decision making in health care.

Other factors that affect the decision-making process are presented in following chapters. Enumeration of the philosophy that underlies bioethics as presented in chapter 1 is intended as a beginning point for the reader. Further reading is suggested for a more comprehensive understanding, but the content of this first chapter provides a basic understanding of bioethics that may begin to "level the field" when discussing end-of-life decisions with other members of the healthcare team.

Due to increased media attention to end-of-life issues, several issues have become prominent, not the least of which is, When does death occur? Chapter 2 delineates the complexity of issues that social workers will encounter in healthcare settings. The definition of death and when exactly it occurs is critical to assess as various end-of-life care treatments and options are considered. Life-sustaining treatment brings up several tough choices that require elaboration, such as when to utilize CPR, mechanical ventilation, dialysis, or artificial nutrition and hydration. Decisions to forgo life support are influenced by our concepts of medical futility, quality of life, and cultural, religious and spiritual beliefs.

Other well-known controversial issues include euthanasia and physician-assisted suicide. Social workers must understand the conflicting viewpoints behind the issues, arguments for and against, and be prepared to face questions about these practices from patients and families. These issues may require social workers to confront and clarify their own personal values so that they may keep them in proper perspective in the practice setting.

Advance care planning is the focus of chapter 3. An overview of federal and state policy on advance directives is presented, including the Patient Self-Determination Act (1990) and its implementation, definitions of advance directives and suggestions for effective documents, and problems with advance directives. Beyond merely filling out a document called an advance directive, ongoing discussions about preferences for care at different stages of an illness, including the end of life, will need to be held among the patient, family, surrogates, and care providers. Social work intervention in advance care planning can ease the burden when end-of-life care decisions become necessary.

Chapter 3 also addresses other factors that can create ethical dilemmas regarding the appropriate course of action. Poor family relationships and disagreements among family members are perhaps the most challenging. Discussion of a range of possible scenarios provides insight into the role of social workers as they attempt to forge a solution that respects the viewpoint of all concerned and also honors the primary right to self-determination of the patient/loved one. Cultural, religious, and spiritual beliefs will factor into these care decisions. Strongly held beliefs and conflicting values of patients, family members, and surrogates can seriously hinder the decision-making process.

Hospice and palliative care are the topics of chapter 4. While hospice uses a palliative care model, not all palliative care is hospice. The decision to choose hospice care at the end of life is not an easy one, for this means that they must "give up" the curative/aggressive phase of medical treatment in favor of palliative care that promotes comfort to the dying in all areas of their life: biological, social, psychological, and spiritual. Particular attention is paid to relief of suffering. Palliative care can and should be mentioned as a choice early in the disease process as well as at the end stage. Social workers are integral to the interdisciplinary teams that are the norm in hospice and palliative care, so social workers must understand the pros and cons of aggressive treatment versus palliative care, to be able to assist families deciding what course of treatment is best for them.

Chapter 5 addresses the process of decision making that social workers encounter in health settings, beginning with informed consent. This concept is familiar to social workers in all fields of practice, but takes on greater importance in end-of-life care. Competence and the capacity of patients to make sound decisions must be determined beforehand so that full informed consent can be given. In the case of incompetence (a legal determination) or incapacity (a judgment by professionals), surrogates may make decisions on behalf of patients. Guidance may come through the enactment of advance directives, or use of the subjective standard, substituted judgment, or the best interests standard. These concepts are examined within an appropriate ethical framework. Where the law fits into decision making in end-of-life care is important, as there may be a legal course of action (or judicial precedent) that must be followed.

Chapter 6 focuses on organ donation, and the controversial debate over when it is appropriate to procure organs for transplant. Adding to the material on the definition of death presented in chapter 2, this chapter discusses the changing definition of the exact moment of death and questions about Non-Heart Beating Organ Donation (NHBOD). The NHBOD policy of the University of Pittsburgh Medical Center was one of the earliest established in the country and serves as an example for others attempting to establish policy. The contributions and ramifications are examined.

Methods of resolution of ethical dilemmas (as they inevitably will arise) are the focus of chapter 7. This includes a discussion of clinical ethics, a practical discipline that assesses the ethical qualities of each clinical encounter, as well as ethical dilemmas that may arise periodically. Clinical ethics provides a structured approach for "identifying, analyzing, and resolving ethical issues in clinical medicine" (Jonsen, Siegler, & Winslade, 1998, p. 1). A model of organizing data such as the medical record, patient preferences, quality of life assessment, and contextual features is introduced. A parallel to the social work profession's commitment to a holistic view as a precursor to problem solving is recognizable in this model. In addition, commonly seen social work ethical decision-making models are introduced.

Primarily in hospitals, but in other health settings as well, professionals have access to institutional ethics committees and/or ethics consultation services. The primary purpose of ethics committees is to protect patients' rights and interests (Hoffman, 1993). These committees developed initially as a result of new technologies in medicine, dating back to the development of hemodialysis for patients with chronic kidney disease in the 1960s. The early deliberations concerned the appropriate allocation of what was a scarce resource at the time. Later, committees were formed at the encouragement of legal entities faced with cases of comatose individuals dependent on life support, such as the case of Karen Ann Quinlan in 1975. Today, the primary functions of these committees focus on more than consultation around individual cases or case reviews, but also include the education of committee members, the institution, and the broader community, as well as policy development and review.

Ethics consultation teams are an even more recent development. Several types exist, but most often the teams are comprised of subgroups derived from the membership of the ethics committee in a particular institution. This chapter reviews the development of ethics committees, the role of these committees in the healthcare setting, and the potential role of social workers in their interactions with ethics committees and consultation services. As ethics committees are multidisciplinary, social workers often serve as members of these forums so an understanding of how best to contribute is imperative.

In chapter 8, the concepts of privacy, confidentiality, truth telling, and medical error in healthcare settings are discussed. In recent years, privacy and the confidentiality of our health information and medical records has gained attention. Federal regulations regarding disclosure of this information are covered by the Health Insurance Portability and Accountability Act (1996). How this law affects the practice of healthcare social workers is discussed. The role of social workers in maintaining the privacy and confidentiality of patients and families is significant.

Ethics and End-of-Life Decisions in Social Work Practice provides a foundation for social workers to build continuing knowledge of trends in health care that will affect our practice. Among these trends are the continuing financial constraints of managed care, medical advances, particularly in genetics, and the focus on quality of services and evaluation of patient outcomes. Especially when we are considering end-of-life care, all of these issues demand that we define what "quality of life" really means. These issues extend beyond the scope of this book, because they are ever-changing. Social workers must keep current on advances in health care and the ethical conflicts inherent in them by continuing to read respected and current professional bioethics literature and attending educational seminars and meetings that cover emerging issues.

In addition to introducing important concepts, each chapter contains case examples that illustrate the associated decision-making processes, potential ethical dilemmas, and questions for examination of the situation by the reader. Except where indicated, all case examples have been derived from actual cases encountered by the authors. Legal cases are designated as such. Recommendations for appropriate practice are suggested.

We believe and hope that you will find the information in this book useful in practical situations. Whether you are at the beginning of your social work career or later, it is a valuable resource that you may refer to whenever you encounter difficult or controversial end-of-life decisions in your practice setting.

Chapter 1

MEDICAL ETHICS:
THE ROLE OF PHILOSOPHY

At the inception of biomedical ethics, a foundation was formulated by combining several schools of thought, not the least of which was philosophy, and the application of philosophical and ethical theory to moral principles. Devettere (2000) enumerated these factors eloquently when he stated that ethics is about evaluation, assessment, and reasoning. Evaluation and reasoning through moral dilemmas can be done successfully by reviewing how philosophers define what is right, exploring how ethical theory is applied, and by affirming that philosophy and morality remain at the foundation of bioethics today.

Within this chapter numerous writings are synthesized into a synopsis of the founding tenets of the field of biomedical ethics, emphasizing the importance of philosophy, the connection of philosophy to morality, and how bioethics grew as a discipline from this connection. First, the chapter reviews basic philosophical principles. Second, the relationship among philosophy, morality, and law is discussed, and how the transformation of principle into moral code and law is essential to "doing the right thing." Exemplary cases demonstrate how philosophy can help to consider dilemmas and, in some situations, how the law can be utilized to bring a moral conflict to the surface. Some cases are primary health law cases, while others represent everyday healthcare cases, each chosen to clarify specific points.

PHILOSOPHY IN MEDICAL ETHICS

Basic Ethics Theories

Philosophers such as Plato, Aristotle, Socrates, and Kant sought to explore and define what is good, right, and just for the individual as

1

well as society, while trying to cultivate virtues and encourage development of sound moral principles. Philosophy as a discipline was strongly linked to the practice of medicine in ancient Greece. For medicine to evolve as a profession it was necessary to separate medicine from the arts. Yet in order to solve some of the dilemmas faced within medicine, a return to the roots of philosophy from which medicine was born is required (Pellegrino, 1993). Some philosophers state that the founding principles of biomedical ethics were constructed through the extrapolation of ethical theory (Beauchamp & Childress, 2001), while others say the reverse: that ethical theories "attempt to articulate and justify principles that can be employed as guides for making moral decisions and as standards for the evaluation of actions and policies" (Munson, 1988, p. 2). Regardless of how principles evolve, philosophy forms the foundational points of healthcare ethics.

Philosophical principles are not solely sufficient (Beauchamp & Childress, 2001). Ethical constructs have been formulated on many theories. A few are outlined here, specifically those that best serve to resolve the types of dilemmas faced most often in the provision of health care.

Consequentialism. Consequentialism judges the rightness or wrongness of an action or decision based upon the consequences that result. Within medical ethics, this might mean how the action affects the personal, social, psychological, economic, familial, or other aspects of the patient's life (Kelly, 1991). *Utilitarianism* is a form of consequentialism that points to social consequences, discussed below. Actions taken in a particular case can have a significant long-term impact upon societal viewpoint. This is clearly seen in the 1976 case of Karen Ann Quinlan.

The Case of Karen Ann Quinlan

Karen Ann Quinlan was a 21-year-old college student who was found unresponsive by friends after she attended a party where she consumed two gin and tonics and 5 mg of valium. She was taken to a local hospital where she was placed on a life-support ventilator then transported to a large community hospital.

2

Her parents were faithful Catholics whose priest informed them that they were not required to provide extraordinary care to their daughter once her condition was declared hopeless. In 1975, Quinlan's father, Joe, petitioned the New Jersey lower court to be named his daughter's guardian so that he could legally have her disconnected from the ventilator that was keeping her alive. The judge was not prepared to grant such a request and named an outside guardian for Karen Ann. The case was then sent to the New Jersey Supreme Court on appeal.

The Quinlan case gained national recognition because it was the first case of its kind to discuss these profound ethical issues on a national level: How is death defined? Who decides what medical treatment to accept or refuse if the patient is incompetent? Is the withdrawal of life-sustaining therapy the same as euthanasia? Is all medical therapy the same?

The Quinlan case resulted in a legal ruling that all competent patients have the right to refuse any and all life-sustaining interventions, even if such refusal might result in death (Meisel, 1989). This right passes to family or surrogate decision-makers when the patient is deemed incompetent to decide. The ruling in this tragic case concluded that all life-sustaining interventions are to be considered the same; for example, ventilators are the same as tube feedings under the law (Meisel, 1989; Pence, 1995; *In re Quinlan*, 1976).

The debates that occurred as a result of the Quinlan case brought to the national forefront the moral question of whether the withdrawal of life-sustaining treatment is tantamount to euthanasia. The utilitarian (wide-reaching social) consequences have been widely debated ever since. This case still provides a basis with which to address the ethical, moral, legal question of our right to die.

Utilitarianism. The theory of utilitarianism was best articulated by Jeremy Bentham (1748–1832) and John Stuart Mill (1806–1873), two classical utilitarian thinkers. Mill spoke of "the principle of utility," which holds that "actions are right in proportion as they tend to promote happiness, wrong as they tend to produce the reverse of happiness" (Munson, 1988, p. 3). In other words, the rightness of any one action is determined by the degree to which the action produces the best overall result (Beauchamp & Childress, 1994). No single action or response is right or wrong based upon the intention or hope; it can be right one time and wrong another based upon the extent to which it produces the best possible outcome (Munson, 1988).

Bentham utilized a "calculus of pleasure and pain in which characteristics of pleasure such as intensity, duration, and number of people affected are measured and assigned numerical values" (Munson, 1988, p. 4). The right action is the one with the highest numerical score. This type of thinking is the basis for risk/benefit analysis, often utilized in medical ethics to consider the best course of treatment. In utilitarian theory each individual counts the same as another and the interests of each person are considered when discussing an issue. The right action produces the greatest number of goods for the greatest number of people (Garrett, Baillie, & Garrett, 1993; Munson, 1988). A majority of utilitarians believe that we should produce *intrinsic goods*, goods of value to the most individuals (Beauchamp & Childress, 2001).

Utilitarianism is a goods-based theory that focuses on the end point and is therefore considered to be a teleological ethical theory (from *telos,* Greek for end or goal). The theory is separated into act and rule utilitarianism. *Act utilitarianism* states that this theory should be applied to particular acts, while *rule utilitarianism* discusses how this theory should be utilized to test rules, which, in turn, are utilized to assess the rightness of the acts themselves (Munson, 1988). Act utilitarianism is sensitive to the consequences of specific acts upon specific cases. According to Beauchamp and Childress, the classic utilitarian has great difficulty defining a strict distinction between *morally obligatory actions* and those seen as *supererogatory actions,* which Beauchamp and Childress define as those actions that are above the call of moral obligation and are performed for the sake of personal ideals (1994). Neither viewpoint can be analyzed or applied without criticism.

The German philosopher Immanuel Kant (1724–1804) put forth a contrasting view to the utilitarian notion that the rightness of an action or decision is determined by the consequences of this action. In *Fundamental Principles of the Metaphysics of Morals*, Kant wrote that consequences are an irrelevant aspect of evaluating rightness of any one action. Instead, Kant offered the *categorical imperative*, which prescribes what ought to be done in certain situations each time, regardless of consequences. Maxims are rules under this imperative that guide an individual to react in a given circumstance. One type of maxim that could be applied to health care would be to always *choose the action most likely to bring about greater benefit than risk to the patient* (Macklin, 1987). Kant's categorical imperative states that you must only act on a maxim that you can will to be a universal law. The true test of such a command is the ability to generalize it. In the example given above, this maxim, choosing the action that is most likely to bring about greater benefit than risk to the patient, is often generalized in the medical field and is frequently referred to as the *risks/benefits ratio*.

Two principles form the basis of this maxim. The development of principles is the next step toward formulating a moral code or rules that serve to direct moral or right action. The two principles that support the above maxim, *always choose the action which is most likely to bring about greater benefit than risk to the patient* are: the principle of *nonmaleficence*, the duty to do no harm (based upon the Hippocratic Oath), and the principle of *beneficence*, which states that one should do what is of most benefit and least risk to the patient (Devettere, 2000; Macklin, 1987; Munson, 1988). However, there are times when these principles clash and it is this clash that creates ethical dilemmas. One such dilemma is well illustrated in the Dubreuil case.

The Dubreuil Case

Mrs. Dubreuil was a young woman who suffered from a blood clotting disorder. She was admitted for the delivery of her fourth child and signed a consent form agreeing to the required cesarean section but withheld consent for any blood transfusion that would be required to save her life due to her values and conviction as a practicing Jehovah's Witness. Due to severe loss of blood from the operation, she was going to die without a transfusion but the patient continued to refuse this treatment. The hospital contacted Mr. Dubreuil, who was not a Jehovah's Witness, and he gave consent. The patient's two brothers were not Jehovah's Witnesses either, and supported the choice made by Mr. Dubreuil. However, the patient's mother was a Jehovah's Witness and intervened to advocate for the right of her daughter to refuse blood.

The hospital sought an emergent legal judgment in case further transfusions were necessary. No testimony was given during this hearing, for the attorney received a call informing him that the patient had regained consciousness. Mrs. Dubreuil was approached again for consent to transfusions, and again refused. Despite this fact, the judge verbally announced judgment in favor of the hospital stating that they could administer blood if physicians deemed it necessary.

A few days later, the written court order backed this decision based on the fact that no testimony was given as to how the minor children would be cared for in the event of the death of Mrs. Dubreuil. The court ruled that the State's interest in protecting the rights of innocent third parties outweighed the patient's right of refusal. The Florida Supreme Court heard this case on appeal despite the fact that it was moot. The Florida Supreme Court reversed the judge's ruling, stating there is a duty on the part of the State to prove that abandonment of minor children would occur if the patient's refusal of care were honored (Meisel, 1989; *Dubeuil*, 1992).

The conflict between the duty to do no harm and the desire to do what is of most benefit to the patient is clearly present in the Dubeuil case. Such cases are indicative of the ethical conundrums frequently faced within health care. Such conflicts require principle-based or rule-based thinking in order to achieve reasonable resolutions. These rules embrace personal moral codes of conduct, societal norms, and cultural beliefs of the patient, family, and clinical practitioners, as well as hospital policies and procedures and state and federal laws.

For a philosopher such as Kant, resolution of conflict would rely on the categorical imperative (or ultimate personal law). Kant had only one true categorical imperative: All individuals should be treated as an end, never only as a means. This emphasizes the basic value of all individuals. According to Kant, the worth of an individual lies in the fact that he/she is capable of rational thought. The ability to reason is demonstrated in Man's "autonomous, self-legislating will," fundamental to the concepts of self-determination and autonomy (Munson, 1988, p. 12). Kant would have favored and advocated for the self-determined choice of Mrs. Dubeuil to refuse blood based on her categorical imperative, which could be stated as, "I will follow the tenets outlined and practiced within my faith as a Jehovah's Witness."

Consequentialism and Utilitarianism. The English philosopher W. D. Ross (1877) attempted to combine aspects of utilitarianism and Kantianism in his book *The Right and the Good.* Ross rejected the belief that utilitarianism focused only on the consequences of an action, and had difficulty with the Kantian notion of absolute rules or commands. In Ross's view, the right thing to do is not always obvious and the development of rigid rules does not increase our ability to determine right action. There are always several ways of acting in any given situation. How to act is guided by discriminating between *actual duty* and *prima facie duty.*

Ross describes prima facie duty as one that dictates what should be done when other relevant factors are not being considered. For example, I promised to attend my son's school concert but just as I am leaving work to drive to the concert, my sister telephones to tell me that her husband had a heart attack and is in the emergency room in the hospital where I work. I have two prima facie duties: one, to go to my son's concert because I promised, and the other is to support my sister. To resolve this dilemma, I need to determine the difference between both duties to determine which one is prima facie (Munson, 1988). The following lists a few of the duties outlined by Ross (Munson, 1988, p. 19):

1. Fidelity: telling the truth, keeping actual and implicit promises, and not representing fiction as history
2. Reparation: righting wrongs done by us to others
3. Gratitude: recognizing services done for us by others
4. Justice: preventing the distribution of pleasure or happiness that is not in keeping with the merit of the people involved
5. Beneficence: helping to better the condition of others with respect to virtue, intelligence, or pleasure
6. Self-Improvement: bettering oneself with respect to virtue or intelligence
7. Nonmaleficence: avoiding or preventing injury to others

Ross does not see this as a complete list of prima facie duties that everyone will recognize as true and self-evident. He recommends that we deal with conflict between these principles on an individual basis.

Ross's first principle addresses conflict between two overarching principles. *One should act in accord with the more stringent prima facie duty.* His second principle assists when there is conflict among several prima facie duties and this principle states that *One's duty is to act where there is the balance of prima facie rightness over prima facie wrongness* (Munson, 1988; Beauchamp & Childress, 2001). Applying Ross's theories to bioethics, one gains the benefits of utilitarian reasoning while acknowledging the moral force that may conflict with these duties.

Rawls's Theory of Justice. Harvard philosopher John Rawls (1971) developed a theory of justice that drew upon the strengths of utilitarian thought in combination with the deontological position expressed by Kant and Ross. *Deontology* perceives the rightness or wrongness of a decision or action by examining the properties of the decision or action. Some acts are good or evil in themselves despite the consequences; the deontological view looks at the basic rules by which we live. Kant was a deontologist who believed that there are moral imperatives by which we all should live. For example, lying is wrong. In the deontological view of Kant, even if a lie results in a good, the act is wrong because it goes against the categorical imperative that lying is wrong. In this category of moral theory the focus is on the individual over and above the needs of the group or society. Under this theory, an individual's place, responsibility, and role within society are not considered. Some believe this is a critical fault of deontology. This system suggests that any ethical dilemma can be clarified with reason, however modern society is more complex than that (Garrett, Baillie, & Garrett, 1993; Rawls, 1971).

Rawls views the primary responsibility of government as the preservation of liberty and the promotion of the welfare of individuals. His principle of justice serves as a standard for evaluation of social practices (Rawls, 1971). His theory presents ways to resolve conflicts while preserving the legitimate interests of individuals. He developed a hypothetical stance termed the *original position*, which is occupied by all individuals who make up society. No single individual in this view is considered based on age, race, sex, social position, deficits, intellect, or economic status. Individuals reside behind "a veil of ignorance," which increases the likelihood of fairness and the rendering of justice in decisions presented to the group (Rawls, 1971). Rawls argues that people in the original position would agree to two principles of justice designed to "govern the distribution of all social goods: liberty, property, wealth, and social privilege" (Rawls, 1971; Munson, 1988, p. 23):

1. Each person is to have an equal right to the most extensive total system of equal basic liberties compatible with a similar system of liberty for all.
2. Social and economic inequalities are to be arranged so that they are both:
   a. to the greatest advantage of the least advantaged and,
   b. attached to offices and positions open to all under conditions of fair equality of opportunity

These two principles are applied in combination with Rawls's natural duties to support and comply with just institutions, to help those in need, to do no harm, and to keep our promises. Together they provide a mechanism for to considering complex bioethical quandaries such as the rationing of organs or of health care in general.

The case of Baby K provides an example of obstacles to be considered when discussing rationing of care.

The Case of Baby K

Baby K was delivered on October 13, 1992. During her pregnancy Ms. H was informed that her fetus was encephalic and would be born with only the brain stem intact. An abortion was recommended as an option but Ms. H preferred to carry the pregnancy to term. At the time of birth, Baby K experienced respiratory distress and was placed on a respirator. After several days, physicians informed Ms. H that continued ventilatory support would not be of much assistance to Baby K's overall health and that to continue to provide this support would be medically inappropriate. The physicians recommended that the ventilator be withdrawn, but she refused.

A three-person subcommittee of the ethics committee reviewed the case and recommended that the ventilator be withdrawn because the care was seen as "futile" in nature. It was also recommended that legal recourse be taken if the mother refused to withdraw care.

By November 1992, Baby K was able to breathe on her own without the ventilator and she was transferred to a nursing home. It was understood that the hospital would accept the baby back if she required the ventilator again.

Baby K was returned to the hospital on February 12 and readmitted again on March 3, where she remained a patient until April 13. The hospital sought a ruling to allow the withholding of ventilation from Baby K if she was returned again to the emergency room, as it was thought to be ethically inappropriate to provide this level of care when the case was futile. A guardian *ad litem* was appointed and the guardian agreed that provision of continued ventilatory support was inappropriate, as did K's father (who was never married to Ms. H). However, Ms. H. continued to insist that Baby K receive the ventilator whenever she required this care, based on her strong religious convictions.

The judge supported Ms. H, stating: "When one parent asserts the child's explicit constitutional right to life as the basis for continuing medical treatment and the other is asserting his nebulous liberty interest in refusing life-saving treatment on behalf of the minor child, the explicit right to life must prevail" (*Matter of Baby K*, 1994).

Major Moral Principles

The principles referred to most often in the consideration of ethical dilemmas are *autonomy, nonmaleficence, beneficence*, and *justice*. These four principles were first described cohesively in a primary bioethics sourcebook entitled *Principles of Biomedical Ethics*, written by Beauchamp and Childress (2001). They have remained the mainstay of ethical problem solving for thirty years (Beauchamp & Childress, 1994), and are generally accepted and still utilized in primary ethical analysis in the field of bioethics.

The principles are a guide to help begin the intellectual process of considering, evaluating, and solving bioethical dilemmas, however, they cannot be automatically applied to every situation. In a complex case, the ethics consultant only begins the evaluation of the dilemma by considering that the problem may be one in which autonomy has been eroded through the actions of another. Resolution of the issue requires that one understand the role of autonomy in medicine and how the law views the individual autonomy of patients. A paradigm of possible issues and solutions related to the erosion of autonomy in similar cases must be reviewed.

In some circumstances these principles may conflict and several principles may need to be balanced in order to determine which principle takes precedence over another and in which situations that might occur (Beauchamp & Childress, 2001). The context of individual cases, applicable health law and review of hospital practice and policy, and insight into the physiological, cultural, spiritual, and psychosocial needs of the patient and family is the way to determine which principles may be appropriate or applicable.

Caution must be exercised, as the importance of principles can be oversimplified, especially the principle of autonomy. Autonomy, or self-determination, is one of two primary principles that form the foundation of the informed consent statute. *Informed consent* is the basis of communication between patient and doctor (see chapter 4). Autonomy is a principle that social workers should reflect on most because of the high regard placed on self-determination within the profession, however, no right is absolute and dilemmas often occur because of competing rights.

Autonomy. The word comes from the Greek *autonomos*, or self-rule, and refers to the right of all competent individuals to accept or refuse any and all medical therapy, even if such a refusal could result in death (Meisel, 1989). Plato, Aristotle, Socrates, and Kant all discuss the importance of seeking knowledge to increase self-rule. The work of these philosophers has greatly influenced our understanding of the self and the definition of right and the good within each individual, as well as our definitions of individual and social justice.

Application of these philosophical theories progressed into the principle of respect for self-determination and has evolved over time, via the interpretation of secular law, into a right. The right of autonomous individuals to accept or refuse care has its basis in ancient philosophical theories. Reading additional works on the role of philosophy in ethics will lead to a fuller understanding of its influence on biomedical principles.

The move from principle-based problem solving to the idea of perceived rights in health care has not been a smooth transition. Several principles discussed in this chapter, especially autonomy and beneficence, have been debated in the legal system for decades in the hope of settling once and for all the question of whether we have the "right to die." This question has never been fully answered because the question itself is ever evolving. The two paramount questions of the right to health care and the right to die have defied resolution, as no right is absolute and each right carries with it a corresponding responsibility. At times, individuals may want the right but not the responsibility. For example, for a patient to exercise the right of refusal of a medical procedure or test, a healthcare provider is required to respect that right, and herein lies the quandary. It is not unusual for the refusal of treatment to be in opposition to what the physician believes is the correct choice for the patient. Not all such cases involve patients who are terminally ill. One such complex case of refusal of care is that of Elizabeth Bouvia.

The Case of Elizabeth Bouvia

In September 1983 Elizabeth Bouvia checked herself into Riverside General Hospital in California for treatment of depression. Her father stated that she was suicidal and she was admitted to the psychiatric ward for treatment. Ms. Bouvia was a 25-year-old woman afflicted with cerebral palsy, which left her totally paralyzed. She had no use of her legs and only minimal use of her right arm, which helped her to use a power-controlled wheelchair and to smoke.

Her parents were divorced and Elizabeth lived with her mother until the age of 10 and then with her father until the age of 18 when he announced that he could no longer care for her. She lived in her own apartment cared for by a live-in nurse with the support of state assistance. Ms. Bouvia completed general high school equivalence as an adult and then went on to complete a bachelor's degree in 1981. She subsequently entered into a masters program in social work but dropped out due to difficulties related to her field placement work. She had done some volunteer work but was never gainfully employed for wages.

12

Elizabeth was married to an ex-convict, Richard, whom she met via correspondence. She became pregnant by him and suffered a miscarriage in 1982. She and her husband had some financial difficulties. Elizabeth asked her father to assist them, but he declined. Richard could not find work and subsequently abandoned his wife.

Ms. Bouvia suffered from chronic severe pain due to degenerative arthritis. When she entered Riverside General in 1983, she requested that she be permitted to starve to death. Her attending psychiatrist did not agree and Ms. Bouvia telephoned the American Civil Liberties Union (ACLU). Elizabeth petitioned the court to prevent the hospital from force-feeding her. Despite the fact that Judge Hews stated that Ms. Bouvia was "rational, sincere, and fully competent," he chose to allow the force-feeding.

This case became a nationally reviewed medical ethics nightmare. Lawrence White, California Medical Association Director at the time, eloquently stated, ". . . her first amendment rights may hit somebody else's medical ethics rights right between the eye." A legal standoff continued until April 7, 1984, when Elizabeth signed herself out of Riverside and went to a hospital in Mexico where she hoped they would be more sympathetic and allow her to die. They were no more sympathetic so she returned to California. She disliked the force-feeding at Riverside and checked herself into a private care facility where she began eating.

In September 1985, Ms. Bouvia checked herself in to USC Medical Center in Los Angeles and a morphine pump was started to control her increasing pain. She ate and was transferred to another recovery facility where it was determined that she was not "eating enough" and was again force-fed. She again appealed and the California Court of Appeals found in her favor (Pence, 1995; Meisel, 1989; *Bouvia v. County of Riverside,* 1983).

Ethics cases such as the case of Elizabeth Bouvia clearly outline the fact that there can be more than one right viewpoint and case points can be interpreted in more than one way with no single correct response or resolution. The reality is that rights overlap and are conflictual at times with no clearly observable reasonable option. The right of this competent woman to refuse to be force-fed is in conflict with what physicians see as their duty not to participate in her death. The quandary of Ms. Bouvia's autonomy versus another's right or duty (such as the State's right and doctor's duty to preserve life and prevent suicide) is a highly complex issue. Cases such as these frequently are reviewed by medical ethicists and can lead to a request for legal discourse, as occurred in this case. Most cases, even highly complicated ones, are solved at the bedside through endless communication and careful negotiation.

At times a physician does question the decision-making capacity of a patient who refuses what appears to be reasonable care, not out of malice but out of sincere conflict and a desire to make sure that the facts are clear, because death is not reversible. Hypothetically, all individuals have the right to accept or refuse care, but when treatment is refused, especially if the "no" is unanticipated, healthcare providers may become uncomfortable. "No" is always one of the treatment options presented within the informed consent process.

If autonomy is respected as a principle, the cost of this respect for the self-determination of others is that at times patients may appear to die too soon, for no good reason, while at other times patients may appear to linger too long; at the cost of the loss of individual freedoms, the right of refusal still remains with the patient. A physician may disagree with the choice a patient makes but ultimately the individual freedom of each patient to make such a choice must be respected (Beauchamp & Childress, 2001).

The clinical social worker can be of great assistance at times when the refusal of care by a patient is at odds with what a physician believes to be reasonable, or if the refusal risks death. When such disagreements occur, the assistance of a clinical social worker or medical ethicist can help sort out what lies at the basis of the refusal. It is important for any healthcare provider to remember that the choice made is not what determines the capacity of an individual to give informed consent but the process utilized to make this decision that is important (Pellegrino, 1991). Even if the clinical social worker or medical ethicist believes like the physician that the patient might benefit from a recommended therapy, the right of the patient to choose differently based upon his/her own autonomy or self-determination must be respected.

Social workers carry an obligation to foster the autonomy of their patients and to increase autonomy if it is compromised. Information gained from assessments by the clinical social worker adds depth to an assessment of the patient's capacity for informed consent. Simple factors that social workers should pay attention to are making sure that patients are interviewed with hearing aids in place, teeth in, and family present. Social workers may be aware of when the patient last ate or when medication was last given. They can help to assure that decisions are self-determined merely by participating in developing a plan through which the highest level of capacity can be gained (see chapter 4).

Autonomy should be respected *unless* the actions taken in the name of autonomy cause harm to others. Professionals have the duty to tell the truth to patients, gain informed consent before treatment or any procedure is performed, respect informed refusal of unwanted treatment, and protect confidential information. The principle of autonomy does not cover individuals who may be immature, mentally incapacitated, coerced, or exploited, including, for example, infants, drug-dependent patients, or suicidal individuals (Beauchamp & Childress, 2001). However, when someone is not considered autonomous, all efforts are made to support those who serve as surrogate decision-makers for that patient. Then choices are made based on the value structure of the patient when they used to be autonomous or whatever is in the best interest of the nonautonomous patient. The clinical social worker can often be a pivotal part of support for informed decision making by the surrogate speaking for the silent or incapacitated patient. When defending patient autonomy is no longer possible, the focus is on preserving the human dignity of the patient (Berg, Appelbaum, Lidz, & Parker, 2001). Preservation of human dignity is a primary principle, which undergirds the statute of informed consent (see chapter 4).

These principles represent a Western philosophy of medicine, which may not apply in all cultures. Respect for value structures that fall outside of Western philosophy is paramount, and frequently it falls upon the social worker to assist the healthcare team in determining how to best abide by the values, principles, and social norms that formulate the philosophy by which the patient contemplates and solves dilemmas. The team should function according to a standard that acknowledges that "respect for persons is fundamental to the ethical provider-patient relationship" (Joffe, Manocchia, Weeks, & Cleary, 2003, p. 103). Within bioethics, respect for persons is seen as equal to respect for autonomy (Beauchamp, 1994; Beauchamp & Childress, 1994; Cummings & Cockerham, 1997).

Nonmaleficence. The principle of nonmaleficence holds that professionals act in ways that do not intentionally cause harm or injury to others. Several obligations arise from this principle: Avoid disabling another, avoid unnecessary suffering, avoid risk of injury (in the case of research subjects), and avoid killing another. In medicine, the assertion of nonmaleficence can be found in the Hippocratic Oath: *I will use treatment to help the sick according to my ability and judgment, but I will never use it to injure or wrong them.* The obligation here is to not inflict evil or harm onto another individual (Beauchamp & Childress, 2001). Professionals should strive to prevent or remove unnecessary harm. Ineffective interventions should be avoided. If benefits and burdens are equally balanced, it is best to err on the side of not intervening (Lo, 2000).

Injury and harm are used to explain the principle of nonmaleficence. These terms may have many interpretations. Injury may refer to harm or to an injustice. Wronging may involve a violation of individual rights, but harming may not mean that such a violation has occurred. To clarify the principle, Beauchamp and Childress (2001) refer to physical harm, which may include pain, disability, and death; intending, causing, or permitting death; or risking death. Violation of this principle might include performing painful procedures without premedicating, unnecessary sedation, and unwarranted or uninformed withdrawal of treatment. Inflicting mental harm and interfering with the individual's other interests may also be interpreted as violations of this principle.

Other concepts associated with discussions of nonmaleficence are the *standard of due care* and the *rule of double effect.* In cases involving imposition of risk, both the law and morality recognize a standard of due care in medicine. To meet this standard, the goals of care must justify the risks imposed to achieve those goals (Beauchamp

& Childress, 2001). Negligence refers to a case where this standard is not followed and unwarranted risks are intentionally imposed or are unintentionally but carelessly imposed. It also includes knowingly failing to guard against the risk of being harmed; for example, some interventions may produce both benefits and harms. An intervention that involves truth-telling, such as a DNR discussion, can sometimes create unintended harm.

> Joe is a 33-year-old-male recently admitted to the intensive care unit with PCP pneumonia and AIDS meningitis. Because of these diagnoses, Joe is on a ventilator and unable to communicate his wishes. This patient has been cared for by Dr. Johnson for the past eight years. Joe chose not to inform his family of his HIV status due to his fear of rejection. He has asked Dr. Johnson to discuss all his healthcare issues with David (Joe's life partner). However, Joe has never executed a legal document naming David as his power of attorney and now that Joe is unconscious and seriously ill, Dr. Johnson believes it would be wrong "not to sit with the whole family to discuss Joe's prognosis." Dr. Johnson feels morally obligated to keep Joe from harm and believes that revealing his diagnosis of AIDS will help his family to "do the right thing."

Clearly, it is not Dr. Johnson's intention to hurt Joe by breaking his confidence at this time but it may cause unintended harm from the release of this confidential information. Dr. Johnson risks the loss of Joe's trust, the potential rejection of Joe by his family, and the social and economic repercussions of discrimination against persons with AIDS. In this case, there are laws that do not permit the revelation of such information. There are also principles that serve the individual faced with such a quandary. One such principle or rule is the rule of double effect.

The rule of double effect refers to one specific act that may have two foreseeable effects, one good and one harmful. If the harmful effect is unintended, the act is not always morally prohibited (Beauchamp & Childress, 2001). This rule is discussed within Catholic moral theology in detail. For example, according to the rule, treating a terminally ill person's pain by administering high doses of opioids for pain relief may be acceptable, even if the medication might cause respiratory depression and the individual's death. However, the rule does not sanction euthanasia or physician-assisted suicide (Quill, Dresser, & Brock, 1997). In a time when the public and many professionals are fearful that they may be engaging in euthanasia if a patient's death is hastened unintentionally in an attempt to ease pain, the rule of double effect provides moral reassurance (Sulmasy & Pellegrino, 1999). The foreseen beneficial effect (symptom relief) must be intended to be equal to or greater than the foreseen harmful effect (possible respiratory depression/death). This is distinguished from euthanasia, where the direct intent is to end life.

Beneficence. Beneficence is the act of providing benefit; acting in ways that promote the welfare of other people. It implies a moral obligation to act for the benefit of others. Duties associated with this principle are: protection of the rights of others, prevention of harm, removal of conditions expected to be harmful, and rescue of those that are vulnerable from imminent danger. These duties are often fulfilled and associated with the principle of nonmaleficence. Though we are morally obligated not to cause harm, there is not an obligation to help or benefit those with whom we do not have a special relationship. It is not possible to act beneficently toward all persons, and we are not morally required to do so. Some norms of beneficence may be morally recommended, but not required. One example of the beneficence obligation, which can override nonmaleficence, occurs when a significant benefit for many can result from a minor harm to a few, as is often seen in the public health arena, for example, vaccinations (Beauchamp & Childress, 2001). Advocates of general beneficence, utilitarian theorists, and some Christian moralists believe that we should act to benefit individuals we don't know and whose views may not be our own. Ross (1930, cited in Beauchamp & Childress, 2001) held that such an obligation rests on the mere fact that there are other beings in the world whose condition we can improve. Others contend that this isn't practical, as it is too demanding to fulfill at all times. Most of us can be reasonably expected to act beneficently toward persons with whom we share a relationship, such as with children/family, friends, or patients.

Beneficence is one of the primary obligations specified in the Hippocratic Oath, which physicians are bound to uphold. However, the conflict over whether autonomy or beneficence should take priority has become a central focus in bioethics. Some argue that the best interests of patients depend upon their preferences, and this is what should be upheld by professionals (Pellegrino & Thomasma, 1987). Others contend that beneficence is the primary goal and rationale of medicine, whereas respect for autonomy (and nonmaleficence and justice) sets moral limits on the professional's actions in pursuit of this goal (Beauchamp & Childress, 1994, p. 273). Beneficence is to be carried out according to the usual goals of medicine and also in terms of patients' value systems, which is a potential source of conflict.

The concept of *paternalism* in medicine is normally included in a discussion of beneficence. Paternalism is not simply guidance of a patient through medical decision making but implies the intentional overriding of an individual's preferences or actions, the justification being that the individual will benefit or be prevented from harm (Beauchamp & Childress, 1994). According to Dworkin (1971, p. 108), paternalism interferes with a person's liberty of action, which may be justified by referring to the welfare, good, happiness, needs, interests, or values of the person being coerced. According to Pellegrino & Thomasma (1987), medical paternalism perhaps makes a false assumption that medical good is the greatest good and supersedes all others. Acting under the guise of paternalism can put vulnerable individuals at risk of harm and coercion, as with patients in pain or nearing death.

In social work, paternalism is often considered in discussions of self-determination and of beneficence (noting that the principles overlap often and cannot be considered independently). The 1996 NASW Code of Ethics Standard 1.02 states, "Social workers may act to limit clients' right to self-determination when, in the social worker's professional judgment, the patient's actions pose a serious, foreseeable, imminent risk to themselves or others." According to Reamer (1998), it is incumbent upon social workers to understand two concepts in interpreting this standard: professional paternalism and protection of third parties. In cases of professional paternalism, a patient's well-being is the primary concern.

> Mary is a 23-year-old woman who comes to the outpatient clinic with severe depression. During an hour-long interview Mary informs the social worker that she has been having trouble functioning at her job

and feels life is not worth living. In her purse she has three bottles of medication which she has been hoarding, and she plans to kill herself after this appointment. The social worker chooses to commit Mary involuntarily to a psychiatric hospital for an emergency evaluation.

Health law supports the actions of the social worker through what is generally referred to as states' rights. The state (government) must uphold a certain level of rights, which can compete and at times override the rights of the individual. The four rights of the state that are exercised most often in specific medical situations are the state's right to:

Preserve life.
Prevent suicide.
Protect the interests of innocent third parties.
Preserve the ethical integrity of the practice of medicine.

The debate over the rights of the individual versus the rights of the state are seen when cases are taken to court. The social worker acknowledges the state's rights, for example, when a client wants to commit suicide, thereby justifying a reason to interfere with a client's actions. What may appear at first to be professional paternalism is in fact imposition of the competing right of the state to intervene (Csikai, 1999; Foster, Sharp, Scesny, McLellan, & Cotman, 1993; Reamer, 1998). In situations where a client poses an imminent threat to someone else, social workers who become aware of this have a legal obligation to warn the third party, thus limiting the client's right to self-determination and breaching confidentiality. This obligation is based on a widely known health law case called the Tarasoff case (Meisel, 1989).

Justice. The principle of justice is comprised of many principles regarding the distribution of benefits and burdens in society. In the provision of health care, the benefits and burdens (or risks) of health care should be described to patients in a fair manner. In upholding this principle, professionals must ensure the right to a decent minimum of health care, fair and equal access to scarce resources (such as organs), and nondiscriminatory treatment based on race, religion, or gender. Justice is violated when subgroups of patients (e.g., the elderly, women, minorities) receive less than adequate pain management, for example.

> Suzanne is a 75-year-old African-American female with breast cancer that has spread to her liver, spine, and lungs. The patient also has a history of mild dementia. The night nurse notes that Suzanne moans more often at night. The medical resident is called and he telephones the family and requests that they come and sit with Suzanne because "she seems to be more confused at night." The patient has been prescribed only darvocet (a non-narcotic pain medication) for pain, without consideration for whether or not the patient's pain is controlled.

Many challenges arise in today's healthcare system, including the notion of the need for universal health care, maintenance of high quality of care, and management of the rising costs. A complication is that there is no agreement regarding the meaning of justice in health care. Nor are there means to enforce justice in many cases. As discussed earlier the views of John Rawls make a reasonable starting point for considering how to distribute scarce resources most equitably. In his classic text *A Theory of Justice* (1971), the starting point for justice is ignorance of one's position in the world. Behind the veil of ignorance you do not know your age, race, sex, or degree of illness. You are unaware of your economic position in life and have no idea when you will require health care. In this condition you might consider the fair distribution of healthcare resources in a much more just way.

In an attempt to uphold the principle of distributive justice, several standards of fundamental or material needs have been proposed (Beauchamp & Childress, 2001, p. 330):

> To each person an equal share
> To each person according to need
> To each person according to effort
> To each person according to contribution
> To each person according to merit
> To each person according to free-market exchanges

Casuistry. This is a practical focus to moral decision making that considers the specific case characteristics and situation (Beauchamp &

Childress, 1994, pp. 92-94). It is appealing to healthcare providers since case-based teaching is the primary method of learning in many health professions. The goal of a casuist form of case review is to search for a complex case that clearly demonstrates a principle and then create argumentative dialogue among the students, using the case example as a base of discourse (Pellegrino, 1993, pp. 1158-1162). The cases are ranked from clear solution to much more complex and are ordered by paradigm or case example. The paradigm cases become the guide for behavior rather than the principles themselves. These paradigm cases are used to assist in the resolution of future cases of a similar type (Devettere, 2000, p. 15; Pellegrino, 1993, pp. 1158-1162).

Casuistry is the movement up from the cases to the principles, the direct opposite of the traditional application of moral principles to the problem (Beauchamp & Childress, 1994, pp. 92-94; Pellegrino, 1993, pp. 1158-1162). The problem with this approach is that there is no strong consensus as to the moral viewpoint of Western society regarding what constitutes a moral dilemma, much less a resolution of that dilemma. Casuistry is derived from the practice of problem resolution utilized in medieval times when there was a consensus regarding certain moral principles. However, we are a pluralistic society, which struggles with such issues. Casuistry is a strong "method of case analysis" but is not very strong as a "reliable guide to moral theory or practice" (Pellegrino, 1993, pp. 1158-1162).

Chapter Conclusion

It would be of great benefit if solutions to the complex ethical quandaries faced daily during the provision of health care could be resolved simply by identifying which moral principles were violated. However, each dilemma requires not only the identification of the potential principle of concern but also the negotiation of a solution. Labeling the principle, which is at the base of the quandary, does not serve to answer any of the complex moral issues, but merely provides the point from which one begins the ethical discourse.

The next several chapters discuss other factors to consider when resolving complex ethical dilemmas. Because they provide the foundation, philosophical constructs and aspects of morality will continue to be discussed as part of this problem-solving process.

Chapter 2

ETHICAL ISSUES AT THE END OF LIFE

At the end of life, it is not unusual for multiple, equally complex issues to arise when planning for treatment. End-of-life planning and decision making requires a working understanding of these complex ethical dilemmas. Social workers, particularly those in healthcare settings, require some knowledge of these issues. They also need to be aware of how such concerns are discussed with patients who have a life-limiting illness, their families, and the friends who care for them.

Among the questions that will be explored in this chapter are: How is death defined? What constitutes life-sustaining treatments: mechanical respiration, cardiopulmonary resuscitation (CPR), dialysis, medical nutrition and hydration? What is the importance of Do Not Resuscitate (DNR) orders and how are they established? Is the withholding or withdrawal of life-sustaining therapies paramount to euthanasia? What does the term *medical futility* mean? What is the difference between euthanasia and physician-assisted suicide?

Within this chapter, as in chapter 1, pertinent historic health law cases will be used to clarify points and add to your knowledge of how society has historically chosen to respond to ethical concerns.

HOW IS DEATH DEFINED?

With continual advances in life-sustaining technology, it is not always clear anymore when death is imminent. Wider use and need for organ donation has made it increasingly difficult to stipulate the criteria for pronouncing a person dead. The definition of physiological death has changed drastically with the invention and implementation of pressure support ventilation. Once physicians learned how to restart the human heart using cardiopulmonary resuscitation (CPR) and defibrillation, and machines were able to breathe for patients whose lungs were no longer able to function on their own, it appeared as if death could be kept "at bay," at least mechanically. Thus life could seemingly be sustained indefinitely (Youngner, Arnold, & Schapiro, 1999). It quickly became apparent, however, that individuals could be physiologically sustained but at the same time be viewed as dead in the eyes of those who loved them, as in the case of Nancy Cruzan.

The Case of Nancy Cruzan

Nancy Cruzan was a woman in her thirties who suffered irreversible brain damage as the result of a car accident in 1983. She had remained in a persistent vegetative state for six years when her parents requested that their daughter's feeding tube be withdrawn. In the state of Missouri a court order was required before a feeding tube could be withdrawn. The probate circuit court granted the parent's permission but the State of Missouri appealed this ruling, based upon the clear and convincing evidentiary standard. The case was then moved from the lower court to the Missouri Supreme Court (Kelly, 1991). There are three standards of evidence, which go in sequence from the most permissive: a preponderance of evidence, to clear and convincing evidence, to the least permissive: beyond a reasonable doubt (Pence, 1995).

The Supreme Court of Missouri overturned the first decision in a 4–3 decision. This ruling was based upon the belief that the State of Missouri is a right-to-life state and, as such, it would be wrong for the state to allow a feeding tube to be removed from a non–terminally ill patient without clear and convincing evidence of her wishes related to such treatment (Meisel, 1989; Pence, 1995).

The Cruzan case was then sent to the U.S. Supreme Court for ruling, where it became the first case of its kind to go before the nation's highest court. The U.S. Supreme Court voted 8–1 to uphold the right of all competent persons to refuse any and all life-sustaining interventions, including feeding tubes. This right was said to be based upon the liberty interest present within the 14th amendment of the Constitution (Meisel, 1989). The Supreme Court also permitted, but did not require, that each state could pass, but *was* not required to pass, a law stating the necessary standard of proof before an incompetent individual could be withdrawn from any life-sustaining treatment. Since Missouri had such a statute and it was not viewed as unconstitutional, the ruling of the Missouri Supreme Court was not overturned. The Missouri Court felt the Cruzans had failed to provide clear and convincing evidence of Nancy's wishes, and therefore her feeding tube could not be removed.

Seven months after the Supreme Court ruling, the same county probate court heard additional information on the Cruzan case and ruled again that the feeding tube could be removed. This time the State did not appeal and Nancy Cruzan died eleven days later (Pence, 1995; Kelly, 1991; Meisel, 1989; *Cruzan v. Harmon*, 1990).

The Cruzan case became an interesting historic case after the 1976 case of Karen Ann Quinlan (discussed in Chapter 1) for many reasons, not the least of which was that the Cruzan case asked the same questions posed by Quinlan but asked them in the United States Supreme Court. One such question was, When does death occur?

WHEN DOES DEATH OCCUR?

According to Devettere (2000), it is important to make the distinction between the concept of death and the criteria for determining death; in other words, the evidence that verifies that death has occurred. The evidence examines two separate elements: circulation and respiration, which have a long history in medicine, and brain function, a new criterion developed fairly recently. Cessation of either the cardiac system or the pulmonary system will in turn cause the cessation of the other. Death occurs when there is an irreversible cessation of cardiopulmonary function. Temporary cessation does not mean that the person is dead; however, after twenty minutes it is unlikely to be reversible. Without the use of life supports, cardiopulmonary and brain functioning will cease almost concurrently. With the use of life supports, such as supportive ventilation, medication to support cardiac function and blood pressure, dialysis to support kidney dysfunction, and nutrition and hydration, persons may now be kept alive according to the old cardiopulmonary criteria. However, lower brain stem function may have ceased (Youngner, Arnold, & Schapiro, 1999).

Harvard Brain Death Criteria

In 1968, an ad hoc committee of the Harvard Medical School was formulated to examine and define brain death. This committee, chaired by anesthesiologist Dr. Henry K. Beecher, published a report in the *Journal of the American Medical Association*, which outlined criteria that could be used by physicians to determine permanent loss of brain function (Youngner et al., 1999). The Harvard committee recorded that its purpose in clearly defining the neurological criteria for death was twofold: "First, it was to decrease the burden on family and society that continued therapy would produce," and second, the criteria were designed to "update obsolete (i.e., cardiac) criteria for death that led to controversy in obtaining organs for transplantation" (Arnold, Youngner, Schapiro, & Spicer, 1995; Beecher, 1968). According to Arnold et al. (1995, p. 40), three criteria for brain death include: (1) "severe coma of known cause, (2) absent brainstem reflexes, and (3) sustained apnea." Before evaluation of brain death is started, all other physiological causes for the coma must be excluded. Before settling on the diagnosis of brain death, the treating physician must look for all reversible medical complications that could have caused the coma, such as the presence of any anesthetics, muscle relaxants, sedatives, shock, electrolyte imbalances, and/or endocrine problems (Youngner et al.). This exclusionary testing can take from several hours to several days and be a cause of emotional stress for the family and loved ones of comatose patients.

The criteria for the determination of brain death are defined clearly by Youngner et al. (1999) as:

> (1) No spontaneous or responsive cranial nerve activity can be identified after stimuli delivered anywhere in the body. No spinal activity can be elicited by stimuli delivered above the foramen magnum. (2) Brainstem reflexes must be absent. Pupils must be: (a) unresponsive to bright light, (b) usually midposition (4-6 mm) or dilated (9 mm). Pinpoint pupils can accompany lethal pontine hemorrhages or infarcts. (3) Oculocephalic reflexes to repetitive head turning must be absent. (Sometimes this test is referred to as doll's eyes). If so, the test must be followed by 50 ml of cold water irrigated against the tympanum on both sides. At least a 5-minute interval should separate the two irritations, neither of which should induce eye movement. (4) No corneal, jaw, or laryngeal reflex or pain response involving cranial nerves can be elicited. (5) A failed apnea test is crucial and imperative. The apneic test

is conducted only after all other signs of brainstem function have disappeared and should not be applied until all reasonable amounts of anesthetic or paralytic drugs have dissipated to nonconfounding levels. . . . The apnea test represents the ultimate physiological-clinical test to diagnose brain death (pp. 41–42).

This apnea test is done according to strict standards, which are further outlined by Youngner, Arnold, and Schapiro.

There are other confirmatory tests to assist in the diagnosis of brain death: electroencephalography (EEGs), brainstem auditory evoked potentials (BAEPs), somatic evoked potentials (SEPs), motor evoked responses (MEVs), and arteriography. It is a misnomer that EEGs are a part of the required testing for the determination of brain death. In the ICU environment, an EEG is susceptible to artifact interference and is less than 100% sensitive, whereas BAEPs are 100% sensitive. The completion of an EEG is not a requirement to determine brain death and in many institutions this test has been replaced by BAEPs or some of the other tests discussed above (Youngner, Arnold & Schapiro, 1999).

There was much debate over the establishment of death criteria for those with significant neurological impairment, especially from individuals who believed such legislation would cause discrimination against the handicapped. Their argument was that this form of severe neurological injury was always followed by death, but the injury itself was not death (DeVita, Snyder, & Grenvik, 1993). Efforts to carefully develop clear standards for devastating neurological impairment culminated in the Uniform Determination of Death Act (UDDA) in the early 1980s, which was approved by several prestigious organizations, including the American Medical Association, American Academy of Neurology, and American Bar Association. The act reads: "An individual who has sustained either (1) irreversible cessation of circulatory and respiratory functions, or (2) irreversible cessation of all functions of the entire brain, including the brain stem, is dead" (Devettere, 2000). Despite the establishment of this criteria, the determination of brain death has not been widely accepted socially. Because of this continued controversy, it has been stipulated that the neurologically impaired person who met brain death criteria must be declared dead prior to the removal of the respirator, thereby avoiding prosecution for causing death via removal of the ventilator (DeVita et al., 1993).

The President's Commission

The President's Commission for the Study of Ethical Problems in Medicine and Biomedical and Behavioral Research (1983) drafted similar criteria and also supported the Harvard Ad Hoc Committee in recommending that loss of all brain functions be accepted as a criterion for death. It has been speculated that the move toward establishment of a brain death criteria was motivated by practicality, namely a need to pronounce a person dead so that their organs could be removed for transplantation. Dr. Beecher was reportedly also concerned with the use of vital resources, thereby connecting the new definition of death in some fashion to the allocation of ICU resources. Physicians had long been making decisions and choices privately in order to determine when such treatment was no longer of benefit, and the brain death criteria simply provided a formal mechanism by which their decisions could be supported (Youngner et al., 1999). The Karen Ann Quinlan case (see chapter 1) and the Cruzan case both relied upon these established criteria to determine whether these women were physiologically dead or alive.

WHAT CONSTITUTES LIFE-SUSTAINING MEDICAL THERAPY?

Cardiopulmonary Resuscitation

What is CPR? Among the most common end-of-life discussions that social workers will have with patients and families regards the provision of cardiopulmonary resuscitation (CPR). Often this discussion occurs when patients are hospitalized with a potentially terminal or irreversible illness; when they are admitted to a nursing home or long-term care facility, inpatient palliative care, or hospice; or when being enrolled into home health, home palliative care, or home hospice care. Ironically, CPR is the only medical treatment provided automatically; consent is required *not* to provide this treatment. In all other aspects of medical therapy, informed consent is required before the treatment can be rendered (Meisel, 1989).

It was not until 1974 that the American Medical Association came forth with a proposal that stated that Do-Not-Resuscitate (DNR) decisions needed to be formally documented on the patient's medical record and communicated to all staff caring for the patient (Burns, Edwards, Johnson, Cassem, & Troug, 2003). In 1974 the Massachusetts Supreme Court ruled that with the concurrence of the patient or family, a physician could enter a DNR order without previous court approval based upon common law and the federal or state constitutional right of refusal (Burns et al.). As case law has continued to develop in relation to when it is appropriate to invoke an advance medical directive, the requirement became, in some states, that the patient must be terminally ill, with death imminent; less stringent requirements were developed in other states (Burns et al.).

The 1983 President's Commission on Deciding to Forgo Life-Sustaining Treatment advocated for the right of competent patients to refuse all life-sustaining treatments through an advance directive to be implemented in the event of loss of future decision-making capacity. The commission also advocated for the right of surrogates to speak on behalf of incapable or incompetent patients (Burns et al., 2003).

After the successful development of CPR, it was seen as something that should be done whenever a person's cardiopulmonary system stops functioning. However, the provision of CPR is not statistically a highly successful intervention. Success of CPR varies in the medical literature: Immediate survival rates range from 3% to 55%, with a 4% to 26% chance of being alive at the time of discharge (Robinson & Mylott, 2001). Survival until discharge is considered to be dismal if the patient suffers from metastatic cancer or has one or more comorbidities such as pneumonia, decreased renal function, sepsis, or congestive heart failure (Robinson & Mylott, 2001). "Additional factors associated with poor survival after CPR include hypotension prior to cardiac arrest, asystole at the time of arrest, a high severity of illness, and a longer length of hospitalization before arrest" (Robinson & Mylott, 2001, p. 71). Brymer, Gangbar, O'Rourke, and Naglie (1995) examined the records of over 264 patients who had been resuscitated while hospitalized in the cardiac care unit. They reported that survival after CPR was 30% and survival until discharge was 17%. This data demonstrated that CPR increased the chances of survival until discharge following resuscitative efforts (Brymer et. al., 1995). Another study completed by Murphy, Murray, and Robinson (1989) reported a survival rate until discharge of only 6.5% in patients older than 69 who were resuscitated in the acute care setting. Finally, a large, national multisite study, the SUPPORT study (1995), enrolled a total of 2,505 subjects, 514 of whom received CPR. Of these 514 people who received CPR, 18.1% survived hospitalization and 63.6% of those who died received CPR again within the last two days of life (Goodlin, Zhong, Lynn, Teno, Fago, Desbiens, et al., 1999).

CPR is an emergency procedure provided by a team of healthcare professionals, including physicians, nurses, respiratory therapists and various technicians, that requires a high level of activity and is accompanied by a certain level of violence. Intravenous lines are inserted (sometimes into the large veins of the legs) to administer strong drugs to regulate of heart rate and blood pressure. During CPR, ribs are frequently broken due to the force applied in an effort to restart a heartbeat. During this process the patient may also require insertion of a tube via the trachea into the lungs (called *endotracheal intubation*). Endotracheal intubation connects a patient to a mechanical ventilator to assist respiration. A cardiac defibrillator may deliver electric shocks to correct cardiac arrhythmia. All of these actions are attempts to revive the patient. However, statistically, only 11% of patients who are successfully resuscitated survive to leave the hospital (Robinson & Mylott, 2001), and it is not uncommon following resuscitation for a patient to be left with brain damage. This damage is caused by a lack of blood flow to the brain (often referred to as anoxic encephalopathy), which may leave the patient persistently vegetative (Deveterre, 2000).

Patient preferences are sought, but if the patient cannot express preferences a surrogate can state these wishes if they are known. Advance medical directives are of benefit during such discussions, for they are viewed as the best evidence of the patient's wishes (Meisel, 1989). Frequently, such discussions take place during planned family meetings when the physician is asked to consider not only the physiological state of the patient but also the psychosocial history, including value structure, belief system, and how the patient would define quality of life.

Do Not Resuscitate. Do-Not-Resuscitate orders consist of a handwritten physician's note in patients' medical records that alerts all providers not to attempt CPR. Normally such an order follows a discussion between the patient or family and a physician. Some facilities may refer to these as DNAR orders or Do Not Attempt Resuscitation, which is more accurate, so the attempt at resuscitation will not be made.

If there is no such order in the medical record, it is assumed by providers that CPR will be administered if a cardiac arrest occurs. Occasionally the Code Status orders are contained on a single sheet in the front of the medical record. This sheet is no more legal than chart notations of orders; it is simply a more organized format that assists the staff in determining what should be done in case of a sudden patient decompensation. Without such written orders, there is an assumption of treatment. Therefore, it is important for providers to discuss CPR and other treatments that may provide a limited benefit so that patients may have a choice in their own medical care.

DNR orders are not restricted only to the terminally ill; resuscitation can be declined by anyone who possesses decision-making capacity. The presumption of treatment always applies in the emergency room unless it is clear that the patient or surrogate does not want it. If CPR has already been initiated before information about the patient's (or family's) desire to refuse CPR is made known, the procedure may be stopped.

CPR Not Indicated. Many hospitals speak openly these days with the patient or surrogate to gain their consent before withholding CPR, which is consistent with case law in this area. However, some institutions have enacted policies that permit the establishment or withholding of CPR orders by the attending physician. This decision is made unilaterally by this physician, who then informs the family of his recommendation so they can transfer care if they disagree with the viewpoint (Burns et al., 2003) Situations where CPR-Not-Indicated orders would be written include provision of care to cases defined by the institution as *futile*. Determining when care is futile is subjective, but it usually refers to treatments with a very low probability of physiological success, where the chance of successful regeneration of the total physiological functional ability of the patient back to his/her pre-admission level is not likely.

There has been a great deal of debate in the literature recently as to whether futility should still be considered a reasonable descriptive term to use in the field of ethics. Traditionally, what is physiologically possible and what is psychologically reasonable or desirable is debatable. Great disagreement exists as to whether there should ever be a policy that permits the unilateral decision to stop treatment without input from the patient or the surrogate decision-maker, for the value judgments of the patient must predominate all other choices in this society (Burns et al., 2003).

Intubation and Mechanical Ventilation

In 1928, Philip Drinker developed the first respirator. Patients were placed in iron tanks and air was pushed in and out of the lungs through cycles of positive and negative pressure. These "iron lungs" were widely used during the polio epidemic in the 1920s and 1930s. Later, smaller machines were developed that supplied positive air pressure through tubes inserted in patients' throats. Today, the more common term used for such machines is ventilator, although respirator and ventilator are sometimes used interchangeably (Devettere, 2000; Hite & Marshall, 1995). Ventilators are most often used to support breathing temporarily while a patient heals from pneumonia or some other form of reversible pulmonary illness. Ventilators are also utilized to assist breathing during surgery when respiration is depressed due to anesthesia. However, when a patient cannot breathe without support from the ventilator, it is considered to be a life-sustaining treatment. When the need for ventilatory support is long-term, difficult decisions must be faced.

Endotracheal intubation and mechanical ventilation are beneficial in supporting the respiratory system in the short term, but, when a patient requires mechanical ventilation for longer than a few weeks the ICU physician or pulmonologist may suggest a tracheotomy, a surgical procedure where a tube is inserted into the trachea and feeds down the throat to the top of the lungs. This procedure is suggested because long-term endotracheal intubation can erode the trachea and increase the chances of infection. A tracheotomy is normally recommended in cases where extubation is not anticipated within a few weeks.

Withdrawal of mechanical ventilation. The withdrawal of the mechanical respirator or ventilator can be an emotionally difficult process for families because of the sense that this action may cause the death of their loved one, or that the withdrawal of air will cause their family member to suffocate. The decision is so emotionally charged because it is often easier to make a crisis plan not to initiate something than it is to stop something already in place. Some sort of limitation of care precedes 51 to 91% of all ICU deaths, and the withholding or withdrawal of life-sustaining therapy is common within most intensive care units (Sjokvist, Berggren, Svantesson, & Nilstun, 1999).

That it is common practice does not mean that the process is rote or routine. The mechanisms or processes utilized in withdrawal of the ventilator must be clearly discussed with the family. These might include how the ventilator is to be weaned to assure the highest level of patient comfort, medications to decrease respiratory distress, exactly how and when the endotracheal tube will be withdrawn, and the approximate time it will take between weaning and extubation. Families frequently ask the healthcare team how comfort is assured, especially during the dying process. Increasingly in many hospitals a palliative care or pain service is in place, or the services of a person who deals with pain and symptoms at the end of life are provided. The presence of such a team, person, or mechanisms can be very comforting to patients and their families as they face the end of life.

Dialysis

Dialysis is a form of renal replacement therapy and under most circumstances is considered a life-sustaining treatment. Research on this method of removing waste products from the body was started in 1913 and further perfected in the 1940s. Hemodialysis did not become a reality until the 1960s (Devettere, 2000). In the late 1960s, dialysis became a realistic possibility for patients who suffered from end-stage renal disease. Renal failure can be caused by any number of illnesses. With dialysis, some patients can have their life lengthened indefinitely, though dialysis is by no means a cure. For those for whom acute renal failure is part of a multi-organ system decline, dialysis merely delays the dying process (Devettere, 2000).

In the late 1960s, there were more patients than dialysis machines. In an effort to fairly choose who was eligible to receive dialysis, committees were developed. Termed "God squads" they were the forerunners of today's ethics committees (see chapter 5) (Devettere, 2000).

Hemodialysis and peritoneal dialysis were perfected during the 1960s and 1970s, but more patients continued to require the treatments than was possible to provide. Finally, in 1972, Congress amended the Social Security Act to guarantee dialysis to all who needed it regardless of their degree of infirmity or age (Meisel, 1989; Devettere, 2000).

It is possible to maintain physiological functioning with the use of hemodialysis and a form of low-level fluid removal at a continuous rate, called CVVHD (Continuous Veno-Venous Hemodialysis). This form of low-flow dialysis can provide the type of fluid withdrawal that can give a critically ill patient the time needed to recover from shock or a significant illness affecting multiple organ systems. However, this physiological functioning exacts a great price. Dialysis has a series of side effects that make this process extremely uncomfortable to undergo. At times, patients find the side effects so bad that they choose to stop treatment rather than continue with such discomfort (Meisel, 1989). It is speculated that approximately "10% of the deaths of patients who receive long-term dialysis for end-stage renal disease are preceded by [the] discontinuation of dialysis" (Cohen, McCue, Germain, & Kjellstrand, 1995).

The question of what issues should be discussed when a patient initiates dialysis as well as when is it reasonable to suggest discontinuation has been a source of ethical debate with nephrologists for years. Countless articles attempt to lead the practitioner as to how to consider the specific ethical dilemmas of dialysis. Ethical issues faced by kidney physicians were so prevalent at one time that the Renal Physicians Association/American Society of Nephrology developed a working group to formulate guidelines that addressed initiation and withdrawal of dialysis (Dash & Mailloux, 2001).

Withdrawal of dialysis. Emotionally, this form of life-sustaining therapy can be similar to ventilatory support in that it is easier to refrain from starting than it is to withhold the therapy. However, with long-term dialysis, it is not unusual for the nephrologist to discuss the option of discontinuation up front before it is instituted as well as during the process. The reason is that dialysis can have unpleasant and even life-threatening side effects and complications. Because of these potential problems, a kidney specialist carefully considers the medical indications for dialysis, the patient's preferences for such therapy (if known), the quality of life that may be experienced as a result of the start of dialysis, and any economic or social burdens that may arise from this choice. In 2002, the American Society of Nephrology and the Renal Physicians Association published a set of guidelines entitled "Shared Decision-Making in the Appropriate Initiation of and Withdrawal of Dialysis." This publication recommends that dialysis be withheld or withdrawn if a patient has acute renal failure or end-stage renal disease and meets any of the following criteria (pp. 10–11):

> Patients with decision-making capacity, who are fully informed and who refuse dialysis or request discontinuation
>
> Patients who no longer possess decision-making capacity (refer to chapter 3), who have previously indicated their desire to refuse dialysis in an oral or written advance medical directive
>
> Patients who no longer possess decision-making capacity and whose properly appointed legal representative wishes to refuse dialysis or who requests discontinuation
>
> Patients who have irreversible, profound neurological impairment, such as a lack of signs of thought, sensation, purposeful behavior, or awareness of self and environment
>
> Patients who have a terminal illness from a non-renal cause, or whose medical condition precludes the technical process of dialysis

Artificial Nutrition and Hydration

Like a Hallmark image of a mother making chicken soup for a sick child with a cold, giving nourishment to the sick is viewed as a routine and natural part of the provision of care. When nutrition and hydration are delivered via intravenous lines and tube feeding it is no longer natural; it is at times no longer nurturing. The purpose of providing nutrition and hydration via these methods is to build and support the body as it heals. However, whether or not this form of feeding should be provided in every case causes conflict on many levels. Patients may receive artificial nutrition and hydration via a tube through the nose, called a nasogastric or NG tube, or it can be delivered via a gastric tube, called a G tube. Patients can also receive artificial nutrition through a specialized intravenous line (IV) (Devettere, 2000). This form of IV nutrition is called total parenteral nutrition (TPN). TPN is a liquid form of artificial nutrition, designed to meet all the nutritional needs of the patient. These forms of artificial nutrition are costly and carry side effects such as diarrhea. It has long been argued that artificial nutrition is not feeding in the social sense of food consumption. Socially, a great deal of the interactions among family and friends happen around food. In this sense, tube feedings are more medical treatment than food (Devettere, 2000).

Withdrawal of Artificial Nutrition and Hydration. The ethical question that surrounds this form of nutritional support is: If artificial nutrition is considered a medical therapy, then are physicians required to provide that therapy? This form of nutritional support is often given to patients at the end of life who have lost the ability to swallow and developed recurrent pneumonia from the aspiration of food into their lungs. An article published in the *Journal of the American Medical Association* discussed the fact that G-tube placement does not reduce the chance of aspiration in patients with a history, and has been known to increase aspiration in patients with no history of aspiration prior to placement of the G-tube (Teno, 2003). These data only increase the ethical debate over the use of artificial feeding at the end of life.

WITHHOLD OR WITHDRAW THERAPY?

The ethical issues faced by ICU clinicians have remained consistent over the years. End-of-life decision making in the ICU and what constitutes effective communication in that setting have remained well-discussed topics in medical and bioethics journals for the past two decades. Despite growth in medical technology and the increase in patient education via methods like the Internet, communication regarding these complex issues remains problematic. One study revealed that "Patient information is frequently not communicated effectively to family members by ICU physicians." The researchers found that even when conversations did take place, comprehension by the family of the issues discussed was poor (Azoulay, Chevret, Leleu, Pochard, Barboteu, Adrie, et al., 2000). Without adequate understanding of the patient's condition and prognosis, how can a family endeavor to consider any complex issues? Sometimes the presence of a clinical social worker, chaplain, or clinical ethicist at the meetings can help clarify the information and provide the family with another set of ears and supports.

Negotiation of Care

Even when communication between the healthcare provider and the patient and family is perfect, questions surrounding the provision or withdrawal of artificial life support are problematic, and arise frequently. Issues related to respiratory support and CPR formulate the basis of many physician and patient/family meetings. The presence of a clinical social worker is crucial at such meetings, as input from this discipline can make the difference between implementing decisions based on the patient's wishes or upon family emotions or physician desires. The reason that input about the patient's value structure is so essential is that it is through understanding the patient's value structure and belief system, that self-determination can be assured. The preservation of autonomy is one of the two primary values that form the informed consent statute (see chapter 1).

The other primary value undergirding informed consent is the preservation of human dignity. Through advocacy for the rights of the patient, both principles can be upheld. Social workers are often placed in an advocacy role for the critically ill patient and the family. A clear understanding of the issues increases the ability of the clinical social worker to represent the patient's interests effectively. When questioned, ICU personnel are less willing to continue ventilator support than are patients and/or the general public (Sjokvist et al., 1999). However, it cannot be assumed that a patient shares the view of the physician regarding discontinuation of life-sustaining medical therapy. Sometimes an assumption is made as to when the quality of life is unacceptable without complete understanding of the patient's views prior to illness. It is not unusual for conflict to be present between patient caregivers, family members, and friends. In a study done by Abbott, Sago, Breen, Abernethy, and Tulsky (2001), 46% of all individuals who responded to a cross-sectional survey of family members of patients and who were asked to consider withdrawal or withholding of life-sustaining therapy stated that they perceived conflict among healthcare team members. The clinical ICU social worker, chaplain, and clinical medical ethicist are crucial to the resolution of such conflict.

In another study by Curtis, Patrick, Shannon, Treece, Engelberg, and Rubenfeld (2001), it was speculated that a formal family meeting could improve communication. According to these researchers, a decision to withhold or withdraw medical interventions is usually the result of detailed, complex, consistent conversations with patients and/or their families. It is unreasonable to assume that the attending physician or any one physician could achieve this degree of communication. It is erroneous to assume the physician is the most skilled person to gather important family data and effectively communicate in preparation for end-of-life decisions. This responsibility should be shared and members of the healthcare team should assemble information and formulate treatment options before meeting with the family. The clinical social worker, chaplain, or medical ethicist can help provide information and support the family regarding choices. The clinical social worker serves both as an advocate to preserve the silent patient's autonomy and human dignity as well as a negotiator for establishment of ethical consensus. In some situations where negotiation of care has failed, a medical ethicist may be called in to mediate. The ethicist may be asked to resolve a disagreement between the healthcare team and the family, among family members, and/or among healthcare team members.

Mediation

Since ancient times mediation has been used for conflict resolution (Dubler & Liebman, 2004). Mediation is a private and informal process by which a third person negotiates disagreement, seeks resolution, and derives solutions from parties while supporting everyone's autonomy, informed decision making, and confidentiality (Dubler & Liebman, 2004, p. 8–9). Mediation of healthcare conflicts embraces the same three principles while focusing on the two primary values of informed decision making: preservation of (the patient's) autonomy and preservation of (the patient's) human dignity. The types of conflict that occur at the end of life require that the mediator possess full authority from both parties (Goodman, 2001). Medical ethicists are frequently chosen to fill this role.

The ethicists responsibility is to learn the facts of the case from all sides: the medical record, the family, and the healthcare team. In situations when the dispute is among healthcare team members, the ethicist will explore the written record and ascertain the view of all parties before proceeding. The mediator may speak with all concerned before a formal meeting. Such interactions should be neutral and not suggest to any party that the mediator/ethicist has taken sides (Goodman, 2001; Dubler & Liebman, 2004). The job is to move the parties from position-based to interest-based thinking (Dubler & Liebman, 2004, p. 9). This is not an easy task since the opposing positions may come from strong emotions and history, which can be difficult to set aside for the sake of the patient as most people view their emotional connection as being in the interest of the patient.

It may be difficult for an ethics consultant to move in and out of the roles of mediator and consultant. However, the process is flexible and open and lends itself well to a positive result. Effective mediation keeps in mind the obligations of the family as well as the obligations of the healthcare team and the hospital. A successful mediation should include:

1. Access and assessment of the medical facts and decision history
2. Understanding of the nature of the dispute
3. Setting up the meeting (Dubler & Liebman, 2004; Beer & Stief, 1997).

The family meeting is critical to a positive outcome (see chapter 5).

IS WITHDRAWAL OF LIFE-SUSTAINING MEDICAL THERAPY EUTHANASIA?

The term *euthanasia* comes from the Greek and means *good death*. For decades, within medical ethics, euthanasia has been associated with the desire for a peaceful death. A critical delineation is drawn between active forms of euthanasia, where the intention is to cause death, and passive actions such as deferring intervention thus risking death (Ashley & O'Rourke, 1997). Recently, euthanasia has become more readily associated with active purposeful actions to seek death. It is essential to distinguish passive actions from active ones (Koenig, 1993). In this book, refusing life-sustaining treatment means to make choices where death is a risk but is not the intent of the decision. Here, euthanasia is defined as direct action in which death is the sole intent (Kelly, 1979).

Legally, all competent individuals have a right to refuse any medical treatment even if such a refusal might result in their death. Honoring such a request is based upon the principle of autonomy and the legal doctrine of informed consent, which supports this principle. As noted in chapter 1, the principle of autonomy gained force within medical ethics following the 1976 Karen Ann Quinlan case. The ensuing debate focused in part on the right of an individual to accept or reject medical treatment. In the lower court case, discussion of refusal of treatment centered around the State's interest in the preservation of life. Ironically, in the New Jersey Supreme Court hearing of the Quinlan case, the principle of autonomy, exercised within the right to privacy, was seen to take precedence over this State's interest. Respect for autonomy and broad application of the right to privacy became foremost in the final legal decision (Meisel, 1995; Pence, 1990). As a result of this case and others that followed, it is now understood that legally, within secular American society, every competent patient has the right to refuse any and all medical treatment, even if such refusal could result in death (Meisel, 1989).

However, the decision of whether to withhold or withdraw medical treatments often involves patients who are incapable of rendering informed consent or refusal. Under these circumstances the decision about limitation of treatment would be made between the physician and the surrogate decision-makers, normally the loved ones of the patient. The goal is to extend the right to self-determination of the formerly competent patient to the family so that the right of informed consent can be maintained. As a result of cases like Quinlan's, the law supports termination of life-sustaining treatment for patients considered hopelessly ill or vegetative (Emanuel, 1994). In such cases, the decision-makers would be asked to choose between actions that would passively allow the patient to die versus actions that will actively result in death.

From a legal point of view, Meisel (1995) makes clear that the law supports allowing dying but not actively causing death. A clear distinction exists between letting someone die naturally and performing an action that actively ends life. Meisel refers to this as the difference between actions and omissions. This distinction, including the intention of the actor, has been heatedly debated legally and theologically.

Despite the fact that the American legal system was established on separation of church and state, the law still considers the moral consequences of medical choices. This was certainly evident in the Quinlan case. The moral difficulties of individuals often mirror dilemmas of society, and we look to the legal structure for some measure of consensus on what constitutes a right or wrong action (Meisel, 1995).

Regarding the question of whether death can ever be sought, the law, so far, is clear. Meisel (1995, p. 450) outlined this very distinctly when he stated:

> Early in the development of the right to die issue, the courts made clear that 'passive euthanasia'—forgoing life-sustaining medical treatment described by such locutions as withholding treatment, withdrawing treatment, letting the patient die—would not ordinarily be the basis for the imposition of liability, either civil or criminal, assuming that appropriate standards and procedures are followed. However, the courts have drawn a bright line between 'passive' and 'active' means of ending life, generally refusing to legitimate the latter. Therefore, from a secular legal view, what is foremost is maintaining a clear distinction between letting someone die and performing an action which could be considered actively killing. For an action that is direct killing is clearly not sanctioned by the legal system.

Decision to Forgo Treatment

In part, the need for a clear definition of death has resulted from the rise in the number of patients in "persistent vegetative states" or permanent unconsciousness as a result of life-sustaining treatments that prolong life but do not cure. People in these states have permanently lost higher brain function and only the brain stem, responsible for breathing and digestion, works. If cared for properly and supported by medical nutrition, such patients can live quite a long time (Hite & Marshall, 1997). Long-term use of ventilators for patients with life-threatening medical problems may create situations where patients do not wish to prolong life as their suffering is extended as well. When cure of an illness is no longer possible and life-prolonging treatments are being used, decisions must be made on how long to continue to sustain the life. According to Hite and Marshall (1997), "The lifesaving technologies and treatments used to stave off death frequently result in a more agonizing end of life."

In deciding whether to begin a treatment or discontinue it, for example, whether to withhold artificial medical nutrition to someone in a persistent vegetative state, the principle of proportionality should be applied. This principle states that medical treatment is ethically required if the benefits are likely to be greater than the burdens (Jonsen, Siegler, & Winslade, 1998). This principle also applies if removal of treatment will result in death.

The principle of proportionality is closely aligned with the patient's preferences and self-determination. Patients should evaluate what burdens they are willing to accept in exchange for a quality of life that they can appreciate. Medical professionals must also determine the benefit-burden ratio in deciding which treatments to recommend. These decisions may be most difficult for surrogates, especially when the incapacitated patient has not previously discussed his/her wishes (Jonsen et al., 1998).

THE ROLE OF RELIGION AND CULTURE

Factors such as cultural norms, ethnic background, educational level, and religious faith often affect how choices are made at the end of life, just as they play a role in how an individual lives throughout life.

Religion, Faith, and Spirituality

Religious traditions and norms provide core belief structures and the foundation for consideration of difficult end-of-life decisions (Daaleman & VandeCreek, 2000). Faith is a generic term that covers what we believe or feel spiritually (Turner, 2001, pp. 592–593). Faith can encompass diverse beliefs and reflect a multitude of cultures. The degree and ways in which religion, spirituality, and faith interconnect is unique to each individual. Some patients may find no comfort in talking to the priest from their church about their spiritual concerns but may find comfort in speaking to the hospital chaplain; others can only discuss such issues with someone they know well. Spirituality and faith are closely tied to character and should not be left unexplored, especially if true autonomy is a goal. Dr. Harvey Chochinov eloquently stated that "Dignity is a state of the soul. . . . [It] is the sense of peace that passes all understanding" (2002, p. 2253). This is why exploration of the patient's faith is essential to the work of all clinicians who care for the dying. Human dignity is preserved not simply through pain and symptom control. It is comprised of many factors outside of physiology.

Hope and faith are closely linked for many. It is something that all healthcare providers should keep intact throughout the healing and dying process. For some, hope helps us to endure the trials of living and allows us a sense of purpose and meaning as we prepare for our death (Chochinov, 2002). The relation of hope to faith or spiritual belief is private and intimate and as such it may be difficult to define during a clinical interview. Unfortunately, faith and spirituality are frequently neglected in the hospital environment. There are many reasons, including the discomfort some clinicians experience in dealing with this topic. Yet spirituality and faith are critically important aspects of recovery from illness, as well as the acceptance of death.

Faith or spiritual concerns lie close to the surface, and individuals usually give hints during conversation with healthcare providers. Lo, Ruston, Kates, Arnold, Cohen, and Faber-Langendoen, in "Discussing Religious and Spiritual Issues at the End of Life" (2002), provide the most common statements by patients or family members alluding to spiritual or faith issues, such as "I trust that God will decide," "I am leaving this in the hands of God," "I wonder why God is doing this to me," and "We believe in miracles" (2002, pp. 749–750). These are not the only way to inform a listener of a spiritual quandary, but they are examples of what people may say during clinical interviews. Despite the clarity of the individual or family's wish to leave care or withdrawal issues in God's hands, some healthcare providers push for the patient or surrogate to consider a decision.

Pushing ahead with a decisive agenda can be detrimental to the clinical relationship, however, especially if the family is not ready to consider limitations or withdrawal of care. As with all treatment concerns, spiritual or faith-based worries must be addressed openly before moving forward to decision making. Questions that recognize the history, values, dreams, and wishes of the patient permit the true autonomy of the patient's belief system to evolve. Research has indicated that "Patients who believe that the physician has really understood them may no longer feel alone with their distress" (Suchman, Markakis, Beckman, & Frankel, 1997, pp. 677–678).

Taking a spiritual history should be part of the physician admission evaluation. According to Koenig, this inquiry should be based around four general questions, such as: Are your religious beliefs a source of comfort or stress to you? Are your religious beliefs in conflict with the medical care you are receiving or considering? Are there religious beliefs that might influence medical decisions (and how)? Is there a supportive faith community likely to check on and monitor your recovery? (2004, p. 1197). Despite these simple straightforward questions, rarely are these histories taken. Doctors report that they are uncomfortable addressing the subject of faith, despite the fact that they have no problem asking much more intimate questions related to one's sexual history, for example. Physicians also report that they feel such discussion is out of their area of expertise, or that they do not have time to have such complex discussions (Koenig, 2004, pp. 1197–98). This answer is given even in areas of the country where a strong majority of physicians do address such questions in an effort to provide holistic care.

Organized Religious Views

Not all religions view end-of-life issues in the same manner. Some faiths share similarities and views, but they also have distinctive differences in how death is approached and how decisions are to be made at the end of life.

Judaism. In Judaism sanctity of life is paramount. Life is of infinite value, with every second having the same value as every other. Judaism has different sects within it, namely, Reform, Conservative, and Orthodox. The sects do not differ on theological constructs but in the degree of observance to the letter of Jewish law, or the halacha (the way) (Clarfield, Gordon, Markwell, & Alibhai, 2003). Orthodox Judaism is the most observant of Jewish law, and frequently members of this sect seek the guidance of a rabbi to determine how the halacha should be interpreted in relation to specific medical choices.

Autonomy of the individual in Judaism holds value, but is weighed in conjunction with the law that governs the collective. Advance care planning in the Jewish faith varies proportionately in relation to the degree of observance to halachic law. For example, the Orthodox Jewish patient will follow the recommendations of the rabbi, who is charged with interpreting law. It is not uncommon for a rabbi to discuss the medical prognosis with physicians caring for the Orthodox patient and then render advice to the observant patient or family.

The Conservative Jewish patient would most likely balance choices related to end-of-life care with the rabbi's view of Jewish law before rendering any decisions. The Reform Jewish patient may or may not be aware of how such decisions have been made historically according to Jewish law and is not required to seek rabbinic guidance before making a choice about life-sustaining interventions. Despite possible differences in how choices are made at the end of life within the Jewish faith, all Jews share the religious belief that every second of life is as important as the previous second. Therefore, quality of life is not the essential factor when discussing care at the end of life. For Orthodox Jews the focus is on death when it is considered to be impending. A patient very close to dying, within 72 hours despite intervention, is *goses*, and nothing should interfere with the departure of the soul from the body. Terminally ill patients are *telefah* (death within several months to a year) and not required to undertake treatment that would induce suffering or pain at the end of life (Bleich, 1998; Rosner, 1991).

Within the Jewish faith a physician has a duty to heal those who seek care and a Jewish patient has an obligation to care for the body and to seek medical treatment when ill. Autonomy within Judaism has varied levels of importance, balanced with the adherence to Jewish law. The more observant the Jewish patient is to the halacha, the less importance is placed upon individual autonomy (Clarfield et al., 2003). Each sect does permit the execution of living wills. With more observant Jews (Orthodox and some Conservative), these documents usually name a rabbi as part of the decision-making process so that adherence to halacha can be assured (Bleich, 1998; Clarfield et al., 2003).

Catholicism. It is a duty in Catholicism to accept impending death and recognize the human condition and the need to return one's body to God, the ultimate steward (Ashley & O'Rourke, 1997). Neither the patient nor physician is obligated to extend life through the use of extraordinary treatment modalities when it is clear that a person is terminally or irreversibly ill, but is to seek out only ordinary treatment. Ordinary treatment is defined as "all medicines, treatments, and operations which offer a reasonable hope of benefit for the patient and which can be obtained or used without excessive expense, pain or burden; while extraordinary means are all medicine, treatments, and operations which cannot be used or obtained without expense, pain, or other burden" (Connery, 1980).

When considering circumstances under which death can be sought through withdrawal of life-sustaining treatment, an essential consideration is intent. The final result must be death from disease, not from the direct action of a person. This delineation of intentions and the determination of when death is imminent are important factors in most faiths practiced in the United States. Among Catholic moral theorists, the delineation of intentions is sometimes referred to as the rule of double effect euthanasia (Kelly, 1991). According to Kelly, the rule of double effect applies if the act is not intended to bring about death but to relieve pain or end suffering. The death would then be considered an indirect result and morally correct (Kelly, 1991, p. 9). The rule of double effect is widely referred to discussion of ethical dilemmas over withdrawal or withholding of life-sustaining therapy.

The Catholic patient, as the steward of the body, is obligated to seek medical treatment when ill and the physician is obligated to treat the patient. However, when a patient is terminally or irreversibly ill, the Church accepts the fact that life ends and the focus then becomes differentiating between provision of ordinary versus extraordinary treatment.

Islam. Muslims have reciprocity of rights and corresponding duties between them and everything around them. No right exists without duty (Clarfield et al., 2003). Healing comes from God and should be sought; physicians have an obligation to heal those who seek healing. As with Catholicism and Judaism, those who follow Islam believe in the sanctity of life. Each moment of life is as sacred as the preceding moment and as such quality of life holds little value.

The taking of life is forbidden except in rare circumstances. Despite the belief that life is sacred, Muslims recognize that all human life is limited and treatment that prolongs dying is not obligatory (Clarfield et al., 2003). As with Catholicism and Judaism, each Muslim is seen as a steward of the body and is required to accept medical treatment. Muslims and Orthodox Jews share similar beliefs regarding provision of artificial nutrition and hydration; namely, that food and water should be provided if it can extend life unless the provision of such would be detrimental to the patient or would hasten death in any fashion. Muslims are permitted to refuse intubation if aspiration or respiratory failure are part of the final stages of a terminal illness (Hasan, 1994).

Presbyterianism. The main belief structure of the Presbyterian faith emerged after the Protestant Reformation. The glory of God is viewed as the purpose and end of all human life. Salvation is seen to be as much God's plan as is creation and redemption. The faith holds a belief in one God who exists as three entities: Father, Son, and Holy Spirit. Salvation comes to the believer through the belief in the Lord Jesus Christ. Believers are witnesses to the faith and are to minister to other persons in Christ's name. No form of evil is able to separate the faithful from the love of God and resurrection of the body and everlasting life are part of the salvation, which comes to the faithful (Renard, 2001, pp. 152, 160; Bowker, 1997, p. 767; Johnson & McGee, 2003, pp. 170–178).

The Presbyterian and Reformed Church follow the teachings of the Old and New Testaments of the Bible, as well as theology and specific manuals of government that contain the guidelines of the church. The individual is not required to accept all that is affirmed in the doctrinal standards. In fact, there is strong and constant revision within the Presbyterian faith, thereby making the listing of the myriad of churches that have resulted from this division impossible (Renard, 2001, pp. 152, 160; Bowker, 1997, p. 767; Johnson & McGee, 2003, pp. 170–178).

Funeral services are a time when the gospel is reaffirmed with solemn joy for all present. The service is to be dignified and simple and should show the love and greatness of God as he strengthens and supports us as we grieve. Cremation is neither encouraged nor forbidden and there is nothing within the Presbyterian faith that forbids the donation of organs. It is not customary to have the body of the deceased viewed during the funeral service but occasionally before the service is started the casket is opened for those who wish to view the body. Following the funeral, friends and family are encouraged to visit the grieving family and to provide messages of hope, love, and support (Renard, 2001, pp. 152, 160; Bowker, 1997, p. 767; Johnson & McGee, 2003, pp. 170–178). Within the Presbyterian faith there is a strong belief in an afterlife, without that life being fully described or defined. The afterlife is defined for each individual by what has occurred in this life, an extension of the earthly life. The soul leaves the body and travels to God immediately, where it remains forever. The departed individual is felt to be beyond us; so much so, that prayers for the dead are not common. The concept of reincarnation is not part of the faith. The key to salvation is "saving faith." Saving faith is described as "receiving and resting upon Christ alone for justification, sanctification, and eternal life" (Renard, 2001, pp. 152, 160; Bowker, 1997, p. 767; Johnson & McGee, 2003, pp. 170–178).

Lutherans. The Lutheran faith is envisioned as an expression of Christianity and as part of one universal church rather than a separate church. Lutherans are followers of Martin Luther, an Augustinian monk. For a combination of religious and political reasons the Lutheran faith grew quickly (Renard, 2001; Bowker, 1997; Johnson & McGee, 2003, pp. 160-170). Lutherans believe that you cannot obtain salvation through mere beliefs and good works; the key factor upon which salvation rests is the grace of God. Individuals spend their life struggling between good and evil, and salvation from that struggle comes to us as a gift from God (Johnson & McGee, 2003, pp. 160-163).

The typical Lutheran funeral service consists of a processional, which starts what is referred to as the service of the world. The casket is opened for viewing at the entrance of the Church until the processional begins. The procession in to the church is led by the minister leading the service, followed by the assistant ministers, the pallbearers, and then finally by the bereaved. The casket is usually covered with a white cloth (a pall), which serves to remind us that we are all equal by avoiding the showing of expensive coffins. Prayers consist of scripture and other readings, along with specially chosen hymns. Communion can be part of the service, followed by a sermon. The sermon can include information or reference to the deceased but it is not intended as a eulogy as much as a message of hope and comfort. The service is usually concluded with the Commendation, a prayer that asks God to receive the deceased in mercy, "Father, into your hands I commend my spirit." Finally, the Committal is the part of the liturgy performed at the gravesite. Once the body is lowered into the ground, the bereaved throw handfuls of dirt onto the coffin, committing the deceased to their final resting place (Renard, 2001, pp. 152, 160; Bowker, 1997, p. 767; Johnson & McGee, 2003, pp. 170-178).

In the Lutheran faith there is some conflict between the resurrection of the body and the resurrection of the immortal soul. Following death, it is believed that some form of consciousness exists after the death of the body. Prayers for the dead are not common in the Lutheran faith. If there is a reference to those who have passed before us, it is usually a reference of remembrance, thanksgiving for life. Only those to whom God has extended Grace will receive salvation and are to be spared eternal punishment, saved from the fires of hell (Renard, 2001, pp. 152, 160; Bowker, 1997, p. 767; Johnson & McGee, 2003, pp. 170-178).

United Methodist Church. The Methodist Church had its beginning in the 18th century at Oxford University, under the leadership of

John and Charles Wesley. Jacob Albright led the growth of the Evangelical Association in 1816. Eventually, the German-speaking Evangelical United Brethren merged with the English-speaking Methodist Church to form the United Methodist Church. The beliefs of the church arc based upon God as the creator, Christ as savior and example, and the Holy Spirit as guide and the source of power (Warren, in Johnson & McGee, 2003, pp. 224–236).

The major Methodist stance is based upon arminianism, the belief that people possess free will that allows them to respond to God's grace (Warren, in Johnson & McGee, 2003, pp. 224–236). The stance was in opposition to the Calvinist view that contended that God pre-ordained some individuals for heaven, while others were relegated to hell.

The second emphasis of Wesleyan theology is that faith is experiential in nature. The third emphasis of the Methodist faith is that saved life is a gift from God. God not only forgives our sins but gives us power over sin. The fourth emphasis is the social dimension of Christian life, to serve within the society in which they live and worship (Warren, in Johnson & McGee, 2003, pp. 224–236; Renard, 2001).

Four sources are utilized to formulate the basis of Methodist Christianity: scriptures, tradition, experience, and reason. The Christian faith does not deny death; in fact, resurrection of the body forms the basis of Christian beliefs, and predisposes death. Death of the body and the subsequent resurrection are correlated with the concept of rebirth of the soul, with the acceptance of the faith.

The funeral service in the Methodist faith is said to be a corporate act of Christian worship, which is to he both comforting and confrontational. The service is an opportunity to have an awareness of one's love for the deceased as well as the love of one's friends and family and focuses upon Christ's victory over death and sin. The United Methodists commit the deceased body or ashes to the earth or the sea. The service is time to affirm one's faith, to focus upon the goodness of God, and to express gratitude and appreciation for life

United Methodists believe in life after death. This salvation comes through the grace of God, which was provided by Christ's death on the cross. Methodists are recurrently blessed through God's continued grace throughout life, and the consummation of God's love is realized in the Kingdom of God after death (Warren, in Johnson & McGee, 2003, pp. 224-236; Irish & Lundquist, 1993). Life is viewed positively in the Methodist faith, where individuals are viewed as unified in body and spirit.

Baptist. Within the United Slates there are 52 different practices of the Baptist faith. The faith is not based upon strict doctrine but on an intellectual, academic heritage formulated through the combination of scripture, hymnody, confessions of the faith, and historic Baptist theologies (Johnson & McGee, 2003, pp. 31-46; Galanti, 1991). Ironically, a great majority of the initial converts to the Baptist faithful were from rural parts of the country where death was very much part of the daily life of parishioners. Prior to baptism, death was seen as an enemy as well as a cure and a release from life's suffering. In the philosophical sense, death meant spiritual unbelief, which was overcome through the waters of baptism from which life comes. Baptism leads to a new way of life, making the baptized believer born again. This dual view considers death part of the phenomenon of the nature of sin as well as part of the life cycle (Johnson & McGee, 2003, pp. 31-46). Because there are so many different forms of Baptist practice, one must inquire locally as to the beliefs and customs surrounding the dying process as well as the post-death and funeral ritual, to be certain of how to provide support.

Hinduism. The Hindu faith is one of the world's oldest living traditions. Its sacred text, The Vedas, dates back 3,000 years. Historically, the faith was referred to as *Vaidika Dharma*, or the religion of the Vedas. It was the primary connecting religion of India, with 80% of the country's 2 billion inhabitants reporting they are of Hindu faith. However, the faith has now spread throughout the world. Hinduism has no prophet, no founder, and no specific dates of founding.

The Vedas is the most revered of a vast amount of sacred literature handed down to Hindus through the ages. Hinduism is an inclusive and pluralistic faith, which practices historic rituals alongside new ideas. It is a faith of diverse philosophy, and Hindus are free to accept all beliefs and practices of the faith, some, or none of them (Pearson, in Johnson & McGee, 1998, pp. 111-129).

Most Hindus affirm that there is one God, yet we find many forms and names of gods. These formed gods are mere aspects, examples, or symbols of the one formless, eternal God (Bowker, 1997, pp. 430–431; Pearson, in Johnson & McGee, 1998, pp. 111–129). True knowledge of God is possible through development of a special relationship with one of the deities. The chosen deity serves as the "face" or the reality of the one God. This God, whose "true essence is beyond human comprehension," is explained to the individual via the deity who teaches the will and teachings of the one God. Knowledge of God is gained through divine human teachers (Pearson, in Johnson & McGee, 1998, pp. 111–129).

As death approaches, friends and family of the dying patient gather at the bedside to listen to the dying words. The dying may give gifts to Brahmins and to those in need. Following death, the body is wrapped in a white, unbleached cotton cloth, placed on a bamboo bier covered with flowers, and cremated. Cremation usually takes place quickly; embalming is not normally practiced. Some Hindus in North America will have the body sent back to India for full funeral rites.

Death is inevitable and natural. It is not feared but viewed as a transition from one aspect of living to another. Religious life consists of measuring or placing order in one's life according to principles and practices that assure a better rebirth. Reincarnation is the belief that the soul is reborn after death into another physical form in this world (Pearson, in Johnson & McGee, 1998, pp. 111–129). Transmigration affirms physical rebirth after death and also affirms life before death through the concept of pre-existence. Each individual thinks and acts in a manner to best determine the social status and character of the next life (Pearson, in Johnson & McGee, 1998, pp. 111–129). Despite karma, there is the possibility that God's grace will intervene to save a devotee from rebirth. According to the Bhagavad Gita, "the eternal man cannot die," therefore death should not be feared nor should those we love fear our death. Our bodies do perish but our souls continue to endure (Pearson, in Johnson & McGee, 1998, pp. 111–129).

At the time of death, the *samskaras* (sacraments), or ceremonies aimed at purifying, refining, and sanctifying the body, are performed. The funeral rites are called the *antyeshti samskara* and they are complicated, historically requiring the assistance of funeral priests. Emphasis is placed upon ancestors and sacrifice, reincarnation, and the grace of God. Traditionally, these complex rites took an entire year. Today they are usually performed on the tenth day of grieving (Pearson, in Johnson & McGee, 1998, pp. 111-129). Among the rites are prescribed food items to nourish the family of the deceased.

Buddhism. Buddha, Siddhartha Gautama, was an ascetic who lived in India in the sixth century *B.C.* According to Buddha, life is unsatisfactory in its basic presentation. For life to be tolerable one needs to transcend this existence using the eightfold path. "Actions conditioned by a defiled mind full of greed, hatred, and delusion produce suffering and karma resulting in repeated rebirths in unsatisfactory worlds" (Irish & Lundquist, 1993, p. 126; Klein, in Johnson & McGee, 1998, pp. 47-61).A state of enlightenment and the attainment of nirvana are possible for the disciplined mind that seeks to have successfully understood the eightfold path.This path is comprised of the "right understanding, right thought, right speech, right action, right vocation, right effort, right mindfulness, and right concentration" (Irish & Lundquist, p. 127; Klein, in Johnson & McGee, 1998, pp. 47-61).This is not easily achieved, considering that the Buddha lived hundreds of rebirths. The Buddha's teachings on the eightfold path are recorded in the Pali Sutras and are one method by which one can attain nirvana. Other methods of spiritual enlightenment developed after Buddha's death, as in the Mahayana and Vajrayana traditions of Buddhism. One such method is faith in a savior like Amida Buddha, universal Buddha of light, through the work of that savior on your behalf. In Mahayana Buddhism, the saviors help those suffering when death is near; suffering is part of all rebirths. Even if you were born a god, eventually you are torn from that existence and sent to another less favorable rebirth.

Some Buddhists seek to increase good karma through enlightenment. Mahayanists seek ways to help others and gain liberation from the cyclical rebirthing, considered to be the highest goal (Klein, in Johnson & McGee, 1998, pp. 47-61).To achieve complete understanding of the impermanence of life is essential. Klein outlines three principles: the strong desire to leave, the attainment of compassionate insight, and nurturance of wisdom (in Johnson & McGee, 1998, p. 54).

The goal of Buddhist tradition is to attain a state of mind in which the eightfold path is understood and practiced. Part of this is understanding the fleeting nature of life. This need to understand impermanence is so strong that monks are often asked to meditate on the image of a corpse (Irish & Lundquist, 1993, pp. 126–129; Klein, in Johnson & McGee, 1998, pp. 47–61). The purpose of this meditation is to prepare mentally for death while living.

Ultimate truths are within the reach of any dedicated person willing to pay attention and to study. An unclear, anxious mind will effect karma and have a direct negative impact on the rebirthing process (Irish & Lundquist, 1993, pp. 126–129; Klein, in Johnson & McGee, 1998, pp. 47–61; Thurman, 1998). A dying person who is able to attain a calm and clear state of mind surrounding death will have a positive effect on the rebirthing process. Frequently, Buddhists will chant aloud at the bedside to draw evil processes from the dying. Creating a calm environment is important, to say that the patient's death was peaceful.

For Buddhists, there is no intrinsic self. This does not mean that the individual does not exist, but self-determination or autonomy is of no value in Buddhism. Individuals are believed to be comprised of a collection of karma, or lived lives. Conceptually, this is troublesome for some followers, while others take comfort in thinking that they will be reunited at some point with their loved ones (Irish & Lundquist, 1993, pp. 126–129; Klein, in Johnson & McGee, 1998, pp. 47–61; Bowker, 1997, pp. 175–176).

The Buddhist tradition outlines the process of dying by describing how the senses are lost, then the intellectual capacity, and finally breathing slows and stops (Klein, in Johnson & McGee, 1998, p. 55). Instruction in the dying process and the impermanence of life is an essential part of Buddhist training. The Tibetan Book of the Dead instructs and prepares the practicing Buddhist in the transition from life to death and from death to rebirth (Irish & Lundquist, 1993, pp. 126–129; Klein, in Johnson & McGee, 1998, pp. 47–61; Thurman, 1998).

As with most faiths, the family plans the funeral, making sure the body is treated with respect and care. Embalming is not necessary, by belief, since resurrection is not part of the tradition. Cremation and below-ground burial are common practices.

The departed is reborn immediately when the consciousness exits the body. In the Mahayana tradition, one can linger for up to 49 days before being reborn. There is only a mental body at this time, which has all five senses and is able to travel wherever one wishes until, in accordance with one's karma, the place of rebirth is chosen (Klein, in Johnson & McGee, 1998, pp. 47–61; Thurman, 1998).

Bahai faith. Bahai dates from 1892 when the Bab (the "gate"), a merchant named Mirza Ali Muhammad, announced that he was the promised Qa'im who was to prepare for the coming of "Him Whom God Shall Make Manifest." At first members of the Bahai faith were persecuted by Islamic clergy. Between 1853 and 1863 the faith grew in size and was known for its kindliness and honesty (Johnson & McGee, 2003, pp. 14–28). The bab only stayed with the followers for a brief period of time before announcing to all that he was "Him Whom God Shall Make Manifest." Baha'u'llah (the Bab) was exiled twice, the second time to the prison site of Akka, Palestine. He remained in contact with his followers and wrote The Most Holy Book, the book of Bahai laws and instruction (Johnson & McGee, 2003, pp. 14–28).

Bahai is not a sect but a faith that affirms the "oneness of God, the oneness of religion, and the oneness of mankind." Prophets serve as mirrors who reflect in their lives and teachings the reality of God's presence. The presence of successive prophets provides a divinely ordained, historically lived educational system. The belief is that all of the world's religions are one, revealed in stages through the work of these prophets (Johnson & McGee, 2003, pp. 14–28). The individual believer strives to put in physical and social form the spiritual principles of Baha'u'llah. One such teaching is the unity of mankind through the abolition of prejudice and poverty (Johnson & McGee, 2003, pp. 14–28).

Followers of the Bahai faith believe in the continuation of the soul beyond the passing of the physical form. The body cannot be moved further than one hour's journey from the place where death has taken place and must not be cremated (Johnson & McGee, 2003, pp. 14–28). The family and friends grieve for the loss of the relationship or connection they had with the one who has died, but they believe that a reunion will take place in the Kingdom of God.

Jehovah's Witnesses. This faith is based upon the belief that those who follow the word of God will rise to be seated with God at the time of Armageddon. Part of this direct word of God forbids the intake of blood. Many healthcare professionals struggle morally with the refusal of blood because it is viewed as such a routine part of care. But individuals faithful to Jehovah fear the loss of eternal life far more than the loss of physical life. As a result of medical professionals' discomfort with the refusal of blood, Jehovah's Witnesses have developed several mechanisms through which they can advocate for their religious beliefs. For example, most Jehovah's Witnesses have a detailed power of attorney and living will form completed specifically for their faith. These documents outline the belief patterns and the case law that supports their federal right of refusal. In addition to this document, the development of a hospital liaison service comprised of educated temple elders supports the patient and family and provides information on the faith for professional caretakers. The case of Mrs. Brown outlines some issues that arise in the care of Jehovah's Witness patients.

> Mrs. Brown is a 43-year-old female who was admitted to the hospital with fatigue and severe vaginal bleeding following a routine dilation and curettage (d & c). At the time of admission, blood was drawn and she was diagnosed with AML (acute myelogenous leukemia). Mrs. Brown was willing to undergo all necessary treatments to save her life—except the provision of blood and blood products.

Spirituality, faith, and religion are important practices for many. All of the larger organized faiths practiced in the United States have made statements describing what is required of their faithful as they approach the end of life, and this information is readily available. In addition, most hospitals have chaplains who provide spiritual guidance and support to the sick, and all efforts should be made to understand and respect the spiritual needs of patients. Recognition of and attention to the spiritual needs of patients is essential, due to the conflict that can occur when religious freedoms are ignored or disrespected, as in the example of Mrs. Farber.

Mrs. Farber was approached by her family doctor regarding inserting a feeding tube in her husband Seymour, who had stopped eating eight days earlier due to increasing nausea and vomiting. She brought him to the hospital in hope of having these symptoms lessened but he suffered a stroke while being treated. Prior to this, Seymour had been an active 94-year-old man despite a diagnosis of metastatic gastric cancer eight months before. The cancer had already spread to Mr. Farber's lungs and liver at the time of diagnosis. He agreed to undergo a colostomy to remove most of the cancer but refused chemotherapy and radiation out of a desire to "live life to the fullest."

The patient and his wife had three sons and six grandsons. Mr. Farber was a retired businessman and practicing Reform Jew who had executed a power of attorney for health care and a faith-based, detailed living will. These documents clearly described his wishes regarding the use of mechanical ventilation, resuscitation, and feeding tubes.

Mr. Farber had been very lethargic for a few days so the family's doctor, David Smith, chose to speak to his wife and power of attorney to recommend the feeding tube. "He and I spoke of this and I know he wouldn't want a feeding tube," Mrs. Farber replied. Dr. Smith voiced his willingness to respect Mr. Farber's wishes and suggested a referral to the inpatient hospice unit. Mrs. Farber agreed.

Later that day the hospital chaplain, an ordained Orthodox rabbi, spoke to Mrs. Farber and informed her that she was going against Jewish law by refusing to "feed" her husband. She telephoned her sons and they contacted the hospital medical ethicist and the clinical social worker requesting support for their parents' wishes.

The placement of a feeding tube goes against the value structure of Mr. and Mrs. Farber and not placing it goes against the value structure of the Orthodox rabbi. All professionals will have our own spiritual beliefs, faith, cultural norms, and moral value structures and we may find ourselves at times in conflict with the views of patients and families assigned to our care. When such conflict occurs, the values of the patient and family must be respected, for they take precedence over ours. The option of removing oneself from a case for moral reasons is always present for every individual employed in a healthcare environment. Another approach is to meet with the hospital chaplain, social worker, or clinical ethicist to gain insight into the belief structure of the patient and family.

Culture

Individuals are born into their race, gender, and culture, which in part define their personality and the tenets of their personal value structure. During stressful times, individual character and values are tested. Understanding these aspects of character, customs, and value structure is crucial to the provision of respectful care. For example, in the care of a Native American, a nurse could misunderstand lack of eye contact and silence as rudeness or lack of respect. However, in that culture one does not interrupt another who is speaking and the eyes are viewed as the window of the soul; many Native Americans will not disturb the spirit of others by looking them in the eyes when spoken to (Galanti, 1991). This example illustrates how customs of respect in one culture may be misunderstood unless efforts are made to become familiar with the cultural norms of the other.

Americans may be divided into four major ethnic groups: European, African, Asian, and Hispanic Americans. Information on these cultures in this book is not exhaustive, and the reader may wish to explore more deeply how numerous cultures confront the common issue of death.

African Americans. Members of this ethnic group may not respond the same way to serious illness and death as, for example, Caucasians. Each person is exposed to an individual experience of faith, family norms, social norms, and cultural response of the family and neighborhood. African Americans may belong to diverse faiths, come from various geographic regions, and have differing economic and educational levels; therefore, no comprehensive statements can be made as to how individuals in this culture would choose to die and mourn. Even for communities where violence is common, texts rarely mention culture-specific death and dying rituals (Kalish & Reynolds, 1981, p. 95).

Hosea L. Perry conducted a study of hundreds of people in Alabama, Florida, Georgia, and Kentucky. They came from all economic classes and were comprised of African-American ministers, priests, and funeral directors. Death is celebrated here, testament to a life that has been lived and that "the earthly journey has been completed" (Perry, in Irish & Lundquist, 1993, p. 54). However, this does not mean that the deceased is not mourned. Funerals may include strongly expressed emotions, almost as if the degree of grief directly measures the love felt for the deceased during life. All who have witnessed the life are expected, and in many ways obligated, to attend the funeral to express out loud and emotionally their feelings for the person. (Perry, in Irish & Lundquist, 1993, pp. 51–65; Kalish & Reynolds, 1981, pp. 95–98).

The reason for this overt demonstration of emotion so frequently present at African-American funerals is attributed to the fact that, following the Nat Turner revolt prior to the Civil War, black funerals were not permitted to be held during the day and were to be conducted in a white-dictated fashion. As a result blacks created mechanisms for expressing grief through African and Southern traditions, combined with individual faith rituals. In populous areas, the custom of night funerals permitted friends from other plantations and farms to attend. The funeral instilled the sense of combined community. Overt grief was not only for the one who just died, but for all who died under slavery. Communal grief created closeness and numerous cultural death practices from Africa, Angola, and local communities were enacted. Some of these funeral customs carry on to the present day, like throwing dirt on the grave, which is traced to Africa, and decoration of graves with broken earthenware, which is from Angola (Perry, in Irish & Lundquist, 1993, p. 56).

African Americans embrace those who grieve from the moment news has spread that death has occurred. Family members, friends, and "sisters" from the church bring food and help care for younger children. Some may be assigned to walk with the family as they go to view the deceased, or serve as "nurses" if mourners are overcome with emotion. The willingness of the community to allow mourners to let their grief out can be viewed as an effective mechanism to avoid the pathological grief reaction experienced by those who keep grief inside (Johnson & McGee, 1998, pp. 31–64; Perry, in Irish & Lundquist, 1993, p. 54; Galanti, 1991).

The past 50 years has shown a trend toward more stoic expression at public funerals and there has been a concurrent move toward less overt emotional expression at African-American funerals. The funerals of President Kennedy, Bobby Kennedy, and Martin Luther King demonstrated this more stoic style of expression. The media publicly rewarded the emotional control demonstrated by the families without exploring how holding in such profound emotion might affect them. This unemotional reaction to death has mistakenly come to be connected with high economic status and education and is emulated partially for these reasons (Johnson & McGee, 1998, pp. 31–46; Perry, in Irish & Lundquist, 1993, p. 54; Galanti, 1991).

Just as there is no single standard through which one can describe an African-American reaction to death, there is no one standard through which African Americans make end-of-life choices. It has been suggested that these patients, compared to other racial groups, frequently request more life-sustaining treatment at the end of life, based upon numerous research studies. However, the reasons offered are sometimes narrow and stereotyped. For example, in one study, it was stated that African-American patients and their families request more life-sustaining interventions due to their mistrust of the white medical community as a result of past discrimination. This may in fact be a reason why some individuals would make such a request, but as a population, African Americans will have diverse reasons why they may want life-sustaining interventions maintained when the healthcare team recommends a different course of care. These other reasons can include religious beliefs, a strong sense of family, or a notion that quantity of life is linked with survival.

These are some of the values held by some African Americans, but will not apply to everyone (Crawley, Payne, Bolden, Payne, Washington, & Williams, 2000). Healthcare providers should learn about the diverse desires of the multicultural environment in which they work and continue to read, observe, and ask questions. In this way insight may be gained regarding nuances of various cultures, people, history, traditions, and beliefs.

Hispanic Americans. In general, in the Hispanic community death is expected and is to be confronted directly. At times it is welcomed; at other times, feared. Death has always been a conscious presence in all aspects of Hispanic society. During October and November, a traditional celebration combines All Saints' Day and the pre-Columbian Day of the Dead. This three-day celebration stretches from Halloween on October 31 through All Saints' Day on November 1, and ends on November 2, which is All Souls' Day. The prominence of the celebration makes it impossible to avoid the concept of death. "The people of this region of the New World were very familiar with the concept of death and faced it in a dramatic and visually violent way," viewing public displays of human skulls, blood, and the exhibition of dead victims' bodies (Younoszai, in Irish & Lundquist, 1993, pp. 71-72).

Hispanic families tend to be strongly devoted to each other and when one member is ill, it is not unusual for the entire family to congregate at the hospital. When death occurs, the family unites to talk around the casket and about the deceased, recalling events and special memories. Death is not a foreign concept to the Hispanic community and funeral attendance is considered by many to be mandatory. Such a requirement may not be said aloud within the family, but will be a silent command, known at the core of any family member. At the time of death, funeral arrangements are made as quickly as possible, a custom from a time when deaths occurred in rural communities and a prompt burial was desired because the body was historically displayed at home atop a bed of herbs and candles.

During the funeral, an openly emotional response is expected; restrained emotion can signify a lack of caring. There is usually a complete service at the gravesite, with mourners throwing handfuls of dirt on top of the casket, culminating with the men filling in the grave. From a young age, children are socialized in how to behave at funerals as all members of the family group are expected to attend.

Family devotion is demonstrated through procreation and respect to elders. Children are taught to keep family business private and to respect their parents and grandparents (Younoszai, in Irish & Lundquist, 1993, pp. 71-72). To do otherwise is disrespectful of the community at large. The Hispanic community also tends to hold a strong devotion to God. Most Hispanics are strict Catholics and combine their faith with norms of the local community where the family lives. Most Hispanics would not consider withdrawing medial care from a loved one.

According to Caralis, Davis, Wright, and Marcial, Hispanic patients would want their doctors to keep them alive despite how ill they may be, even if it requires use of life-prolonging interventions (1993, pp. 158-159). When asked what to do if a Hispanic patient entered a persistently vegetative state, the patient was most likely to entrust proper decision making to the family (Caralis et al., 1993, pp. 155-165).

For other critical treatments, Hispanic patients might defer to the physician's judgement. They were not likely to have completed an advance medical directive but if one was completed it was due to a higher degree of education and the degree of acculturation to American culture (Murphy, Palmer, Azen, Frank, Michel, & Blackhall, 1996, pp. 108-117). Statistically, members of this population are more likely to choose full ICU care, including intubation (the use of breathing machines), cardiopulmonary resuscitation, and dialysis, generally believing that limiting therapy is a decision for a doctor to make, and that the timing of death is a decision for God.

Asian Americans. Asian cultures typically honor respect, dignity, and self-esteem. It is likely that an Asian patient would respond Yes to a question related to understanding medical information provided by the physician. To admit to a lack of understanding might result in a loss of face for the patient as well as for the doctor. It is considered disrespectful to look someone in authority in the eye and a Western physician or nurse might associate such lack of eye contact with a lack of understanding (Galanti, 1991, p. 16). These examples of cultural mores might easily lead a Western healthcare provider to the wrong conclusion about how to best treat the patient.

The Asian family is often hierarchical in nature. The men tend to live with their family of origin and their obligation remains there. This is in contrast to Western culture, where the family of marriage becomes the family of priority. In Asian cultures, sons are considered superior to daughters, parents to children, teachers to students, and doctors to nurses (Galanti, 1991, pp. 16-17). The healthcare team may be compromised by the power differentials between patients and their families.

A clear discussion about the level of information the patient might desire is one way the physician and members of the healthcare team can clarify the patient's autonomy and respect his/her cultural norms. In Asian society the family, rather than the patient, is informed of the diagnosis. The family (usually the oldest child and preferably the son) then becomes the decision maker and it is not discussed with the patient. The patient may come to know that the medical condition is serious but is never required to admit to illness or weakness, thereby upholding the family's control (Crawley, Marshall, Lo, & Koenig, 2002, p. 675).

When an Asian family member is ill, care is designed around the gender of the patient. For example, if the ill family member is a woman, historically the Asian physician would never touch the female patient. The patient would use a doll to illustrate exactly what part of her body is affected by illness. Modesty is valued in both Asian and Hispanic cultures especially the area below the waist (Galanti, 1991, pp. 57–61). If the ill family member is a male, it is the custom for the man to be fussed over by the family, to the point of providing total care. Such care is a demonstration of the degree to which the male family member is loved and respected. Within these cultures, the male is in control in a male-dominated society. Having people wait on the male patient hand and foot demonstrates his dominance and allows the ill patient to once again feel in control (Galanti, 1991, pp. 57–61; Irish & Lundquist, 1993, pp. 79–100; Johnson & McGee, 1998, pp. 47–61).

Asian Americans are the least likely of the three ethnic groups discussed here to be aware of advance care planning. The reason behind a lack of knowledge is that it is believed that bad news should not be discussed with the patient; such information and talk of death and dying could bring harm. It is also felt that the responsibility for care planning is best handled by the family (Murphy et al., 1996, pp. 108–117).

There is no one standard way to care for patients from all the different cultures of the world, as some practitioners might hope. It sometimes seems as if one's culture is merely to be tolerated or overcome to provide Western patient care (Hern et al., 1998, pp. 27–39). In reality, the patient's culture is to be respected and embraced. In one case a patient may wish to defer his/her autonomy to a trusted family member, while another may be more independent and make choices consistent with a combination of their culture of origin and Western influence (Hern et al., 1998, pp. 27–39). It is most beneficial to take each case on its own merits, embracing cultural uniqueness, rather than search for some way to look past the separate traditions of each culture to design a catchall, Western-based treatment plan. In any culture, tradition, faith, and family are valued, and embracing these traits helps to define the best way of dying for the patient.

The negotiation of care requires consideration of the multitude of factors that define us as individuals, such as our values, principles, culture, and faith. Determining the best end-of-life goals is almost always traumatic for the patient, family, and healthcare providers. It can be a heartbreaking experience. An example of the degree of pain is represented on Nancy Cruzan's grave marker (in Hite & Marshall, 1997, p. 130), which reads:

> **NANCY CRUZAN**
> **MOST LOVED**
> **DAUGHTER—SISTER—AUNT**
> **Born, July 20, 1957**
> **Departed, Jan 11, 1983**
> **At Peace, Dec 26, 1990**

A terrible footnote to the case of Nancy Cruzan is that on August 17, 1996, following the death of his daughter, Joseph Cruzan hanged himself in the carport of his home. His family speculated that the pain of her illness and the challenges of the court fight were too much for him (Colby, 2002).

Medical Futility

The goal of medicine is to heal, restore, "to make whole," or provide a benefit to patients. This does not include offering treatments that do not produce benefits (Schneiderman, Jecker, & Jonsen, 1996). The concept of futility of a medical treatment is not new, and withdrawal of a life-sustaining treatment is part of this conversation. Medical futility is described as "any effort to provide a benefit to a patient that is highly likely to fail and which, except in rare instances, cannot be systematically produced" (Schneiderman et al., 1996, p. 8). A futile action is one that "cannot achieve the goals of the action, no matter how often repeated" (Schneiderman, Jecker, & Jonsen, 1990, p. 10). Futility has been defined by Pellegrino (2000) as a relationship among the effectiveness, benefits, and burdens of treatment. Effectiveness refers to the ability of the treatment to produce a change in the course of the disease. This judgment is made by the clinician/physician on the case. A clinical judgment that a medical intervention is futile provides a sound basis for recommending to decline intervention (Jonsen et al., 1998). Perceived benefits of treatment are to be determined solely by patients and refer to the patients' conception of what the results could mean to them.

Burdens are objective and subjective in nature, and involve consideration of the cost, pain, discomfort, and/or inconvenience of the procedure and the patient's assessment of quality of life. Costs may be financial or not, and patients and physicians may determine them together (Pellegrino, 2000). Other criteria to consider include the patient's age, quality of life, and economics. However, "physicians may not unilaterally decide the quality of another person's life, use age as a sole criterion, or invoke economics without reference to the question of futility" (Pellegrino, 2000, p. 1067).

Medical futility, defined as the use of interventions that will fail to restore patients to health and function, may be the primary consideration in cases where a patient's death is imminent, or the patient is terminally ill or "hopelessly ill" in that the disease will progress until death no matter what interventions are delivered (Jonsen et al., 1998). Any of these situations may result in a decision to forgo life-sustaining treatments.

EUTHANASIA VERSUS PHYSICIAN-ASSISTED SUICIDE

Euthanasia and physician-assisted suicide are profound issues in healthcare ethics because they involve the intentional death of very ill patients, and the relationship between the patient and the physician, who may provide the means for death to occur (Deveterre, 2000). Family members, friends, social workers, nurses, or other health professionals may be involved in discussion of the issues, the decision-making process, the actual incidence of the death, and the bereavement period that follows. These practices are weighed in light of potentially life-sustaining medical advances, media attention, and public support or censure.

Whether one opts for *active euthanasia* or *physician-assisted suicide (PAS)*, the intention is to hasten or cause the death of a competent person who has consented to the act. The distinction lies in who administers of the means of death. Euthanasia involves the physician administering a lethal dose of medication, causing immediate death. In PAS the physician prescribes medication and provides instruction to the patient on how to self-administer the lethal dose (Asch, 1996; Cohen, Fihn, Boyko, Jonsen, & Wood, 1994; Emanuel, 1994). *Passive euthanasia* means withholding or withdrawing life-sustaining treatment, and is the only consistently legally sanctioned measure, which can be enacted via an individual's advance directive or by decision of a surrogate decision-maker.

Whether one is for or against euthanasia and physician-assisted suicide, the issues are likely to produce strong emotional responses and moral arguments. Those in favor of allowing euthanasia and PAS appeal mainly to the concept of patient self-determination and individual rights. The idea that people should choose for themselves how they want to live and die is one that few can easily dispute. The right to refuse medical treatment is widely recognized and accepted in health care today, including in end-of-life care situations. It is argued that if individuals have a right to decide what constitutes a good life and to end life when the level of suffering is not consistent with their view of a good life (Emanuel, 1994), then euthanasia and assisted suicide are not ethically different from honoring advance directives in withdrawing life-sustaining medical care. These practices are thought to be compassionate and offer dignity to people suffering from intolerable pain who should be free to choose when, how, and why they live or die (Hite & Marshall, 1997). A third argument in support of euthanasia and assisted suicide is that these options lie along an evolving continuum of normal medical practice that accepts that death is not an enemy or a failure by the physician; instead, death is welcomed and happens consciously. For proponents, little difference exists between withdrawal of treatment and a deliberate lethal overdose of medication. Mercy killing is seen as an extension of normal care for patients suffering and beyond cure (Deveterre, 2000).

The strongest opposition to euthanasia and PAS centers around the Hippocratic Oath of physicians to do no harm, which may be interpreted as prohibiting prescription of lethal medication. Moral and religious arguments are based on the belief that intentional killing of innocent people is always wrong. Allowing euthanasia or assisted suicide under the right of self-determination is disputed based on the fact that even though a person "may think that the killing is good, and freely choose it . . . that is not enough. Ethical reasoning must show that the killing will be truly good, or the less worse, for those engaging in it" (Deveterre, 2000, p. 439).

Regarding the relief of suffering argument, many opponents believe that if appropriate pain management and palliative care is made available then there should be no need to hasten death (Hite & Marshall, 1997).The notion of the "slippery slope" also receives much attention in literature against legalization of euthanasia or assisted suicide. The term refers to a belief that allowing PAS could lead to coercion to choose the option. Part of this argument is that it would undermine the patient-physician relationship; physicians have tremendous power and do in fact have the ability to cause death (Hite & Marshall, 1997; Miller & Brody, 1995). The idea of the action being voluntary is called into question, as the more patients suffer, the more likely they are clinically depressed or under the influence of medications that may cloud their judgment (Deveterre, 2000).Thus, vulnerable and disenfranchised populations such as the elderly or persons with AIDS (not diagnosed as terminal) may not genuinely have free choice (D'Oronzio, 1997; Emanuel, 1994; Hite & Marshall, 1997; Kamisar, 1993; Koenig, 1993).

Even those who support PAS acknowledge that safeguards may be necessary.These might include psychological/psychiatric consultation to ensure that treatable depression does not exist and the individual is of sound mind; second opinions on diagnoses; agreement of two physicians on the decision; checks to make sure that individuals are fully informed; that physicians prescribing the lethal medication have an established relationship with the patient; and that all available alternatives to hastening death have been fully explored (Cohen et al., 1994; Csikai & Bass, 2000).

Another safeguard is the limitation of PAS to terminally ill patients only. The public is well aware, through the media, of the suicides assisted by Dr. Jack Kevorkian, many of whom were not terminal but suffered from chronic debilitating illnesses such as ALS or multiple sclerosis. Restriction of PAS to the terminally ill only is controversial even to those who support PAS.

Legislative Efforts and Support for Euthanasia and Physician-Assisted Suicide

No state has yet legalized the practice of voluntary active euthanasia. Currently, the only state to have legalized physician-assisted suicide is Oregon. The Oregon Death with Dignity Act was originally passed in 1994 but was not implemented at that time, pending the outcome of legal challenges, including in the U.S. Supreme Court. In 1997, the High Court upheld the constitutionality of two states' laws, New York and Washington, banning the practice of physician-assisted suicide. The ruling, however, kept the rights within each state as to legislation regarding this issue, so the debate continues. Some opponents of legalizing euthanasia and assisted suicide believe that it could possibly undermine the delicate balance between the law and medical decisions to forgo life-sustaining treatments. At this time there is an understanding by the courts of a clear line between choosing to withdraw certain treatments and use of lethal medications to end life. If the law were to be expanded to include the ability to intentionally end life, it would likely be intensely scrutinized in the courts first and would call into question all actions that could cause or hasten death (Deveterre, 2000).

At least 37 states have criminalized the act of assisted suicide through legislation. Several states continue active debate, such as California, Hawaii, and Maryland. In November 1998, Michigan voters rejected a ballot measure to legalize assisted suicide. Efforts to push legalization in Michigan appear to have lost some strength with the conviction and incarceration (in March 1999) of Dr. Jack Kevorkian, a catalyst for the issue, after he performed an act of euthanasia that was videotaped and televised nationally on a segment of *60 Minutes*. Prior to conviction, Dr. Kevorkian assisted in over 100 deaths.

Whether there is agreement with Dr. Kevorkian's actions or not, the controversy over PAS will likely continue, as public favor continues to grow. In one study, 57% of Americans polled believed that PAS should be allowed (Mauro, 1997). Additionally, over the past few years public opinion polls have found 52% and 69% in favor of assisted suicide and as many as 79% supported the Oregon law. In a 1998 study of 1,000 adults conducted on behalf of the organization Compassion in

Dying, regarding legislation of issues related to assisted death, many responses were favorable toward legalization of physician-assisted suicide and the notion that Congress should not be involved in regulating lethal drugs that could be prescribed by physicians. Further, 74% agreed with the statement, "People in the final stages of a terminal illness who are suffering and in pain should have the right to get help from their doctor to end their life if they so choose."

Even though there is fairly widespread disapproval of PAS by various professional associations/organizations, including the American Medical Association (AMA), the American Nurses Association (ANA), and the National Hospice and Palliative Care Organization (NHPCO), multiple studies have reported professional support for physician-assisted suicide (Asch, 1996; Back, Wallace, Starks, & Pearlman, 1996; Cohen et al., 1995; Csikai & Sales, 1998). In a study of Washington physicians, a majority thought that PAS was ethical in some circumstances and that the practice should be legalized (Cohen et al., 1994). Several studies have reported that physicians would consider PAS for the terminally ill (Bachman, Alcser, Doukas, Lichtenstein, Corning, & Brody, 1996; Cohen et al., 1994; Lee, Nelson, Tilden, Ganzini, Schmidt, & Tolle, 1996). In fact, physicians in Washington had further indicated that they had provided lethal prescriptions to 24% of patients who requested it (Back et al., 1996). Seventeen percent of critical care nurses in one study reported that they had received requests to perform assisted suicide and 16% of these nurses had engaged in the practice during their career (Asch, 1996). In a study of 122 hospital social workers, 22% reported encountering requests to discuss assisted suicide with patients. Situations where social workers thought that euthanasia and assisted suicide may be appropriate included when a patient's pain is beyond control, when a patient has a poor quality of life despite adequate pain control, and when an ill patient has a poor quality of life yet a life expectancy that may extend for several years (Csikai & Sales, 1998).

Oregon's Death with Dignity Act

In 1997, a measure to repeal the Death with Dignity Act went before Oregon voters and was defeated, thereby clearly the final hurdle for implementation of the act (Miller, Fins, & Snyder, 2000). Guidelines for the Oregon act are extensive. A terminally ill individual (prognosis of 6 months or less) may request PAS from a physician, and a second physician must confirm the diagnosis and prognosis. A 15-day waiting period from the initial oral request begins, which must be followed by a written request and a second oral request, then a prescription for lethal medication may be given (usually barbiturates taken by mouth). Mental health consultation is not required, but can be requested by either physician. Family is not required to be notified (Miller et al., 2000). Responsibilities of the various healthcare professionals that may be involved are outlined in the act.

Oregon's Death with Dignity Act (DWD) has continued to be challenged in the court system. The barbiturates that are most frequently prescribed for use in Oregon were interpreted as controlled substances by U.S. Attorney General John Ashcroft, who issued a ruling on November 6, 2001, prohibiting their use under the act. The state of Oregon challenged the ruling, and on April 17, 2002, the U.S. District Court upheld the Death with Dignity Act, allowing the use of the medications. Ashcroft sent an appeal to the U.S. Supreme Court on his last day in office in 2004; *Oregon v. Gonzalez* is scheduled to be heard sometime in the fall of 2005. The question is whether the law violated the current federal controlled substances act. Many believe the controlled substances act was intended to control illegal drug traffic and not to control individual prescriptions written by physicians. The opposition to Oregon's law and to physician-assisted suicide by the Bush administration is clear in this challenge, although no abuse of the law is evident.

In the seven years that DWD has been in effect, 208 patients have used it to take their lives, and 326 prescriptions have been written. This accounts for about one-eighth of one percent of the total number of deaths in Oregon during that time. Most patients who used the law had a cancer diagnosis or ALS. These individuals tended to be younger, more educated, and were less likely to be married than others who die from these diagnoses in general. Most (86%) were enrolled in a hospice program at the time they decided to use the law (all were encouraged to enroll). Major reasons given for choosing to use the law to die were loss of autonomy, loss of dignity, and loss of the ability to enjoy life (Oregon Department of Human Services, 2004).

Fewer than one-third of all persons who ingested the lethal medications sought mental health consultations. Because social workers are not sanctioned within the act to be providers, psychiatrists are most often the providers of choice.

The National Association of Social Workers (NASW, 2000) addressed the responsibilities of social workers in assisting individuals with end-of-life decisions in the policy statement "Client Self-Determination in End-of-Life Decisions." The NASW position regarding the practice of assisted suicide is minimally addressed in this statement. According to the policy, social workers are free to choose whether to participate or not in discussions of assisted suicide with respect to their own beliefs and values. The professional obligation exists that if a social worker is unwilling to discuss such issues, the individual should be referred to a competent colleague. Where assisted suicide is illegal, it is not appropriate for social workers to "deliver, supply, or personally participate in the commission of an act of assisted suicide when acting in their professional role." Where legal, social workers may be present during the act if requested by the patient. The *NASW Standards for Social Work Practice in Palliative and End of Life Care* (2004) provides similar general guidelines regarding social work involvement in situations of physician-assisted suicide. In addition, the standards state that NASW does not take a stance on the morality of end-of-life decisions but affirms individuals' rights to determine the most appropriate level of care (NASW, 2004).

Given that this practice is legal in Oregon and has been coming up on state ballots and for discussion in legislatures in several states over the past few years, social workers must be prepared to address the issues. This includes assessing their own personal values, being prepared for discussions with patients and families about the practice, and educating other healthcare professionals and the community about the available range of palliative and end-of-life care options.

Chapter Conclusion

Many of the issues presented in this chapter may be encountered in other fields of social work practice with clients who are ill or have family members with life-limiting illnesses. Social workers must have a solid understanding of these issues to effectively assist in deliberations of treatment options and decision making about end-of-life care that is consistent with optimal quality of life.

Chapter 3

ADVANCE CARE PLANNING

An essential precursor to making decisions about end-of-life care is effective communication. However, death continues to be a taboo topic for social conversation. Such talk is fraught with stigma, complex memory, and specific fears. As a result, the initiation of end-of-life planning can be slow at best. Some fear a direct connection between talk and action, as if mere conversation about death will cause it to happen, even if it is not remotely imminent. Yet no credible evidence exists that open, honest, and thoughtful communication about dying has detrimental effects on either patients or families (Corr, 1998).

Advance care planning (ACP) is a broad term used to encompass discussions about how someone wishes to be cared for at the end of life. Through such discussion, individuals can make plans that will shape how decisions should be made about their health care in the event they become "decisionally incapacitated" (Fischer, Arnold, & Tulsky, 2000). Open discussion with family, significant others, and medical personnel is key to understanding what quality of life means to each individual and how these values might be played out at the end of life. Advance care planning can help us prepare for death, and ensure that death will take place in a manner that is consistent with the values by which we have lived our lives. The conversation itself may enhance a family's sense of control and social well-being and reduce stress in a critical situation because of the increased communication between the patient and family members. This sounds like a simple concept, but in reality advance care planning in health care has been difficult to implement.

During these discussions, decisions can be made about desirable and acceptable types of end-of-life care. These decisions should be put in writing using advance directive forms, and shared with others, including family physicians. If no written directive is completed, any discussion, referred to as an oral directive, still must be respected by medical professionals when people become incapacitated and are not able to speak for themselves (see chapter 5). Some of the most ethically challenging situations faced by social workers in healthcare settings are when no discussion regarding treatment preferences at the end of life has occurred between patients and families or between patients and their physicians (Csikai & Bass, 2000).

In this chapter, different formats for advance directives are defined, along with the policies that support their use. Then, communication in advance care planning will be examined, including types of discussions that are important and necessary. A proposed continuum of discussions between individuals, families, and healthcare professionals at varying points in the trajectory of chronic or terminal illness is presented. Social workers have an important role in ensuring that these discussions take place and empowering individuals to make their wishes known, when culturally appropriate, to their families and healthcare providers.

ADVANCE DIRECTIVES

Only within the last three decades has a concern arisen regarding protecting individuals' rights in end-of-life care situations, as medical advances have created conditions whereby patients may be artificially kept alive almost indefinitely. Mechanisms were created that allow individuals, while still competent, to express future treatment preferences for terminal or "hopeless" medical situations. Documents known as advance directives are accepted as one way to meet this need and have been widely sanctioned under federal and state law, beginning with the California Natural Death Act in 1976. The hope was that unwanted medical interventions at the end of life could be avoided if we could identify these in advance.

Federal and State Policies on Advance Directives

A federal policy known as the Patient Self-Determination Act (PSDA) became effective December 1, 1991. The act was aimed at promoting the use of advance directives. According to Ulrich (1994), this new law gave recognition to the pluralistic and democratic ideals of the United States and secured our right to choose how to live our lives and how to die.

The PSDA requires that all persons who utilize healthcare services paid for by Medicare and Medicaid, such as hospitals, nursing homes, and in-home health care, be asked if they have an existing advance directive. When one is produced, it becomes part of the medical chart and record. Patients must be informed of their right to formulate an advance directive if they do not have one. Education is provided one on one and to the community about what advance directives are and how to go about formulating one.

Most institutions responded to the law by developing pamphlets to be handed out upon admission and further questions were directed to social services or clergy. The PSDA also required that the Department of Health Human Services conduct a national campaign to inform the public about advance directives (Sugarman, Powe, Brillantes, & Smith, 1993). The assumption was that if individuals have sufficient information, they will complete the forms (La Puma, Orentlicher, & Moss, 1991).

Shortly after passage of the PSDA, potential benefits were thought to be many. Intangible benefits included increased autonomy through the expression of medical preferences, decreased suffering as undesired treatments would not be imposed, and emotional comfort due to a perception it meant not becoming a burden to family or loved ones financially or emotionally. For healthcare workers, one expected benefit was that patients would have considered some difficult situations already, and have specified desired care in the advance directive. The Patient Self-Determination Act was an attempt to educate people and increase use of the documents. However, though the concept has been acknowledged as a great way to ensure that future wishes will be followed, evidence suggests that usage rates are as low as 4 to 15% (Cantor, 1998; High, 1993; VandeCreek & Frankowski, 1996). Even if the document exists, it may not be followed by family members or healthcare professionals (Cantor, 1998).

As a tangible benefit for hospitals, the PSDA was expected to reduce costs of care (Sugarman et al., 1993), however, this has not been substantiated (Teno, Lynn, Connors, Wenger, Phillips, Alzola, et al., 1997). The time of admission is not the ideal time to discuss advance directives, as individuals may be too ill to participate in such discussions.

A recent effort to strengthen the PSDA was the Advance Planning and Compassionate Care Act, introduced in Congress in March 1999.

This act, if passed, would require discussion of healthcare decision making with trained professionals; make the advance directive a prominent part of the medical record; strengthen portability of advance directives; provide for Medicare coverage of self-administered pain medications for life-threatening disease and chronic pain; require the Department of Health and Human Services to study ways to improve advance directives and develop measures to evaluate end-of-life care; fund a new initiative to improve end-of-life care; and establish a 24-hour hotline and information clearinghouse regarding advance directives. The act was referred to the Finance Committee in the Senate and to the Commerce Committee's Subcommittee on Health and Environment and Committee on Ways and Means in the House and no action was taken before the end of the congressional session in 2000. This type of legislation, if passed, has the potential to make advance care planning simpler, especially the entitlement of Medicare beneficiaries to discuss end-of-life care issues with trained professionals. To date however, no such legislation has been passed at the federal level.

All 50 states have passed statutes protecting the use of advance directives, although the form of advance directives and what exactly is sanctioned regarding their use may vary. The first state to enact a Natural Death Law was California, in 1976. Although this first statute was stimulated by the situation faced by Karen Ann Quinlan's father, who pursued judicial means to authorize the removal of life supports from his daughter, this law actually would not have applied in her case. The law only covered incapacitated individuals whose death is imminent (a small percentage), not those experiencing a prolonged dying process, which is the fear of many (President's Commission, 1982).

The final impetus for protection of patients' rights and passage of the PSDA was the case of Nancy Cruzan, which was taken before the courts in Missouri (see chapter 2). In this case, Ms. Cruzan was in a persistent vegetative state without hope of recovery due to an auto accident. Her parents wished to remove life-supporting treatments and allow her to die. They stated that their daughter would not have wanted to live in such a condition, that it was not consistent with her values. Although in this case the individual's wishes were not made explicit prior to her injury, surrogates who knew her were able to express them. The courts might never have become involved in the case if an advance directive had been in place. This case also pointed to the importance of surrogates in directing care for individuals who become incapacitated and cannot make decisions about their own medical treatment.

One difficulty in states having separate laws regarding advance directives is that individuals may need to formulate a separate directive for each state where they might possibly have medical treatment. This may be particularly important for patients from rural areas who cross state lines for treatment in large cities, or for transplant patients who must transfer out of state to large transplant centers.

The Nature of Advance Directives

Advance directives are intended to extend patients' autonomy to a time when they become incapacitated or incompetent due to a debilitating illness or condition. The forms vary greatly and there is little uniformity in the information contained within the documents, which has contributed to considerable confusion in attempting to enforce them among medical clinicians, even when they are aware that the documents exist.

Probably the oldest type of advance directive in use is the *living will.* Living wills are considered *instruction directives,* which may specify the type of treatment that an individual wants (or does not want) to receive (President's Commission, 1982). In these, individuals confront only one possibility: that if they become terminally ill and permanently incompetent, they would want all medical treatment withheld or withdrawn. These older forms are often ambiguous however, using terms like "extraordinary" and "heroic measures." The extreme situations addressed by the living will are not likely to raise ethical concerns about whether to continue with treatment when there is no hope of recovery, whereas many other unspecified and complex conditions would (Culver, 1998).

Durable powers of attorney for health care are *proxy directives,* documents where individuals may name someone to speak on their behalf. These named persons are expected to assure that individuals' directives are carried out. As not all situations can be specified in advance, the surrogates are trusted to use a *substituted judgment,* or the best interest standard to make appropriate decisions regarding medical treatment. One challenge with this is that the named surrogates may not even be aware that they have been named to serve and may not have discussed their loved one's wishes with them (Culver, 1998). The President's Commission recommended in 1982 that the preferred form of advance directive be those in which a surrogate decision-maker is named, combined with statements of specific wishes, as these allow broader control in decision making.

Culver (1998) has suggested seven necessary characteristics for useful advance directives:

1. Instructions should correspond as closely as possible to questions most likely to arise in the care of seriously ill, mentally incompetent persons.
2. Instructions should be clear.
3. Future states should be anticipated.
4. Whether individuals would want the advance directive followed if there is a chance of a partial or full recovery versus if recovery seems remote.
5. Whether withdrawal of various types of life support is indicated, if individuals were to encounter a situation where they would want treatment stopped.
6. Whether withdrawal of invasive life-sustaining treatments, such as nutrition and hydration, is desired.
7. Advance directives should only be completed by individuals who thoroughly understand the content and the implications of their instructions.

In 1998, the Council on Ethical and Judicial Affairs of the American Medical Association (AMA) made several recommendations in response to increasing concerns over the seemingly ineffective utilization of advance directives, in their formulation, access, understanding, and use in healthcare settings. These recommendations included: use of both advisory and statutory documents; worksheets to record preferences that would then make up the advisory documents; physicians directly discussing end-of-life preferences with patients and their proxies, ahead of time if possible and not delegated to another member of the healthcare team; establishment of central repositories for completed advisory documents, to allow access particularly in emergency situations; Doctors' Orders Sheets to document preferences so that "covering" healthcare professionals may also have access to patients' preferences if they do not know the patients. In the management of end-of-life care treatment, individuals must be given an opportunity to define what they mean by comfort care in the context of their illness and personal values (Quill, Meier, Block, & Billings, 1998).

Problems with Advance Directives

A major reason that elderly individuals do not complete an advance directive is that they simply put off the decision or defer to others (High, 1993). So when should discussions about advance directives occur? Who should initiate and be responsible for discussions about advance directives? Who else should be involved? According to one study of groups of outpatients and physicians in primary care offices, 91% of patients agreed that these discussions should occur before they become extremely ill, and 84% felt they should take place while one is healthy. A majority of these respondents also indicated that discussions should occur in the office, prior to hospitalization. Both patients and physicians believed that the physician is responsible for initiating such discussions. A majority of patients believed that others (the closest person in their lives) should be brought into the discussions, ranked as follows: spouse or significant other, children, parents, siblings, friends, clergy, lawyers. According to these patients, content of the discussion should include: types and descriptions of life-sustaining treatments, health status at time of discussion, survival chances and likelihood of full recovery, and effects of treatments on the family. The group of physicians ranked discussion of chance of survival higher than patients' health status at the time of the discussion (Johnston, Pfeifer, & McNutt, 1995).

Several problems with advance directives have emerged since they began to be more widely promoted under the PSDA over ten years ago. One very basic problem is that individuals may complete them without consulting their physicians or informing their physicians of the existence of the document. Thus, the document may not be available when it is needed. Also, even if the document was available, the physician often lacked an understanding of the individual's intentions; often directives are too vague to be useful, especially if there has been no discussion regarding the intent. On the other hand, directives can be too specific about treatments or states of illness that patients do not understand well if no discussion has occurred with their physician. Physicians can discuss scenarios with patients, which may make their intentions clearer and the documents more useful. Another problem with advance directives is that if an individual is transferred from the hospital to a nursing home, the directive may not get transferred with him/her (Fischer et al., 2000). Teno and Lynn (1996) actually found that in as many as 1 in 15 cases, advance directives hindered decision making, and they concur that without proper discussion and counseling about treatment options, the documents are meaningless.

Families have found it helpful for advance directives to be honored when available because then the burden of decision making was removed from them. If this is in writing, families want it followed, and they may and often do become angry when wishes are not honored by health professionals (Mick, Medvene, & Strunk, 2003). Social workers can ease the decision-making process by assisting other health professionals to validate and support choices made in the advance directive by the patient or the named surrogate.

Advance Care Planning and Formulation of Directives

According to Goodman (1998), the overall goal of completing advance directives is that preferences are expressed about end-of-life care to caregivers, family, and others, so that self-determination is preserved. In reaching this goal, however, what may be more important is the process that occurs in eliciting preferences. If this process can improve communication between providers and individuals, and between individuals and their families, then even further benefit may result. Advance care planning is a much broader activity than constructing a formal living will or power of attorney for health care. The overall goal of advance care planning is to ensure that medical care is directed by the patients' preferences when patients are unable to participate in decision making themselves and to shape how decisions are to be made (Fischer et al., 2000). A more specific goal is the improvement of healthcare decision-making processes, such as facilitating shared decision making among patients, surrogates, and providers, and encouraging individual and public education about issues of death, dying, and incapacity. Another specific goal is the improvement of patient outcomes and well-being and reducing concerns about creating burdens for families and significant others (Teno, Nelson, & Lynn, 1994).

However, "advance care planning requires that both clinicians and patients do what they are strongly disinclined to do: to think and talk about circumstances in which health declines, curative measures fail, and the process of dying and the ultimate fact of death must be confronted" (Rich, 1998, p. 627). The Study to Understand Prognoses and Preferences for Outcomes and Risks of Treatments (SUPPORT), a two-year study of patients with life expectancies of six months or less, was completed in 1994. The aim was to examine communication in end-of-life care and, in the second phase, to improve decision making and reduce use of mechanical means of life support, or painful and prolonged dying among terminally ill patients. The study revealed numerous inadequacies in communication and physicians' knowledge of patient preferences regarding CPR and timing of DNR orders.

Notably, most patients who died had first spent at least ten days in an intensive care unit and were in moderate pain at least half of the time, according to their families. In an intervention phase aimed at improving communication by the provision of timely information about patient's prognosis, discussion of the directive documents patient and family preferences and understanding of the disease and prognosis. A nurse helped to carry out necessary conversations, including arranging and convening meetings with patients and families (all of which required the permission of the attending physician). The outcome of this phase revealed no improvement in patient-physician communication or other indicators used: timing and incidence of DNR orders written, physicians' knowledge of patients' resuscitation preferences, number of days spent in an ICU, receiving mechanical ventilation or being comatose prior to death, and reported level of pain. Recommendations of the study investigators were that efforts to improve communication should include not only enhancing opportunities and creativity for increased interaction between patient and physician, but also more proactive measures to improve the commitment of individuals and society may be needed (SUPPORT investigators, 1995).

An aspect that has been extensively examined through data obtained in the SUPPORT study was the use of advance directives by participants as the study took place during the passage and implementation of the PSDA. For example, in a qualitative study examining whether advance directives were unilaterally disregarded by healthcare professionals in decision making, the finding was often that in fact the family and physician did not feel that patients were "hopelessly ill," so invoking the advance directive was not believed to be appropriate, thus treatment continued. However, in cases where the advance directive had an impact in care of the patient, open communication and negotiation with surrogates had resulted in a change in the goals of care from aggressive treatment to palliative care (Teno, Stevens, Spernak, & Lynn, 1998).

Another finding in additional analysis of data from this study was that patients preferred to have their family and physician make decisions for them rather than following their stated preferences for resuscitation unconditionally, whether they had a surrogate or not. In determining the level of involvement of patients in planning, patients should be asked, for example, whether they want to exercise autonomy, whether their current views regarding resuscitation apply to future situations, and what they value most. Through these questions, professionals can show respect for the individuals and their relation to personal, cultural, and spiritual beliefs (Puchalski, Zhong, Jacobs, Fox, Lynn, Harrold, et al., 2000).

> James G is a sixty-eight-year-old male who was recently diagnosed with recurrent metastatic prostate cancer, which has spread to his lungs and liver. He has decided that he does not want his wife and two adult children to be burdened with his end-of-life wishes, as he had been a few years ago when his father was dying. Jim asked his physician if someone could help him talk this all out. Dr. Smith sent Mr. G to speak with Suzanne, a clinical social worker trained in medical ethics, and they began to draft Jim's Living Will and Medical Power of Attorney.

It may be helpful to clarify the goals and objectives for conversations in which advance care planning will take place. Many objectives of ACP are shared among patients, family members (or surrogates), and healthcare professionals. However, each group may have its own perspective on what they hope will result from the process. ACP objectives for the patient might include: gaining a sense of control, preparing for aspects of dying not previously considered, and reflecting on personal values and goals for end-of-life care.

> Jim believes that the use of his mind is essential. Therefore, if and when he can no longer think or communicate, he does not want to be "kept alive." Jim also does not want any artificial measures utilized to preserve his body. He believes that his death should be a natural process and prefers to die without the use of a breathing machine or a defibrillator to start his heart. He also wishes to avoid the use of artificial feeding and hydration.

Families' objectives in ACP include describing their role and duties as surrogates for the patient and providing a basis for reflection after the patient's death that the dying process did follow the patient's preferences and values for end-of-life care.

> Mary, Jim's wife, wants to be able to care for him at home as long as possible but fears she will make a mistake. Therefore, they spoke of utilizing hospice nurses at home and inpatient hospice care as his death became more imminent. Jim and Mary's children helped to choose which hospice agency to use and toured the inpatient unit to make sure it would provide an atmosphere of comfort for their father.

As a result of ACP, medical decisions can be facilitated that are consistent with patient values and liability risk decreased. Many more objectives are shared by all three groups: patients, families (surrogates), and healthcare providers. Among these are: facilitation of communication; provision of care consistent with values of patient; clear identification of a surrogate decision-maker; the likelihood that conflict among family regarding patient care would be decreased; assurance of an ongoing conversation; promotion of trust among health providers, patient, and family members; facilitation of appropriate palliative care; and the assurance that the information stated in the advance care process is accessible to decision makers who need it (Kolarik, Arnold, Fischer, & Tulsky, 2002).

Patients, families, and healthcare providers also must realize that the goals for ACP and for care may change as a person's health status changes. Advance care planning is increasingly being supported as an ongoing process. Discussions about advance care planning should begin early when individuals are relatively well so that the foundation exists for later discussions when illness occurs. This foundation should be based on the life goals of the individuals and families and care that may be needed in the final years of life. Teno and Lynn (1996) recommended content for discussion, actions, and communication strategies that might appropriately take place with healthy patients, patients diagnosed with a serious illness, and patients with a limited life expectancy. The content and specificity about which treatment options are discussed should depend on the individual's age and the underlying medical condition, whether it is an acute, chronic, or progressive condition.

> Jim was admitted to the hospital emergency room with severe shortness of breath and abdominal pain. It was discovered that he had formulated a blood clot in his lung and had an obstruction in his bowel. Dr. Smith sat down with Jim and his family and formulated a plan of care based upon Jim's living will. He was transferred to the inpatient hospice unit of the hospital later that day, where he remained until his death.

For in healthy individuals, the focus should be on naming a surrogate decision-maker, (Fischer et al., 2000; Teno & Lynn, 1996); discussing preferences for undesirable end-of-life situations, such as persistent vegetative states; and any uncommon preferences based on religious or cultural beliefs. Those who may have atypical surrogates, such as in a homosexual couple, are strongly encouraged to make this designation more formally using a durable power of attorney. With a healthy individual, the type of discussion needed may only require a few minutes on the part of the healthcare professional (Teno & Lynn, 1996). It is this beginning discussion that may be particularly difficult to initiate as there is no impending need for information about how the individual wants to handle a serious illness and end-of-life care situations. However, it is necessary to begin the dialogue early so that healthcare professionals may develop a sense of the individual's preferences and values.

In those diagnosed with a serious illness, the focus shifts to ascertaining more specific preferences regarding any undesirable outcome states that they may consider worse than death. In these situations, discussion should center on time-limited trials of life-sustaining treatments and should recognize that physicians and surrogates will be attempting to respond to a dynamic medical situation for which there may not be any prior preferences expressed. It is thus important here to be guided by the individual's values and directed by the surrogate (Teno & Lynn, 1996).

> Grace had been losing weight, something she had wanted to do but not so quickly. She also noted some changes in her bowel habits and started having significant back pain. Following a series of tests, Grace was informed that she has stage III ovarian cancer, which has spread to her liver, lungs, and pelvis. She is 41 years old, divorced with one son. Her parents are dead and she has no siblings. Grace only recently relocated to Pennsylvania and her closest friend Judith lives in Washington, DC. Grace's ex-husband is an abusive alcoholic.

In advance care planning the inclusion of a *life values history*, or profile, in discussions and documentation is often suggested (Cantor, 1998; Schonwetter, Walker, Solomon, Indurkhya, & Robinson, 1996; Teno & Lynn, 1996). What may sound like a simple process, however, may be very complicated indeed. Items in a values history, in some formats proposed in the literature, include recording of individual's judgments of the importance of independence, being mentally alert, and the use of life-sustaining measures during a chronic or terminal illness. Cantor proposed a format that uses case scenarios with a list of options from which individuals would choose. For example, "my attitude toward a permanently unconscious state, confirmed by up-to-date medical tests, showing no hope of ever regaining consciousness: 'intolerable—I prefer death'; 'tolerable'; 'tolerable, so long as insurance or other non-family sources are paying the bills' " (p. 649). In most cases, however, responses are open-ended out of necessity, and may serve to further complicate the completion of directives. Discussing life values in addition to life-sustaining treatments requires additional time, which may limit the use of this values history strategy. While limitations seem inherent in incorporating discussion of life values in advance care planning, communication and understanding of end-of-life care treatment preferences may be facilitated by such interaction (Schonwetter et al., 1996).

Grace has always feared death so any discussion of this subject is very difficult for her. Designing an advance directive for her required creativity and recognition of Grace's fears. It was recommended by the medical ethicist that the clinical social worker work with Grace on the formation of a letter to her doctor. This letter should describe Grace's health values in order of importance. The document reads as follows:

I, Grace C,

1. Value the use of my mind over the use of my body, therefore if I lose the ability to communicate or interact with my environment in a meaningful fashion because of a stroke or because of the advancement of my cancer, I would consider myself to be in a terminal state and therefore would not wish to be kept alive by any artificial measures, including artificial nutrition and hydration.

2. I value my independence and fear becoming a burden to my young son and my dear friend Judith Olson. Therefore, I agree in advance to placement in a nursing home or rehabilitation center if I can no longer care for myself.

3. I do not wish to linger as my time of death arrives for I fear a long, lingering death. Therefore, I request that no artificial measures be utilized to sustain me once it is clear that nothing else can be done to help me. This includes palliative radiation and/or chemotherapy, the use of a ventilator, CPR, and defibrillation, the use of any medication to elevate or regulate my blood pressure or heartbeat, and the use of dialysis in any form.

4. I fear dying in pain. Therefore, I request that my physician consult a palliative care or pain specialist as my time of death draws near and that I be admitted to a hospice center until the time of my death. I request that Rev. Charles S be called to my side to provide spiritual support and that my son be provided with ongoing psychological support by the clinical social worker, Suzanne G, during and following my illness and death.

In individuals diagnosed with serious illness and limited life expectancy, or who, due to advanced age, have a limited life expectancy, more specific discussions about prognosis and treatment options and likely outcomes should take place. Care desired during their present situation should be elicited as well as future care plans during the progression of an illness (Fischer et al., 2000; Teno & Lynn, 1996). Preferences for individuals in these situations should be formalized in writing at this time. Rather than stating specific preferences about specific treatments, it may perhaps better serve the patient if individuals can allow physicians and their surrogates to discuss together how to respond to the changing medical condition, based on the individual's values (Teno & Lynn, 1996). Healthcare professionals must be aware that some patients may not want to be involved in decision making at this point and may defer to their family, due to their family's cultural norms, which should be respected. Professionals have a responsibility to ask individuals how much they want to know about their medical diagnosis, treatment, and prognosis, and who they want to be involved in the discussion and decision making. Ideally, if advance care planning begins early, professionals involved will already be aware of this dynamic from the initial encounters.

> Grace had chosen her friend Judith as her surrogate decision-maker and requested that Judith be alerted of the change in her prognosis. The patient also requested that the terminal prognosis not be discussed openly with her. As Grace became more ill, Judy was informed of the downgrade in Grace's prognosis and changes were made in Grace's code status and level of care. Grace was transferred to the hospice unit, where she died. She was peaceful but never openly discussed her dying after the preparation of this document.

The American Medical Association's Council on Ethical and Judicial Affairs (1998) recommends that physicians be involved in two key phases in the process of advance care planning: structuring the central discussion and "after patient reflection, cosigning and insuring that a completed document is recorded in the medical record" (p. 673). Physicians should make discussions of end-of-life care preferences a standard practice (Rich, 1998). However, some have lamented the reluctance and limited ability of physicians to discuss issues of death and dying with their patients. Whether they do not fully appreciate the appropriateness of advance directives (Morrison, Morrison, & Glickman, 1994) or simply forget (Dexter, Wolinsky, Gramelspacher, Zhou, Eckert, Waisburd, et al., 1998), reasons for not discussing end-of-life care preferences are not clear. Goodman (1998) believed that the problem is not with the documents or policies themselves, but with poorly trained professionals. Physicians have not traditionally received training in conducting advance care planning discussions and few receive training in communication skills, even though it is an important aspect of the medical encounter (Fischer et al., 2000).

Training in effective communication and in the ethical, psychological, and legal aspects of death and dying must take place in order to achieve the goals of advance care planning, from laying the foundation when individuals are healthy, to planning for care at the end of life. Improved training in communication skills was one of the conclusions made by investigators in the SUPPORT study (1995). Also, systemic change in the financing of end-of-life care, such as including Medicare reimbursement to providers for communication with seriously ill patients, was recommended. Since this activity requires excellent skills and is time consuming if done properly, it must be recognized as important by the healthcare financing systems. Political advocacy was suggested as key in achieving such a change (Covinsky, Fuller, Yaffe, Johnston, Hamel, Lynn, et al., 2000).

SOCIAL WORK INTERVENTION IN ADVANCE CARE PLANNING

In response to the PSDA, healthcare institutions have developed procedures whereby information is provided to patients about their right to formulate an advance directive upon admission. Also at that time, the presence or absence of an advance directive is to be documented as part of a patient's medical record. In many instances, information is supplied through brief pamphlets explaining the patient's rights under state law to formulate a directive. This process, as can be imagined, can leave much to be desired, especially as admission personnel, particularly in hospitals, are not appropriately trained in the meaning and importance of having an advance directive. Often the information or pamphlet is one of many papers and other documents that a patient may receive upon admission and may not be read until much later, if at all.

If patients have questions, institutions generally have protocols regarding which department to consult. Social services or pastoral care departments many times respond to requests for information or to discuss advance directives with patients and families. Social workers may also be consulted throughout a patient's hospital stay to discuss end-of-life care, including advance directives and to provide assistance in decision making. Often this may occur prior to a risky medical procedure or surgery, which may arguably be the most stressful and least appropriate time for patients and families to discuss such important issues. Including a trained clinician is of greater benefit than having no discussion at all.

Regarding advance care planning, patients and families may discuss issues related to end-of-life care treatment options and their personal values regarding life itself, how they have lived, and also how they wish to die. A range of issues may be brought up, including euthanasia and physician-assisted suicide (Csikai, 1999). Social workers develop trusting relationships and provide a safe environment for patients and families to explore the meaning of various treatment options, as well as their hopes, fears, and other concerns. Social workers prepare by assessing their own values around controversial end-of life care practices and options, as well as knowing the legal and financial aspects. It is essential that clinicians have insight and training on hospital policies as well as an understanding of state and federal laws relating to end-of-life care.

Perhaps the biggest impact that social workers can make in the area of advance care planning is engaging patients and families in dialogue about how to achieve quality and meaning at the end of life. In public opinion research conducted by the National Hospice Foundation (NHF) in 1999, more than 1 of every 4 American adults were unlikely to discuss issues related to a parent's death even if the parent was terminally ill. Fewer than 25% of Americans had thought about how they would like to be cared for at the end of life and put these wishes in writing. Although 36% of the respondents reported that they had told someone about how they would like to be cared for at the end of life, further results from focus group discussion revealed that people often viewed that a passing comment about how they wished to die was equal to informing loved ones of their wishes (NHF, 1999). Also, as revealed by the SUPPORT study (SUPPORT investigators, 1995), an intervention by a professional (in this case a nurse) aimed at examining patient/family wishes in a terminal situation when already in the acute hospital setting may be too late, or the choice of that professional may be short-sighted. Planning for the end of life should begin prior to an emergency when emotions are running high. Encouraging discussion and use of advance directives (even though few people may actually formalize their decisions) may lead to a better understanding of an individual's wishes by families, providers, and the patients themselves. These discussions need to include as many family members and significant others (as the patient identifies them) as possible, as this may empower all involved in the process.

Social workers must be well informed about the options available, including but not limited to living wills and durable powers of attorney for healthcare. They should be able to discuss these options with patients who have capacity for decision making and maximize their ability to make choices about care at the end of life. "The appropriate role for social workers is to help patients express their thoughts and feelings to facilitate exploration of alternatives, to provide information to make an informed choice, and to deal with grief and loss issues" (NASW, 2004, p. 48). Social workers' advocacy skills are important here to help ensure that patients' wishes, when known, are carried out. Among the top-rated services that Americans feel are important for the terminally ill is that there be someone there to make sure that patients' wishes are enforced (NHF, 1999). Patients and families may have fears related to prior experiences with death and dying where preferences were not solicited by providers or wishes may not have been followed. Consistent, effective communication is still one of the greatest unmet needs in the intensive care unit (Azoulay, Chevret, LeLeu, Pochard, Barboteu, Adrie, et al., 2000). In one study completed by Dowdy, Robertson, and Bander (1998) use of early intervention by medical ethicists in high-risk cases resulted in better communication with the family when patients had a change in status that required discussion related to limitation of care, and the family reported greater satisfaction with care. In addition, the study group increased communication among all patients and family members. Social work skill sets mirror the skills of the clinical ethicist more closely than do nursing or physician styles.

Other services felt to be important were emotional support for patients and families and an opportunity for patients to put their lives in order (NHF, 1999), both of which fall under the particular skills and values of social workers. Policy development is another important domain for social work involvement, advocating for policy changes that maximize the individual's ability to express preferences.

One of many demographic changes affecting the dynamics of end-of-life care is that people are living longer and facing a range of chronic illnesses. Some illnesses, such as congestive heart failure or chronic obstructive pulmonary disease, often have acute episodes that require hospitalization and rehabilitative phases, which may include the assistance of home health or nursing home care. Social workers in each of these settings can capitalize on opportunities to engage families about how they might wish to handle a terminal phase of their chronic condition and bring up advance care planning.

Acute medical episodes may certainly present as crises for the individual and the family will experience a state of disequilibrium. Crisis intervention services can provide a turning point opportunity for the ill person and his/her family (Roberts, 2000). The social worker should help the family respond to possible changing dynamics resulting from stress and varying coping styles (Shulman & Shewbert, 2000). Focus can be placed on the quality of life in between episodes rather than on fear about the next episode.

Cultural diversity in end-of-life care planning is another aspect to consider, especially in relation to how to deliver information on a terminal illness and who may be involved in decision making about medical treatment.

> Ms. K is a 23-year-old woman who was admitted to the hospital with an ischemic bowel. The patient is from Korea and is in the United States to complete her doctoral training. She has had a long history of anorexia, which has not responded well to psychiatric intervention. Surgery is not an option due to the extent of her bowel ischemia and the severity of her starvation. Her family does not want her told of her terminal state.

The bedside nurse is very upset and believes this to be "wrong," stating, "If this were me, I would want to know."

Patient autonomy, the right of individuals to make informed decisions, is widely accepted in America. However, examination of the attitudes of various ethnic groups toward this notion revealed that Korean Americans were less likely than African and European Americans to believe that the patient should be told the full truth about diagnosis or a terminal prognosis, or that the patient alone should make decisions regarding life-sustaining technology. Korean and Mexican Americans were more likely to believe that only the family should be told the truth; however, increased acculturation increases the likelihood that they will adopt the autonomy model (Blackhall, Murphy, Frank, Michel, & Azen, 1995).

Being asked to complete an advance directive may also be a sensitive ethnic/cultural issue. For example, in one study of 139 African Americans, Hispanics, and whites from a general medical clinic setting, 10% of African Americans and only 2% of whites felt that signing such a form would mean giving up (Caralis, Davis, Wright, & Macial, 1993). Patients should be asked who they would want to involve in discussions and decision making about their illness and end-of-life care treatment, as there are diverse approaches within ethnic groups.

In order for Ms. K to die without disgrace her cultural values must be understood and respected. Her family provided interested staff with education as to the customs of her village regarding care of the ill and dying. The nurses spent time making paper cranes and filling the patient's room with these cranes and flowers. These familiar vituals allowed her to have hope but also gave her the knowledge that she was preparing for a journey. The family was honored that so many people worked to respect the living and dying of their child.

INDIVIDUAL AND FAMILY ISSUES

Determining Capacity

In family conferences on advance care planning with healthy individuals, in the earliest stage, their capacity for conscious decision making will likely be evident. Exceptions can arise in cases of questionable mental illness or mental retardation. However, when a serious illness is diagnosed and then progresses, causing physical and mental debilitation, capacity for decision making should be continually assessed. Most often this is done informally by care providers, typically social workers.

Social workers are often involved in investigating capacity when providers believe that patients are making harmful decisions or are going against recommendations (see chapter 5). If the person is found capable of making decisions, the primary role of the social worker is upholding the right of autonomy or self-determination. Care must be taken to offer opportunities to discuss decisions fully with family and providers, and that all choices are considered based upon correct and complete information in keeping with the patient's values. Issues as complex as life and death should not be accepted on face value, for patients may be temporarily depressed or change their mind after considering the options more thoroughly. Social workers should be confident that the patient is not reacting to a situational fear or misunderstanding of his/her medical condition (Loewenberg, Dolgoff, & Harrington, 2000).

Managing Conflicts

Conflicts over decisions to limit treatment can be among the most difficult situations that physicians face in the care of patients at the end of life (Goold, Williams, & Arnold, 2000). Family conflict regarding end-of-life care preferences of a patient who has become incapacitated was identified as presenting a significant ethical challenge for healthcare social workers (Csikai & Bass, 2000). A key role for social workers is mediating conflict among all involved. A key aspect to the informed consent process is free voluntary choice, which means decisions must be free from coercion, explicit or implicit. For example, individuals may feel pressured to accept a treatment they really do not wish to have because the family wants them to live.

One factor that could affect family decisions is misunderstanding the medical situation. The individual could have a long history of an illness that progresses into a terminal state. Both individuals and families should be asked what their understanding of the situation is, prior to describing the options and risks of various treatments. They may see the current situation as just another acute episode in a long series and may not fully appreciate that each episode is likely to cause deterioration in the individual's condition, leading toward the end stage of a disease. Families may be psychologically unprepared to hear the patient's diagnosis or prognosis and may project denial. Denial is often seen as an inability to recognize facts because of psychological consequences that may have to be faced if the diagnosis or prognosis is accepted, such as overwhelming grief or guilt.

Family Roles

Families often maintain multiple roles in end-of-life decision making, which makes them important stakeholders. The varying roles and interests of family members arise due to common histories, shared values, and reciprocal obligations. Often these roles are a significant source of tension, particularly over differing perceptions of the roles that individual members should play and how they should act (Levine & Zuckerman, 1999). A primary role is advocate. Families often have fear that their loved one will be neglected or treated improperly, possibly as a result of previous negative experiences with the healthcare system. People often hand over much of their freedom and identity and become vulnerable as patients. Families then may identify with professionals and approach them with concerns. "Even for the competent patient, the family is the link to an identity beyond the illness and to a world in which one makes choices about daily living without the constraint of institutional rules" (Levine & Zuckerman, 1999, p. 149).

In addition, families may provide a substantial amount of direct care even while the individual is in the hospital. They are trusted companions as they accompany a relative through the journey of illness and death, sharing and responding to the experience. Family members see their presence as a sign of their fidelity.

One barrier to family participation that is particularly restrictive, in ICUs and other special medical units, are limits to visiting hours. In ICUs, staff may see family members as interlopers and be concerned that their presence will interfere with procedures or limit their use of gallows humor, which is commonly used in such tense situations (Levine & Zuckerman, 1999). There is a double-sided issue here in that, on one hand if families do not visit they are seen as not caring, and if they want to visit too much they are seen as intruders on the medical turf.

Families also serve the role of surrogate decision-maker for a relative facing the end of life. According to many health professionals, the ideal (and the simplest) decision-making process is one that proceeds in a cerebral world of intellect, without the complications of culture, religion, personal history, and beliefs, and without the involvement of relatives, friends, or others with whom the patient has shared many good and bad experiences (Levine & Zuckerman, 1999). However, the ideal does not exist. Individuals and their families are influenced by all these factors. Families may be unclear about choices or how to participate meaningfully, and often do not even know the precise wishes of their relatives. Even when they have not specifically discussed end-of-life care wishes, usually no one else is a better judge of what the patient would have wanted.

Other sources of potential conflict include the biases of the healthcare professionals, who may unfairly believe that family members who face financial or care burdens will put their own self-interest above that of the patient. Healthcare professionals become frustrated when family members disagree with their treatment recommendations or make decisions contrary to recommendation. This is a time when the social worker is consulted and expected to help sway the family's decision back to the health team's point of view.

The extent of family cohesiveness is often a necessary factor to examine in end-of-life care situations. Under the stress of a family member's illness, tensions may erupt that may be long-standing, but normally hidden. A family that has been in turmoil prior to diagnosis will likely not only remain in turmoil but difficulties may intensify. In an emotional situation, rallying around the individual is only seen on television medical dramas. However, in some cases, new alliances may be forged and forgiveness and closure may be achieved.

Professional Reaction

Reactions of healthcare professionals vary widely. Rather than acknowledge the impact of the illness on the family, some may distance themselves from the emotional atmosphere. Families often seek solace from friends and medical staff, while physicians often see their role as ending when "there is nothing more to be done." They may view a terminal diagnosis or cessation of curative treatment as a failure, wish to avoid emotions, or feel they need to devote their time to others where their expertise is useful, thus the family may feel abandoned.

Another source of tension between healthcare professionals and families is the fear of litigation. Families may be perceived as a challenge to authority in institutions, as they are often the watchdogs or agents of quality control; they observe the care being provided very closely and may act threateningly. This can push families away from direct observation of care, or professionals may capitulate too quickly to unwarranted demands. When communication is direct and honest, litigation occurs less.

Decision-Making Factors

Families and professionals do not always speak the same language metaphorically, due to religion, cultural, or ethnic background, or literally, due to a language barrier. The patient's role in the family, such as caregiver or scapegoat, also influences the family's decisions. This is particularly pertinent when a patient has been in an authoritative role and then others must step in during illness. In addition, other structural characteristics, such as problem-solving style, openness, assertiveness, age, or gender must be considered, as well as whether anyone is experiencing denial, guilt, and/or anger.

The developmental stage of the family may influence decision making as well. Families of older, more chronically ill persons may have an easier time letting go than families of younger persons. Older families or those that have been together longer may cope better with the stressors of a terminal illness.

Families can actually affect how soon a patient dies. Patients from intact families may die sooner, allowed to go with less ambivalence than in dysfunctional families. They are often better prepared and at peace, more able to let go.

The definition of the family according to the patient is crucial. The traditional definition of family has long been altered, due to gay and lesbian relationships or other situations where patients may be estranged from blood relatives and prefer to put their trust and confidence in a close friend or neighbor. Identifying who the spokesperson is for the family is crucial if the patient is not able to speak for him- or herself. The social worker can assist the family in coming to agreement and reinforcing this agreement when a designated spokesperson or an estranged member comes into the picture.

INTERVENTION WITH INDIVIDUALS AND FAMILIES

Interventions commonly provided by social workers in palliative and end-of-life care include: individual counseling and psychotherapy (cognitive-behavioral interventions, for example); family counseling; family-team conferences; crisis intervention counseling; information and education; multidimensional interventions to address pain and symptom management; support groups; bereavement groups; case management; discharge planning; resource counseling (including financial and legal aspects); and client advocacy (NASW, 2004). Family-team conferences occur frequently in health settings and social work skills can be invaluable here.

Family-Team Conferences

John C is a 56-year-old male who was admitted to the hospital with shortness of breath. He was diagnosed with an acute leukemia. John is a practicing Jehovah's Witness and refuses blood and blood products. He has a strong and very supportive family as well as strong community support. John's physician has known the patient for over 25 years and states, "I like this guy. He was one of my original patients. I don't want to lose him because of something so simple as blood." The social worker schedules a family meeting at the request of the patient. John wishes to execute a living will and durable power of attorney.

Family conferences can serve as an important intervention in initial advance care planning and throughout the spectrum of end-of-life care decisions, especially as individuals encounter new medical situations, including serious and terminal illnesses. These conferences can occur in any healthcare environment, including the home when patients are using home health or hospice care. A family conference has been defined as "a meeting which involves a number of family members, the patient, and hospital [or other healthcare] personnel in discussions concerning the patient's illness, treatment, and plans for their discharge or their care" (Hanson, Cornish, & Kayser, 1998, p. 58). Most commonly, family meetings are conducted in one session. The purpose is to ensure a clear exchange of information among the patient, members of the family, and healthcare team, and that everyone hears the same facts about diagnosis, prognosis, and treatment and care options. They are a vehicle to correct misinformation, discuss patient and family wishes, make treatment decisions, and plan for the future (Blacker, Cohen, & Sormanti, 2002; Hanson et al., 1998).

There are three phases to holding family conferences: a pre-conference preparation stage, the conference itself, and follow-up work, to be completed after the conference. Social workers can and should play a key role in all stages. In the pre-conference phase, the social worker should take the lead in identifying issues that will need to be addressed, identify appropriate members of the healthcare team to include, prepare patient and family, and develop objectives in relation to the overall goals of the plan. During the conference itself, care should be taken to ensure that the patient and family understand all the information being provided and that health team members obtain needed information regarding the patient and family's values, care wishes, and conception of quality of life. The social worker should monitor reactions and emotions, and respond by engaging in empathetic communication, clarify ambiguous medical terms, and explore concerns. When decision making is taking place during the conference, social workers must act to expand choices where possible, so that the individual who desires it maintains control over decisions; at the same time, they should make explicit what options will be implemented by the care team if immediate action is called for in a crisis. Social workers should model and encourage shared decision making during the meeting.

Another advantage of holding these family conferences is to normalize fears and concerns. If the conference goal is to initiate advance care planning, appointing a surrogate for the individual is appropriate and formally documenting the named surrogate should take place. After the conference, social workers should follow up to be clear that decisions made during the conference are being implemented. These may range from filling out durable power of attorney documents to agreeing to provide comfort care only in the intensive care unit. The social worker should address any other issues that may have been raised, particularly as they relate to the emotional response of the patient and family to the conference discussion (Blacker et al., 2002; Hanson et al., 1998).

To summarize, elements of successful family meetings include: commitment of team to the use of family conferences as an important intervention; identification of individuals important to the patient to involve in decision making; clarification of the purpose; establishment of a coordinator/facilitator; communication with professionals prior to the conference; preparation of the patient and family; skillful facilitation; and documentation of the outcomes of the conference, including the decision or plan to be implemented (Blacker et al., 2002).

In one study (Hanson et al., 1998), a small sample of family conferences held in a hospital setting were examined in depth. Disagreement between family members and hospital staff occurred in 50% of cases; more than with any other of the key people involved. Another difficulty found was that the conference time was too short to achieve many objectives. In most cases, more time was needed to consider the array of options and, on the other hand, choices that may feel very restricted. As a result, families ended up feeling that they did not have the amount of control that they would ideally like.

Along with insufficient time, other barriers may include lack of reimbursement (which has value implications), scheduling difficulties, and insufficient training of professionals in the type of facilitation and communication skills needed for successful family conferencing. Benefits for the team are that they provide an opportunity to gather information and disseminate it efficiently, and can be an important means for consensus building when tough decisions are needed. A sense of teamwork can be created that is extremely helpful as professionals work together toward common goals (Blacker et al., 2002).

In situations involving ethical issues and dilemmas, the psychosocial perspective that social work brings to the situation provides a context for examining and resolving the relevant issues. The perception of illness is expanded through the social work lens to include "socioemotional suffering" and also assesses cultural values, beliefs, and rituals associated with death and dying. The bioethical perspective in clinical ethics, on the other hand, is based on normative ethics involving specific ethical norms, principles, and moral rules such as veracity, confidentiality, autonomy, beneficence, and others discussed in chapter 1. In supportive counseling, advance care planning, and decision making with families, social workers will often be faced with families in moral distress. Exploration and assessment of the context of the distress must be complete so that intervention may be effective. (For elaboration and an example of family conferences, see chapter 5.)

WORKING WITH TEAMS

Yet another point where social workers can have a major impact in end-of-life care is through working as members of various types of teams in healthcare settings. Social workers may (and should) serve as leaders or coordinators of these committee or team efforts, as they bring trained skills in facilitating communication to the table. Part of effective functioning and leadership in these groups entails knowledge of one's own professional values as well as insight into the value structure of those from different disciplines. Social workers may be part of interdisciplinary, multidisciplinary, or transdisciplinary teams. Since health care is a host setting for social workers (rather than being the primary discipline, as in child welfare services, for example), social workers must be flexible in their practice here.

Interdisciplinary teams are composed of representatives from more than one field of study and there is a coordinated team effort. Each member performs discipline-related activities, and is also responsible to contribute to the group effort and common group goals. Fluid boundaries and flexible roles exist (Dhooper, 1997). An example occurs in the hospice setting. Each discipline and service offered to patients in care planning is on the team and responsible for the overall care of the patient and family. If the social worker goes out to the home and a family member needs help with changing soiled sheets on the patient's bed, then she assists in the role of the certified nurse's assistant (CNA). Likewise, if a patient becomes upset while the CNA is bathing the patient or any time during the nurse's visit, then the CNA or nurse should provide emotional support. Not that the disciplines are interchangeable, but turf issues are minimized as the patient's needs are being met.

Multidisciplinary teams include individuals from various disciplines who are responsible for their own specialty. Work is done independently and relationships between disciplines are not clearly specified (Dhooper, 1997; Schofield & Amodeo, 1999). An example of a multidisciplinary team is a hospital ethics committee. Each participant is expected to provide input on the issue before the committee from the viewpoint of a particular discipline. The differing perspectives add to the richness of the discussion and more informed deliberations by the committee. The team as a whole will agree on final recommendations.

Transdisciplinary teams are used increasingly as a preferred model. On these teams, members of several disciplines work together in the initial phases of assessment, evaluation, and care planning, however, direct services may only be provided by one or two team members (Dhooper, 1997; Halper, 1993; Schofield & Amodeo, 1999). Two reasons why these teams are being utilized more often include limited availability of resources due to cost-containment (personnel and financial) and that not all disciplines may be needed in every situation.

As liaisons among the patient, family, and other healthcare providers, social workers can help team members understand patients' and families' fears, hopes, and wishes. As social workers assess and intervene on multiple levels, information gained regarding patients' values, pressures, and preferences can be shared with the team. Helping other professionals understand the context of the situations faced by patients and families and providing a broad systems perspective is important. Social workers can arrange family conferences to discuss advance care planning, stressing the importance of involvement from all the health professionals, including physicians.

Behaviors such as active listening, exploration, and empathy can be modeled and are important skills to use when encountering difficult conversations with patients. These behaviors should be modeled consistently in every encounter that involves another team member, teaching opportunities that may enhance understanding of the social work role. In another act of modeling, social workers should not only execute their own advance directives and engage their loved ones in discussion about end-of-life care, but should encourage team members to do the same in order to heighten self-awareness and sensitivity to others (Soskis & Kerson, 1992).

End-of-life care discussions can bring out deeply held emotions that may have previously impeded effective work with patients who need a great deal of support and intervention at this time in their life. If this dialogue can be structured by the social worker to occur after a traumatic or emotionally charged situation involving difficult decisions or death of a patient, it may be more meaningful; sensitively conducted, growth may occur naturally.

Conflict may arise on the team around when advance care planning and end-of-life care discussions should occur, how frequently, who should be involved, and what depth of information should be provided. Physicians or others on the team may be uncomfortable with prognostic uncertainty in limiting treatment decisions so may be hesitant. Discussion of death may signal medical failure to them or bring about unspoken and unresolved anxiety about their own mortality.

Attitudes toward the chronically ill may vary. The quality of life of chronically ill patients is often misjudged. Professionals are more likely than patients or families to think that patients would choose to forgo life-sustaining treatment. Other attitudes that may affect the decision-making process include religious tenets about the sanctity of life, beliefs regarding the proper role of families in end-of-life decision making, misunderstanding of radically different value systems, or insecurity about competence or skill. Social workers can assist team members in exploring and gaining insight into their own limitations and beliefs around death and dying. This may help a physician to understand feelings of anger or frustration with certain families and be able to discuss the areas of disagreement with the family more clearly.

In the social worker's role as educator, knowledge or skill deficits of individual team members may be addressed. For example, some may be unaware of the prognosis or treatment options and misinform the family. Misunderstanding regarding the legality of withdrawing ventilatory support or artificial nutrition can lead a physician to refuse to accede to the family's wishes. Lack of training in pain and symptom management may lead to inappropriate care, such as not prescribing adequate doses of pain medication. Health professionals may be overworked, fatigued, frustrated, stressed, or have competing concerns that impede their ability to access the information they need to provide quality interventions. Economic and peer pressures, lack of reimbursement for time-consuming conversations with patients and families, and the culture of hospitals impose other challenges.

Hospital policies may exacerbate conflicts. In ICUs and other units with restricted visiting hours, for example, contact between patients and families is minimized and may seriously impair communication, preventing families from seeing their loved ones and understanding what they might be going through.

Social work departments may want to engage in providing education within their own facility so that a greater comfort level with discussion of end-of-life care is achieved. In a study of social workers on hospital ethics committees, both social workers and committee chairs felt that social workers should have greater involvement in educational activities than was occurring, so there is an opportunity for social workers to take the lead in this area (Csikai & Sales, 1998). Social workers can engage professionals in their service area within the hospital or their agency around issues that they encounter often, such as pain management, withdrawal of feeding tubes, or termination of ventilatory support.

WORKING WITH THE COMMUNITY

Social workers can play a significant educational role in advance care planning and end-of-life care practices. In the larger community, they can provide leadership in increasing the number of people who are properly informed about advance care planning and end-of-life care decisions that they may face at some point in their lives. Part of PSDA mandated that healthcare facilities provide education to the community on the importance of advance directives. Social workers can be involved in planning community seminars with local organizations such as NASW local chapters or the local AARP group, or may be invited speakers at such seminars.

Chapter Conclusion

Social workers need to participate in all aspects of advance care planning. As the population ages, it is increasingly important for social workers to examine these issues and to intervene, when necessary, in their implementation. Involvement must take place on the interpersonal level with patients, families, and providers (including clinical intervention), and also on organizational, community, and societal levels in terms of policy and education in the wish to fulfill our professional mission of enhancing the lives and deaths of all people.

Chapter 4

Hospice and Palliative Care

Mr. Miller is a 70-year-old man who was recently diagnosed with advanced non–small cell lung cancer two years ago. His original symptoms were fatigue, shortness of breath, raspy voice, and a general sense of feeling poorly for several months. His only previous examination was by the company physician for his yearly work physical exam. Because of the symptoms, the physician suspected lung cancer and ordered a chest X-ray and later a chest CT scan. Mr. Miller then underwent a biopsy of the tumor in his left lung, and it was found that a malignant form of lung cancer had spread to the surrounding lymph nodes. Radiation therapy was recommended and began shortly after his discharge from the hospital. Chemotherapy was initiated after the course of radiation was completed.

Mr. Miller was told that things "looked good." He tolerated the radiation treatments well, but discontinued chemotherapy due to the side effects; he did not want "to be so sick." He had been a strong, active, and outgoing man who had emigrated to the United States from Eastern Europe at the age of 13. The family settled in eastern Pennsylvania and he immediately found work at the steel mill. He spent most of his life working around the furnace systems (a very hot and smoky job). He smoked cigarettes nearly all his life.

After Mr. Miller stopped chemotherapy, he began to feel better. Although he did not completely regain all of his strength, he went back to daily activities and other things he enjoyed. After six months, his energy level began to decline until he finally went back to the hospital with increased shortness of breath and pain in his right side. Preliminary testing revealed that the cancer had returned in his lungs and metastasized to his liver and bones.

Mr. Miller was hospitalized due to intractable pain. He had repeatedly discussed his desire to stay alive as long as he "could enjoy life" but if he could not live a full life he wanted to "die comfortably" with his family at his side. He went into respiratory distress a few days after admission and was placed on a ventilator. His family never had a chance to speak with him again and he died eight days after being placed on life support. His family was in shock that he died "so quickly." They felt unprepared by medical professionals to face his death and wished that things had been done differently. They all wished he had been given a chance to go home to die.

Arguably, one of the most difficult concepts and decisions for patients, families, and members of the healthcare team to reconcile involves the choice of hospice care, palliative care, or full technological treatment support at the end of life. Often what is presented to patients and families, if the hospice option is presented at all, is a choice between hospice care or continued treatment of their condition. Hospice is seen by some as "giving up" on the person's well-being and future and giving in to the illness. Failure is what some patients and families hear when hospice is presented as an option. Physicians and other health professionals have come to believe that their academic preparation and the science of medicine can "save" everyone, and that taking a comfort-based approach means giving up or giving in to the illness. Mention of the word hospice may evoke a negative reaction in a culture of denial of death, as in the modern healthcare environment. Refusal to face our own mortality makes us retain hope that there's a treatment out there that will cure or at least hold back the illness. Thus there is resistance to refer patients to hospice until it is late in the course of illness, preventing patients and families from benefiting fully from the range of services. These include management of the patient's physical pain and preparation of the patient and family for the idea and reality of death (Lamers, 2002).

Accurately predicting a prognosis, particularly for chronic conditions, may delay a referral to hospice. End-of-life care options for people with limited and deteriorating cognitive abilities can be complicated, particularly if no advance care planning has taken place. For example, to predict death for patients with end-stage cardiac disease is exceedingly difficult because they can appear as if they have still have two weeks to live, even 24 hours before death occurs. Advance care planning for this population is essential. Unlike cancer, which has a clear and progressive line of decline in most cases, those who suffer from chronic lung, renal, and cardiac disease have an unclear illness progression.

This chapter examines the models by which palliative care is delivered to those with life-limiting illness. These models include: hospice at home, inpatient hospice, palliative care in long-term care facilities, hospital-based palliative care programs, and palliative care provided by primary care medical professionals. The philosophy and elements of care provided by hospice and palliative care programs, along with the critical role that social workers play in decisions that are made in the provision of care in these programs, are discussed.

DEFINING HOSPICE AND PALLIATIVE CARE

The National Hospice and Palliative Care Organization (NHPCO) defines *hospice* as a program that provides palliative and supportive care (2004). The central concept in the provision of hospice care services is palliative care, which is provided by an interdisciplinary care team. Palliative care focuses on caring for patients' total needs, not on curing or eliminating the disease. Palliative care allows the patient to continue with current therapies while seeking comfort and control of pain and other symptoms associated with a life-limiting illness. These patients face suffering on many levels. Physical pain may be present and must be alleviated, and many complex, personal factors contribute to suffering. According to Cassell (1991), "suffering occurs when an impending destruction of the person is perceived; it continues until the threat of disintegration has passed or until the integrity of the person can be restored in some manner." Among the arguments against legalizing euthanasia is that it could undermine commitment to providing the best possible care to dying patients, particularly those who decline to choose euthanasia or assisted suicide (Deveterre, 2000).

Palliative care has been defined by the World Health Organization (WHO) as the

> . . . active total care of patients whose disease is not responsive to curative treatment. Control of pain, of other symptoms, and of psychological,

social and spiritual problems, is paramount. The goal of palliative care is the achievement of the best quality of life for patients and their families. ... Palliative care affirms life and regards dying as a normal process, neither hastens nor postpones death ... provides relief from pain and other distressing symptoms (Doyle, Hanks, & MacDonald, 1998, p. 3).

Palliative care broadly applies the central concepts of hospice care to individuals earlier in the disease trajectory. It should be integrated into treatment plans of individuals with serious illness as they pursue life-prolonging and curative treatments. The goal is to support and comfort individuals who have reached a terminal phase (prognosis of six months or less) in the disease process (Fine, 2004).

HOSPICE CARE IN THE UNITED STATES

The first modern hospices in the United States appeared in the late 1960s and 1970s and were patterned after St. Christopher's Hospice in London. Initially, many were inpatient facilities where patients could receive basic care until they died. Patients who could be cared for at home remained there, with services to support death at home. Since the addition of hospice care as a covered service under Medicare in 1983, hospice services have grown tremendously, to over 1,800 agencies in the United States.

The standards set forth in the Medicare guidelines defined how hospice care should be delivered in order to receive medical insurance reimbursement (Brenner, 1997). To be eligible for the Medicare Hospice Benefit (MHB), the following must be in place:

The individual is a Medicare (Part A) beneficiary.
Physician certifies a prognosis <6 months.
Individual agrees not to pursue curative treatment.

After the individual chooses coverage under the MHB, a per diem (daily) reimbursement is paid to the hospice agency. Among the services that are provided to the patients and families (depending on their plan of care) are as follows:

Physician visits
Skilled nursing
Physical, speech, occupational therapy
Home health aide visits
Social work/supportive services
Medical equipment/supplies
Bereavement support (up to 1 year after death)
Spiritual counseling
Volunteer services
Prescription pain medications
(or other medications related to the terminal diagnosis)
Short-term inpatient and respite care

According to Cicely Saunders (1998), founder of the hospice movement in England, the work of the interdisciplinary team in providing palliative care is aimed toward enabling the dying person "to live until he dies, at his own maximum potential, performing to the limit of his physical activity and mental capacity with control and independence whenever possible" (p. viii). She goes on to say "if he [the dying person] is recognized as the unique person that he is and helped to live as part of his family and in other relationships, he can still reach out to his hopes and expectations and to what has deepest meaning for him and end his life with a sense of completion" (p. viii).

THE HOSPICE POPULATION

In 2003, an estimated 950,000 patients were served by hospice programs. Fifty-four percent of hospice patients were female and 46% male. Sixty-three percent were age 75 and older. Eighty-one percent of all hospice patients were white, 9% were African American, 4% Hispanic, 1% Asian or Hawaiian/Pacific Islander, and 5% were classified as multiracial or another race. Fifty percent of hospice deaths took place at home, 23% in a nursing facility, 7% in a hospice unit, 9% in a hospital, 7% in a free-standing inpatient facility operated by the hospice, and 4% in a residential care setting (NHPCO, 2004).

Close to half of all individuals enrolled in hospice programs had a cancer diagnosis in 2003. The top five other causes of death in hospice programs were end-stage heart disease (11.0%), dementia (9.6%), lung disease (6.8%), end-stage kidney disease (2.8%), and end-stage liver disease (1.6%) (NHPCO, 2004). Hospice patients with a diagnosis of dementia represent about 1/10 of all deaths of persons with dementia. Barriers to effective end-of-life care for people with dementia include: dementia is not seen as a terminal illness; the nature of advanced dementia and treatment possibilities; the psychological and emotional challenges of withholding treatments such as antibiotics and tube feeding; assessment and management of pain in cognitively impaired individuals; management of behavioral problems and psychiatric symptoms; the challenges of caregiver stress and bereavement issues; and economic and systemic disincentives for providing excellent end-of-life care to patients with dementia (Sachs, Shega, & Cox-Hayley, 2004).

INTERDISCIPLINARY PRACTICE

"Interdisciplinary practice refers to people with distinct disciplinary training working together for a common purpose, as they make different, complementary contributions to patient-focused care." (McCallin, 2001).An interdisciplinary team is critical in the provision of hospice care, as no one discipline has the expertise to meet the wide range of issues and physical needs that patients may have at the end of life. The core of these teams is normally composed of physicians, nurses, social workers, chaplains, and volunteers. Other disciplines may be brought in as needed and available for consultation. Each patient and family are assigned a core team with whom they normally interact. The core team communicates regularly to coordinate the patient's plan of care as the illness progresses; extended members of the team are kept informed of the situation so they may step in if needed.

All team members support family caregivers. Social workers can provide education, informally at interdisciplinary team meetings, or formally in organized seminars for staff, regarding family stressors and family dynamics particular to terminal illness, along with interventions that may be used. Ferrell (1998) identified eleven issues of concern for families caring for patients with cancer: emotional strain, physical demands, uncertainty, fear of the patient dying, altered rules and lifestyles, finances, ways to comfort the patient, perceived inadequacies of services, existential concern, sexuality, and nonconvergent needs among household members. Major issues related to family communication were found to be: acquiring information, concealing feelings, and coping with helplessness (Vachon, 1998). Communication skills are emphasized in social work programs, and the social work team member takes responsibility for training in this area, particularly among nonprofessional team members such as volunteers.

SOCIAL WORK'S ROLE IN HOSPICE CARE

Medical social work is one of the oldest "specialties." It began in 1905, first in the dispensaries (outpatient clinics) of Massachusetts General Hospital, and later in 1914, social work was introduced into the inpatient system. Soon social workers were an integral part of the healthcare team in hospitals and outpatient health settings. Medical social workers often maintained continuity between hospital and home by seeing patients in the community. Home visits were made to follow up on treatment plans and to assess obstacles to treatment that may exist in the patient's environment. Under the current healthcare system, medical social workers in increasing numbers are finding themselves in the "field," in home health and hospice settings.

Hospice Medicare guidelines require social workers to be a fundamental part of the interdisciplinary team approach in caring for terminally ill individuals. In the hospice setting, social workers' special skills and knowledge are essential. Social work values and principles have influenced hospice theory and practice from its early beginnings in England (MacDonald, 1991). Cicely Saunders, considered the founder of the hospice movement, was a nurse, medical social worker, and a physician, and she included aspects and values of each of these disciplines in her conceptualization of the modern hospice (Kulys & Davis, 1986).

Hospice philosophy recognizes a holistic perspective on care, consistent with traditional social work values, skills, and knowledge base. Unlike the other disciplines in health care, social work champions the concepts of self-determination, person-in-environment or ecological perspective, and a strengths perspective that address the whole person (Reese & Raymer, 2004). Biological, psychological, social, and spiritual aspects of the person are considered and respected. Social workers can assist in the following hospice objectives (Cowles, 2003, p. 300):

> Relief of suffering
> Preservation of relationships
> Facilitation of anticipatory grief
> Resolution of residual conflicts
> Supporting the client's sense of integrity and control over decisions

Social workers form relationships intended to maximize the quality of life that remains. After the death, social workers counsel families through their bereavement and adjustment to the loss of someone important in their lives.

Only a small amount of literature and few studies have examined social work roles and functions in hospice. In a 1982 study of social services provided in the hospice setting, nurses, social workers, and volunteers reported that regardless of their other functions, counseling and emotional support were the primary focus of their care. Nurses were more involved than social workers in a number of other areas, including program development. A limitation to assessing the level of social work involvement was that not all of the hospices surveyed (n=34) employed full-time social workers (Kulys & Davis, 1986). Mac-Donald (1991) suggested two areas for strengthening the social work role in hospice: conducting applied research, and developing specific interventions. According to a study of 122 hospice social workers, the activities they performed most often were psychosocial assessment, counseling patients and families, connecting patients and families with concrete resources, and interdisciplinary planning. Activities in which they were least involved included research, volunteer training, and education of staff regarding therapeutic interventions (Csikai, 2004).

According to Monroe (1998), three elements influence the social work role in palliative care: the nonmedical social goals, teamwork and multidisciplinary skills needed to meet those goals, and the expectations that patients, families, and other members of the team have of social workers. Nonmedical goals can be pursued once the patient's physical pain and other disease-related symptoms causing discomfort have been alleviated. Among nonmedical needs are expression of the emotional pain of terminal illness, exploration of spiritual pain, and assistance with practical tasks, such as making a will or other legal or financial decisions.

The interdisciplinary team's effectiveness in meeting nonmedical needs is essential. Members have overlapping roles: Medical needs are met by those in the medical disciplines; nonmedical needs may be addressed by anyone on the team. Patients and families should expect "a consistent, careful, and effective approach to be adopted by all of them" (Monroe, 1998, p. 867). All members of the team are involved in listening, talking, and sharing information. Social workers should model good communication skills in their interactions with the team, and act as a safety net for tasks that are hard for other team members to fulfill (Monroe, 1998).

A thorough assessment of the situation takes place upon admission to the hospice program. Normally a nurse takes care of the medical aspects and may identify areas where coordination with other team members is needed. A detailed psycho-social-spiritual assessment may be required and routinely completed by hospice services. Assessment considers the individual, family, physical resources, and social resources, including support from family, friends, and church.

Interventions that may be needed are identified through this thorough assessment of the patient and family situation. Common interventions used by social workers in hospice include information and communication, to increase confidence of patients and families to control their situation. Provision of practical resources may be delivered through linkages with community agencies. After death, bereavement services are offered. Social workers may choose to intervene one-on-one, in family meetings, or in group settings (Monroe, 1998).

In a recent study conducted in conjunction with the Social Work Section of the National Hospice and Palliative Care Organization (Reese & Raymer, 2004), a majority of social workers surveyed (through a retrospective review of 330 patient charts) provided input to the interdisciplinary team regarding psychosocial, cultural, and spiritual issues. Social workers provided education about the importance of an ecological perspective, served as advocates for self-determination, and provided emotional support to other team members. Social workers help in solving conflicts arising from differences in values among the disciplines, boundary issues, self-determination, and turf issues. Social workers serve as educators in volunteer training, public education about hospice, and outreach, particularly in the medical community, to increase awareness of hospice services to dying individuals and their families.

The main goal of the Reese and Raymer study (2004) was to show, empirically, the value of social work in the hospice setting. It showed that social workers with the most experience and masters degrees had better patient outcomes. Supervision by a social worker, rather than by a professional of another discipline, was also related to better patient outcomes. Participation in intake interviews was associated with lower overall hospice costs. When families are initially admitted to hospice, social workers can apply their skills to identifying problems in the environment, family dynamics that may contribute to difficulties in caregiving or lead to complicated grief processes, and devise a plan of care that incorporates strategies to pre-empt potential problems.

Preventing crises can lead to lower rates of hospitalization, pain costs, and number of nursing visits. The use of psychosocial interventions by trained, experienced social workers at the beginning of a case can ensure that all options are explored "before less effective, higher-cost options are used," such as continuous care and inpatient treatment. Other beneficial outcomes of increased social work intervention were fewer hospitalizations, fewer home health aide visits, fewer nights in continuous care, and better client satisfaction (Reese & Raymer, 2004).

HOSPICE AND PALLIATIVE CARE IN LONG-TERM CARE FACILITIES

Long-term care facilities are responsible for a large portion of care given at the time of death. More than 20% of all deaths in the United States occur in nursing homes. Of nursing home residents, more than two-thirds of permanent residents will stay there until they die. In spite of this, the emphasis in nursing homes is on rehabilitation rather than provision of exceptional end-of-life care (Reynolds, Henderson, Schulman, & Hanson, 2002).

Increasingly, hospice and palliative care is being offered to residents of long-term care facilities. When residents choose the Medicare hospice benefit, hospice becomes responsible for residents' plan of care. Similar to other hospice patients, nursing home residents must choose to forgo curative treatments. Residents are responsible to pay their room and board either privately or through Medicaid, if eligible. Hospice in the nursing home is considered as providing care in the home as the facility is the patient's home environment. Residents are eligible for all services that traditional home patients receive.

Perhaps the most significant contribution of hospice services for residents in nursing homes is the attention to pain management in terminal illness. It is well documented that nursing home residents with cancer and other terminal conditions often do not receive adequate pain medications. In one study of nursing home residents with cancer, 26% had documented daily pain and did not receive any analgesic medication; 26% of residents with a known cancer diagnosis received morphine. The presence of pain was associated with several factors: age, gender, race, physical function, depression, and cognitive impairment. Undertreatment was prominent among minority residents (Bernabei, Gambassi, Lapane, Landi, Gatsonis, Dunlop, et al., 1998). Not only is there a benefit to the identified resident for services, it is an opportunity to improve pain management for other residents through education of nursing home staff by hospice workers (Miller & Mor, 2002). The day-to-day care needs of the nursing home residents are met by nursing home staff, but the addition of hospice services adds a second level of support. Recent studies have suggested that higher-quality assessment and management of symptoms and fewer hospitalizations are associated with hospice care (Baer & Hanson, 2000; Miller, Gozalo, & Mor, 2001).

The nursing home environment presents unique problems for professionals involved in service delivery. These include the working relationship with the immediate family and nursing home staff and the patterns of communication that exist in this setting. Among nursing home staff issues that hospice professionals may deal with are high rates of burnout and turnover. Also, the usual standard of care focuses on custodial care rather than on psychosocial and spiritual needs of residents. Open communication about death and bereavement is encouraged in hospice care, while this is minimal in the nursing home environment (Amar, 1994; Jones, Nackerud, & Boyle, 1997). Hospice professionals should keep in mind that the nursing home is the resident's home. Since the nursing home staff are providing direct care, they should be included as part of the hospice interdisciplinary team and be involved in the hospice plan of care. The facility's staff should be considered the resident's extended family and should be treated as such, including addressing the staff's bereavement needs after the resident's death.

Managing end-of-life care for residents diagnosed with dementia or Alzheimer's disease may be particularly difficult in the nursing home environment. Because of deteriorating cognitive abilities, these persons are not able to communicate when they are in pain or experiencing discomfort.

INPATIENT PALLIATIVE CARE SERVICES

Though the notion of palliative care grew out of the hospice movement and the national movement to reduce pain and symptoms experienced at the end of life, it is most often associated with inpatient or in-home hospice services. Recently an effort has been underway, mainly in large urban hospitals, to create special palliative care units and services for hospital inpatients. Often teams of palliative care specialists consult on pain and symptom management for patients suffering from a life-limiting illness. These services are being offered in response to critics who have identified poor management of pain and other kinds of suffering for dying patients within hospitals. The criticisms have included: that the primary concern has been with those who have a good chance of cure, emphasis on the illness rather than on symptoms, devalued family needs, and negating the attitude of fighting death until there is nothing left to do (Hite & Marshall, 1997). The philosophy and techniques of comfort care can be easily transferred to the hospital setting. Proper training and attention to all the symptoms of pain and suffering must accompany any effort to provide successful palliative care in the hospital, as it requires a vastly different attitude.

DECISION MAKING IN HOSPICE AND PALLIATIVE CARE

After the initial choice to receive hospice care is made, other decisions may arise up until the death of the patient.

> Mary was a 75-year-old woman with end-stage renal cancer. She was frail and weak after her two-year battle with the disease, which included surgery and chemotherapy. She was receiving hospice care in the home of her son and daughter-in-law. A hospice nurse visited weekly to monitor Mary's pain level. On one occasion, the family noted that the pain seemed to be worsening. The nurse recommended a change in morphine dosage. This worked temporarily but the pain would worsen again every few days. The family was worried that Mary was not comfortable and efforts to control the pain were not successful. The nurse recommended an inpatient stay. Mary stated she didn't want to go because she didn't want to die in the hospital, but her son and daughter-in-law convinced her that it would be temporary and that she could come home again. They felt guilty not being able to keep her at home for care and also because they felt relieved to have a break from caregiving.

There are times that pain cannot be adequately controlled in the home setting and an inpatient hospice stay specifically to address pain control is warranted. When the pain is better controlled the patient may return home. Early exposure to palliative care management can allow the patient and family to feel more comfortable asking for help when needed. This is often a difficult situation for the caregivers in that they may feel like they have failed.

Inpatient stays are also allowed as a respite for caregivers. This may involve acknowledgment of fatigue and the need to care for themselves. This can be difficult as well and also experienced as a failure. Social workers help to normalize those feelings and to see that they must take care of their own needs to effectively care for the patient.

Another instance when inpatient hospice stays can be appropriate is when a patient is actively dying. The active phase of the dying process is typically characterized by severe agitation, coma or semi-coma, long pauses in breathing, cool extremities, and cyanosis; it still may be difficult to predict exactly when the patient will die. Families sometimes do not feel comfortable with their loved one actually dying in their home. They may not feel prepared for their reactions at the time of death. Upon admission to hospice care, families should discuss the possibility of transferring the patient to the inpatient unit when near death; while not encouraged, it is acceptable, especially since the MHB will cover the costs.

Home care is the primary model, and throughout the hospice stay the social worker will work with the family to consider whether the patient is able to remain at home until death.

Mrs. S, age 70, has been caring for her 88-year-old mother, Mrs. R, who was diagnosed with Alzheimer's disease seven years ago. Mrs. R has had very little support or help from her two other daughters who live fairly close by. They have not been able to handle it when they visit, and Mrs. R doesn't recognize them. The patient is now bedridden and believed to be in the terminal phase of the disease. She was referred to hospice care by the primary care physician after a recent hospital stay for pneumonia.

Upon initial assessment by the social worker, Mrs. S appeared fatigued and broke into tears when asked if she needed assistance in caring for her mother. It has been a struggle but the daughter is proud that she has been able to care for her mother at home up until now. The hospice social worker suggests that nursing aides come in to bathe Mrs. R three to four times per week and that a volunteer come once a week for a few hours so that Mrs. S can grocery shop or just have time to herself. Mrs. S agrees to this. The social worker will reassess care needs after two weeks.

At the follow up visit Mrs. S still described how difficult it was to have total care of her mother and that she got little sleep at night. Mrs. S stated that at a recent visit to her family doctor, her blood pressure was very high and the doctor had increased her dosage of medication to treat it. He also prescribed Xanax, for her feelings of anxiety that she wasn't doing enough for her mother. The social worker suggested the options of hiring paid caregivers to come in to give Mrs. S a break or placing Mrs. R in a nursing home with continued hospice care, and that Mrs. S should discuss these possibilities with the rest of her family.

Providing care for someone at the end of life can be both comforting and stressful. While care provided to Mrs. R was excellent, her caregiver's physical and emotional health was compromised. The situation was not optimal. Alternatives do exist. Social workers in hospice service may find that discharge planning is a useful skill at times like these. Awareness of resources that can assist patients and families with care in the home (paid caregivers) or placement outside the home is essential.

Social workers must also be aware of the disease trajectories for various medical conditions served by hospice care. For example, in late-stage Alzheimer's disease a severe decline in cognitive and functional abilities is typical. At this stage complete care is required, including help with eating and toileting as the patient may become incontinent. Further medical complications may arise from falls or episodes of pneumonia (Cummings & Cockerham, 1997). Trajectories of functional decline before death were described by Lunney, Lynn, Foley, Lipson, and Buralnik (2003). Before a sudden death, individuals can be highly functional, even one month prior to death. Cancer deaths are characterized by a high degree of functional ability during the last year and increased disability three months prior to death. In the case of organ failure (CHF), there is a fluctuating pattern of decline, with lower functioning during the final three months. In deaths due to frailty, individuals are more disabled during the final year, especially during the final month.

Much discussion took place over two social work visits with Mrs. S. During the second visit, one of the other daughters was present. Mrs. S agreed, with the support of her sister, to consider placing Mrs. R in a nursing facility. The social worker suggested three nursing homes and the daughter agreed to look at them and decide with her sister which was best. As it turned out, one was close to Mrs. S's home (about 1 mile away), which they felt would be appropriate.

Mrs. R was transferred to the nursing home with continued hospice care. The nurse in charge of Mrs. R in the nursing home was different, but the social worker was able to continue to work with the family until Mrs. R died six months later. Mrs. R died peacefully and Mrs. S's blood pressure and stress level decreased over time. The entire family viewed this change of environment as beneficial to all, including the patient.

That care can be given outside the home is hard for caregivers to accept due to feelings of guilt caused by being unable to do it themselves or because of promises they made to the loved one. The idea of death at home is often represented as oversimplified and overdramatized. It is essential that social workers consider how at-home care of a patient with a life-limiting illness will affect the entire family. In the case of dementia or Alzheimer's disease, the individual will not be able to make end-of-life treatment decisions due to cognitive impairment. If the impaired individual does not have an advance directive and has not discussed wishes with the family, questions about care are not easily resolved.

ETHICAL ISSUES IN HOSPICE AND PALLIATIVE CARE

Ethical issues can arise when care is provided in the home because of advancing medical technology that may prolong life almost indefinitely and an increased focus on transferring health care to community settings. Even though patients and families have made a decision to accept hospice services, everyone may face ethical issues during the palliative care stages until death occurs. Sensitive management of ethical issues as they come up can ensure a good experience and influence the way people handle future deaths. Social workers are an integral part of the hospice team and can be valuable resources in assisting with resolution of ethical dilemmas.

Cummings and Cockerham (1997) identified seven ethical issues in the provision of palliative care: clinical ethics, confidentiality, competence, research, resource allocation, withholding or withdrawing therapy, and euthanasia. Hospices may additionally face organizational issues, such as access to services by people of diverse economic and racial backgrounds (Byock, 1994). People with dementia and chronic diseases also face barriers as some hospices view themselves as unprepared to provide services in these cases, particularly with dementia. Some may be reluctant to admit individuals with mental illness, developmental disabilities, or who are homeless or have a history of drug and/or alcohol abuse (Jennings, Ryndes, D'Onofrio, & Baily, 2003).

Ethics committees in hospice settings provide excellent forums for healthcare professionals to engage in discussion of difficult cases, educate staff and community, and formulate agency policy that can minimize the occurrence of ethical dilemmas. Policies that offer guidance for provision of care in difficult cases can be fully considered and plans made. Few such committees exist, so interdisciplinary team meetings often serve as the outlet for discussion of ethical problems in specific cases (Csikai, 2004). Education and policy formulation may be assigned to small task groups of agency personnel.

According to social workers in one study (Csikai, 2004), the situations with potential for ethical problems had to do with the medical condition of the patient, uncontrolled pain, progression of illness during hospice stay, re-examination of curative care versus palliative care, involvement of family, and family denial of terminal illness. Least discussed were issues related to euthanasia, assisted suicide, and completion of suicide by the patient. However, 32% of the social workers indicated that they'd had a request from a patient to discuss assisted suicide and 17% reported that they had received such a request from a patient's family member. Four percent of respondents indicated that they had witnessed active euthanasia and 2% had witnessed assisted suicide during the course of their work as a hospice social worker (Csikai, 2004).

With respect to physician-assisted suicide, the strongest objection among many hospice workers to legal sanction to hasten death is a belief in the potential for personal and family growth through sharing the experience of dying; if death is hastened, this opportunity is lost (Saunders, 1998). Some proponents of legalization of assisted suicide maintain that hastening death should only be considered as a last resort, after full utilization of hospice services (Brody, 1992; Quill, 1991 a, b; Miller, 1997).

Chapter Conclusion

Social workers in a range of healthcare settings, and in other fields as well should understand the extent and limits of support and care that palliative and hospice care programs can offer to patients and families at the end of life. They will have a role in assisting patients and families in the transition from pursuing aggressive treatments aimed at curing disease to accepting that death is near. Their role is to offer comfort, physically, emotionally, and spiritually at this time. In hospice programs, social workers are an invaluable part of the interdisciplinary team. How likely it is for programs to increase the number and involvement of social workers in intakes and other preventive interactions and day-to-day activities with patients and families, as is called for by Reese and Raymer (2004), remains to be seen.

Chapter Five

THE PROCESS OF END-OF-LIFE DECISION MAKING

Medical decision making, especially at the end of life, is a carefully orchestrated process that takes place between a patient and doctor. Informed consent forms the basis of these interactions, and is usually a straightforward two-step process. In step one, the physician informs the patient about proposed treatments, clarifies risks and benefits, and describes the options. In step two, the competent patient considers all this and decides whether to consent or refuse. Obtaining informed consent is not always such a smooth exercise, however, and problems can occur for many reasons. Add the emotional anxiety often attached to end-of-life choices and the decision-making course becomes even more complex. The case of David is an example of the types of complexities that can arise for someone who is terminally ill and who may not be capable of fully participating in the informed consent process.

The purpose of this chapter is to describe the informed consent process, address the standard of competence required to assure informed consent or refusal, and discuss the complexity of choices. The role of the clinical social worker is paramount and most critical at the end of life, where choices may be painful and require so much of the patient and their surrogate decision-makers. David's case will be referenced throughout the chapter to illustrate key problematic areas in medical decision making.

> David is a 39-year-old male diagnosed with stage IV malignant melanoma. He has metastases to his lungs, abdominal cavity, spine, and bilateral femurs, which leave him in severe pain (score 10 out of 10) most of the day. He was first admitted to a large academic medical center for treatment of a small bowel obstruction. After considerable testing

it was determined that the obstruction is inoperable. His pain remains poorly controlled and his physicians state that he is terminal.

David has a flat affect, discussing little of how he feels, physically or emotionally. The physicians treating David are not sure he truly understands how ill he is. They are concerned that his request for surgical intervention, despite the almost certain odds of death, are a wish on David's part to die. He has refused to take radiation treatments. He has a documented history of anxiety and depression, has provided little family information, and no family was present when he arrived from the outside hospital. The patient's sister, from whom he has been estranged until recently, informed the attending physician, via telephone, that David was a victim of early childhood neglect. He has executed no living will or power of attorney for health care.

HISTORY AND DEFINITION OF INFORMED CONSENT

The concept of informed consent began to emerge from court involvement early in the 20th century. In 1914, the court responded to the case of a woman who had a tumor removed without her consent while undergoing an examination for a uterine growth, under anesthesia. Following the procedure the patient developed gangrene and suffered from a serious long-term illness. In response to the question of consent in this case, Justice Benjamin Cardozo stated, "Every human being of adult years and sound mind has a right to determine what shall be done with his own body." This case brought to the public eye the right of an individual to self-determination in the context of informed medical consent (Boyle, 1995; *Schloendorff v. Society of New York Hospital*, 1914). In 1957, legal requirements began to be defined by the courts by declaring that physicians violate their duty to patients if they withhold any facts necessary to give consent (*Salgo v. Leland Stanford Jr.*). Still, this ruling emphasized disclosure and not the right of the patient to make the decision (Boyle, 1995). Also in 1957, the American Medical Association (AMA) recognized that voluntary consent was needed for involvement in medical research, however, it was not until 1981 that the AMA (in "Current Opinions of the Judicial Council") addressed the decision aspect of true informed consent in the organization's code of ethics. "The patient's right of self-determination can be effectively exercised only if the patient possesses enough information to enable an intelligent choice. The patient should make his own determination on treatment." Other influences that formed the impetus for informed consent during this era were the civil liberties revolution, consumer rights and advocacy movements, and increasing media coverage and public awareness of medical issues, treatments, and alternatives (Boyle, 1995).

Types of Consent

Several different types of consent are discussed in the literature: tacit consent, implicit or implied consent, presumed consent, and informed consent.

Tacit consent. This is expressed passively by omission or lack of objection. It assumes an understanding of the proposal and the need for consent or objection. An example of tacit consent occurs when a phlebotomist enters a patient's room and says, "Do you mind if I draw blood now?" If there is no objection, the blood is drawn. There is minimal interaction or discussion of the procedure beforehand.

Implicit or implied consent. This is inferred by an individual's actions. For example, if you agree to have anesthesia for a surgical procedure, then you implicitly agree to be on a respirator for that time as well. The assumption is that, under anesthesia, respiration is depressed and assistance in breathing will be necessary.

Presumed consent. This is based on a general theory of human goods, social norms, or beliefs about a group. One example is emergency treatment in which consent is not sought specifically but it is generally believed that most people would want medical treatment in a crisis situation. Other examples include (in some states) HIV testing of newborns or routine procurement of corneas; procedures that are thought to be a benefit to all.

Informed consent. This requires respect for informed and voluntary treatment choices made by competent individuals (Buchanan & Brock, 1990) and based on individual decisions. According to

Kuczewski (1996), central to the doctrine of informed consent is the legal principle of the right of a competent person to refuse medical treatment. This legal right is expressed in two aspects of the law, *tort law* and *constitutional law*. A tort is described by Faden and Beauchamp (1986) as "civil injury to one's person or property that is intentionally or negligently inflicted by another person and that is measured in terms of, and compensated by, money damages" (p. 23). The other relevant aspect of the law in the informed consent statute is the right to privacy, which is "imbedded in American constitutional law" (Faden & Beauchamp, 1986, pp. 23–24). The right of privacy is the aspect of law most reflected upon when considering issues at the end of life. This right allows all competent patients to refuse any and all medical interventions, even if such refusal could result in death (Meisel, 1989). To carry out this right, the individual must receive and comprehend comprehensive information and decide independently either to undergo or forgo medical treatment. Beauchamp and Childress (1994) discussed the two aspects of informed consent: *autonomous authorization* and *social rules of consent*. Autonomous authorization is needed from patients for medical treatment to be administered or for involvement in a research protocol. This is the "process" aspect of informed consent. The second aspect is "paperwork," whereby institutions must obtain legally valid written or otherwise documented consent before proceeding with the treatment or research. "Informed consent" is what happens in the interaction between physicians and individuals; it is not the document itself.

Exceptions to Informed Consent

There *are* situations when it is ethically appropriate to provide treatment without consent. One such incident is in an emergency when the patient is incapable of granting consent, a proxy cannot be located, and delay of treatment could cause death. There are also other situations, called waivers, when treatment can be rendered without consent (Devettere, 2000). All exceptions to informed consent are discussed here.

Emergencies. These are usually defined as situations under which "there is not time to disclose the necessary information for an informed consent" (Devettere, 2000, p. 108). Some situations may be defined as emergent when consent has been obtained but overlooked due to the emergency. For example, a patient is dying at home and on home hospice. He is found to be very short of breath and his wife panics and calls 9-1-1. When the paramedics arrive they insist on intubating the dying patient despite the fact that his previous wishes were not to receive heroic care. It is not unusual for paramedics to express a moral need to provide care because of the emergency status of the care that paramedics provide (Devettere, 2000).

Waivers. According to Devettere (2000), there are times when patients choose to give up their right to consent, preferring not to be informed of their diagnosis or prognosis. Patients are permitted to waive their right to give consent. However, according to Meisel (1989), "For a waiver to be legally effective, the patient must know of the right to be provided with information about treatment by the attending physician and the right to make a decision about treatment, including the right to decline it. In addition, the waiver must be voluntarily signed" (Meisel, 1989). Other times patients may request that others make medical decisions for them; for example, wives who request that their husbands make the medical decisions, or elderly parents who request that their children make their medical decisions, or patients from certain cultural groups may ask that family be informed of the diagnosis, prognosis, and treatment options, and make the decisions. Some patients prefer that their physicians make their medical choices. In the current litigation-driven healthcare environment, this type of request is more than morally complicated, and few physicians are willing to make choices for their patients (Devettere, 2000). Patients can waive their right to make decisions and transfer their autonomy to someone they trust; however, autonomy should not be transferred to the physician treating the patient (Devettere, 2000).

Therapeutic privilege. This exception was discussed in one of the initial informed consent cases, *Canterbury v. Spence* (1972). This case discussed the therapeutic privilege of a physician to "withhold part or all of the material information from a patient, because of the harmful effects of disclosure" (Faden & Beauchamp, 1986, pp. 35–38).

This privilege is ambiguous at best (Faden & Beauchamp, 1986). According to Devettere (2000), "There is no evidence that informing patients of their situation when the diagnosis and prognosis are not good is more dangerous to them than pretending everything is fine" (pp. 107–113). Such a "privilege" forces all who care for this patient to enter a conspiracy of silence, which complicates the moral integrity of all and far outweighs whatever benefit was to be gained by executing therapeutic privilege (Devettere, 2000).

INFORMED CONSENT PROCESS

Informed consent is best conceptualized as a conversation, normally initiated by a physician, healthcare provider, or someone in a position of power or authority due to specialized knowledge of the illness and treatment options. During the conversation, the clinician reveals his or her thinking, knowledge, concerns, and advice. The patient or surrogate has the responsibility to ask questions and state concerns and preferences rather than be a passive participant. Engagement by both parties is encouraged. Consent should be obtained at each step for all care provided, delivered over time and withdrawn at any time. Informed consent is an ongoing process when practiced under the best of standards and circumstances (Roth & Meisel, 1977).

Two values undergird the informed consent statute: preservation of autonomy and preservation of human dignity. In the best situation, informed consent occurs between the patient and doctor, with both providing and obtaining information about proposed medical treatments or procedures. The goal is to create the best environment for the patient to execute an informed, self-determined choice. When patients are unable to render informed consent or refusal, the process assures that the patient's human dignity is preserved through the use of a surrogate decision-maker. Over the past thirty years, the legal system has helped to outline the role of the surrogate as well as the best process to assist in making end-of-life choices (Meisel, 1989). Issues specifically related to surrogate decision-making are discussed later in this chapter.

By law, all competent patients have the right to refuse any medical treatment, even if such rejection could result in death (Meisel, 1989).

It is essential to gain consent of the patient before rendering medical treatment. To do so, adequate disclosure of the following information is required: the medical diagnosis, a description of the recommended treatment, the risks and benefits of the proposed treatment, and the availability of alternative forms of treatment, including no treatment (Roth & Meisel, 1977). The amount and detail of risk information must be divulged based on the community standard for such disclosure. The standard of disclosure is typically "limited to those disclosures which a reasonable medical practitioner would make under the same or similar circumstances" (*Natason v. Kline*, 1960). According to Berg, Appelbaum, and Grisso (1996), "This standard closely parallels the one used in medical negligence or malpractice cases generally: Physicians are held to the standard of what is customary and usual in the profession, not only the exercise of skill but also in the disclosure of information to patients" (p. 46).

DETERMINATION OF DECISION-MAKING CAPACITY

Informed consent also requires determination of the capacity of the patient to understand the information (Lidz, Appelbaum & Meisel, 1988). Capacity to participate in medical decision making is measured in many ways. Roth and Meisel (1977) outline five tests to measure competency, in order of increasing importance:

> Evidence of a choice
> "Reasonable" outcome of choice
> Choice based upon rational reasons
> Ability to understand
> Actual evidence of understanding

Determination of what constitutes "reasonable" and "rational" is unclear. Who determines what is reasonable and rational? In a later writing, Roth, Appelbaum, Sallee, Reynolds, and Huber (1982) listed only four criteria:

> Evidence of a choice
> Evidence of an understanding of the relevant information

Rational manipulation of relevant information provided
Appreciation of the consequences of the situation

According to Gutheil and Appelbaum (1983), for *general competency* a patient should have the following:

Awareness of the nature of the situation, including level of impairment, if any exists
Factual understanding of the issues
Ability to manipulate information rationally to reach a decision

These factors are similar to the four characteristics outlining what is reasonable and rational above. Whether referring to one, both, or a combination of assessment methods, several factors come into play when one is considering an individual's capacity for informed consent. One is the task in question, or what the patient is being asked to consider. For example, is the patient being asked to consent to open-heart surgery or the cardiac catheterization procedure to determine if such surgery is required? Each procedure requires a different level of understanding as they hold different levels of risk. Another critical factor is outlined well by Schaffner (1991).

In practice, the processes discussed above have been used in a combined fashion, and a shortened process has been devised (see case example of David). Frequently, assessments of capacity are part of an interdisciplinary assessment completed in conjunction with a psychiatrist.

Measurement of decision-making capacity is an essential aspect of informed consent. Decisions must be made by someone who can comprehend the situation and the consequences of his/her choice. Provision of information and evidence of understanding form the foundation of informed consent.

In David's case, the actual declaration of incapacity is left to a licensed physician with the guidance of a psychiatrist. No matter which professional is doing the evaluation he or she is interested in the patient's abilities related to the following: In the case of David, he would need to demonstrate a reasonable *level of understanding* of his illness. His *understanding of the choices* needs to be clear, including the risks and benefits. He should *understand the severity* of his condition. The clinician might be asked to determine how well David *assimilates information* and the *degree of information* he is able to provide to the healthcare team, regarding his current level of illness.

The clinical social worker would need to assess David's emotional age, his coping abilities, and history and current level of depression or anxiety, as well as relevant history of death or serious illness in his family of origin. The clinical social worker might also be asked to outline the level of support required from the healthcare team to assure David's highest capacity for making complex decisions.

In sum, the key factors to look for when assessing a patient's ability to grant or refuse consent are *information*: David's ability to assimilate and provide information related to his current level of illness; and *understanding*: David's ability to evidence understanding of the choices, issues of concern, and severity of his current state.

Two other factors are critical to the capacity for consent: the ability to make a voluntary choice and the ability to render a choice based on issues of concern.

Voluntary Choice

Informed consent requires that decisions be voluntary, made free from internal and external constraints. The exercise of free choice is paramount. Free choice supports the core values at the heart of the informed consent doctrine: the preservation of human dignity and self-determination. Schaffner (1991) describes it as the "volitional component," and characterizes voluntary choice as "intend[ing] to capture those factors which adversely affect free choice but which do not appear to be purely conceptual or 'rational.' "

Factors that adversely affect free choice are coercion, manipulation, and persuasion. Some feel that coercion and persuasion are present in all forms of communication, especially when it occurs between people with unequal power. An example of an unequal, power-based relationship is the one between a doctor and a patient. This relationship was described well by Smith and Pettegrew (1986) when they stated, "The traditional doctor-patient relationship has been characterized by the giving of orders. Communication is [a] directive and the appropriate response on the part of the patient is compliance" (pp. 23–24).

David met with his attending physician one evening after he had been medicated for the treatment of pain. He had been taking the same dose of morphine since admission. He remained alert and well oriented, had a good understanding of his medical condition, and was able to relay and assimilate information. He was seen as being able to voluntarily render a choice.

Evidence of Choice

The final requirement of informed consent is to gain the consent of the patient and render a decision. In the hospital setting, consent to treatment is the typical goal. This is problematic, especially if the patient elects to refuse treatment. Sometimes a decision to decline medically recommended treatment is viewed as a sign of incapacity, or an irrational choice. However, this decision alone should not be seen as the sole indicator of incompetence, because refusal of treatment is always an option and well within the patient's rights. This was described eloquently by Pellegrino (1991) when he stated, "Competence is a capacity; the decision is the product of that capacity. . . .The competence of the decision is not synonymous with the 'competence' of the patient"(p. 33).

In each medical situation determination of capacity or incapacity is considered. Any given decision may trigger questioning of the patient's ability to render choice. The capacity evaluation focuses on the process over the decision. A critical role for the healthcare social worker is to construct a full picture of the patient. This should be comprised of the physiological, social, emotional, and psychological needs of the patient. Delivering this full view assures that the value structure of the patient will be considered.

Several possible case outcomes might be discussed. One scenario calls into question the capacity of the patient, which then demands to know who else is competent to assist the healthcare team with end-of-life choices? Interestingly, assessment of the patient's capacity for consent and to designate a surrogate are distinctly different conceptual viewpoints that are "inextricably intertwined in clinical practice" (Meisel, 1989, p. 71). Another case outcome might be a movement from a curative focus to one of comfort care.

David's Case: Outcome #1

As David's condition deteriorated, the treating physician asked David his views on the end of life. "If your heart were to stop or if you had trouble breathing, how far would you like us to go?" David's response was, "Do everything. I want to live and I know that if you do the surgery we talked about I will be fine." His physicians felt this response was "totally unrealistic" and that his optimism about the surgery was proof that he was unable to render a rational choice. They felt he was in denial of his terminal state.

The role of the clinical social worker at this point might be to help determine the thought process that led to David's choices. He or she could assist in constructing the family history of illness reaction as a way to support and understand David's response to his illness.

Social workers can aid the medical team by researching background information on the patient's family, to faciliate understanding the patient's emotional needs. David's history contains crucial information about how he thinks, which may dictate how the social worker approaches David around end-of-life decisions. This data could also help the individual chosen by David to speak for him, or who is legally named as his surrogate, to understand his preferences.

SURROGATE DECISION MAKING

Meisel (1989) defined a surrogate decision-maker as someone who makes a medical decision on behalf of another. The link between capacity and the need for a surrogate decision-maker is clearly discussed in the 1976 case of Karen Ann Quinlan. This case came to national attention because it was the first one to ask the questions: How is death defined when individuals can be maintained on life-support? Is withdrawal of life-sustaining medical interventions the same as euthanasia? If the patient is deemed to be incompetent to decide, who makes the medical decisions? Karen Ann Quinlan was a 21-year-old woman who lapsed into a persistent vegetative state following aspiration of her own vomit subsequent to overconsumption of alcohol and valium. When it became clear that she would not recover, her parents petitioned the New Jersey Supreme Court to remove the ventilator that was keeping her artificially alive.

This court case set standards for end-of-life decision making and started the public questioning about the right to die. The need to choose a surrogate occurs frequently and this can be problematic. Who can or should serve in this capacity can be a legal matter but is often one of clinical judgment instead. If the patient has named someone to serve as power of attorney or proxy, the law supports that person's right to make medical choices on behalf of the incapacitated patient (Meisel, 1989). However, routinely in clinical practice, the family of the incapacitated patient is called upon to render judgment. This is a "deeply embedded and officially approved professional custom which rarely is up for scrutiny" (Meisel, 1989, p. 174). The practice of clinical assessment of capacity followed by seeking out family as surrogate decision-makers, without seeking adjudication of the patient's incompetence or other judicial guidance, is viewed presumptively as legitimate (Meisel, 1989). Probably the most widely known example is Karen Ann Quinlan, a case when New Jersey Supreme Court deemed it important to allow families to make choices on behalf of patients who are incapable of informed consent.

According to the judge, the family was the logical choice to be the surrogate decision-maker as they were most likely to know their relative's value system. In 1983, the President's Commission analyzed the best way to identify a surrogate and stated that in most cases, this should be the next of kin. They gave several reasons why this was reasonable:

> The family is generally the most concerned about the welfare of the patient.
>
> The family is the most knowledgeable about the patient's goals, preferences, and value structure.
>
> The family deserves recognition as an important social unit that ought to be treated as a respected, responsible decision-maker in matters that intimately affect its members.
>
> Participation in a family is generally an important dimension of personal fulfillment.
>
> Since a protected sphere of privacy and autonomy is required for the flourishing of this interpersonal union, institutions and the state should be reluctant to intrude, particularly

regarding matters that are personal and on which there is a wide range of opinion in society.

The President's Commission went on to state that the healthcare practitioner was "responsible for determining who should act as the patient's surrogate" (1983, p. 154) and that this responsibility allowed for the definition of family to be extended to close friends. Buchanan and Brock (1990) eloquently summarized what formulated the basis of the right of the family to be chosen as surrogate for the incapacitated patient when they stated, "The family bears the consequences of all decisions that are made" (pp. 89–90).

No matter who is chosen, whether family or a friend, specific standards exist to guide them. The search for a correct standard by which to frame decisions made in relation to incapacitated patients began with the Quinlan case. *Barber v. Superior Court* (1983) provided further groundwork for delineation of decision-making standards, and the case of Clare Conroy brought to light the "potential for the creation of a hierarchy of standards" (Meisel, 1989, pp. 407–409). According to Meisel (1989), the hierarchy of standards began with "the use of the best interests standard in right-to-die cases when there was inadequate evidence to meet the then prevailing primary standard, the substituted judgment standard" (p. 409).

Then there came a more stringent standard called the *subjective standard*; in the media this is referred to as the *clear and convincing evidence standard*. The hierarchy of standards, as it is commonly followed at this time, begins with the subjective standard, followed by the *substituted judgment standard*, and then by the *best interests standard*.

Subjective Standard

This standard advocates for the autonomy and self-determination of the incapacitated patient by demanding proof or knowledge of the patient's actual (subjective) wishes. A written advance medical directive is seen as the best proof of the anticipatory wishes of the patient (Meisel, 1989). This was referred to in the 1990 case of Nancy Cruzan, in which the State of Missouri requested "clear and convincing evidence" of Ms. Cruzan's wishes related to discontinuation of the feeding tube. Through such cases the subjective standard mistakenly began to be called the clear and convincing evidence standard.

Substituted Judgment Standard

In cases where another individual is making medical choices for an incapacitated patient, the standard method for making choices is called substituted judgment. This is invoked when a patient has previously indicated his/her wishes for or against certain forms of medical therapy. The surrogate is instructed to choose as the patient would have chosen if he or she were still competent (Meisel, 1989; Buchanan & Brock, 1990). Normally, the competent patient executes an advance directive in writing, which then guides the surrogate in making medical decisions according to the expressed written wishes of the patient.

When implementing the substituted judgment standard in its purest form, the surrogate is not legally permitted to override previously stated patient desires for or against treatment. This standard is seen as the model for all cases of incapacity, whether or not the patient was ever competent or executed an advance directive.

According to Buchanan and Brock (1990), "where there is no advance directive, there is no one guidance principle appropriate for all cases" (p. 152). Sometimes there is not sufficient evidence of what patients would have wanted because they may never have expressed their viewpoint or may have expressed contrary or inconsistent wishes.

It is impossible to apply the substituted judgment standard in situations where the patient lacked capacity from birth (Buchanan & Brock, 1990). The question then remains how to best help surrogates as they seek to make medical choices for incapacitated patients? Some insight into this decision-making process is seen in the history of the substituted judgment standard.

The standard emanated from estate law and contained within it a provision called the "basic interest" of the incompetent ward. This is similar to the best interests standard outlined below. The basic interest clause of the substituted judgment standard as it related to estates was put into place when conflict occurred, and it obligated the judge to consider the basic interests of the incompetent ward and protect them by law (Buchanan & Brock, 1990).

This clause should be applied proportionately because of the complexity of certain cases. In cases where an oral advance directive is weak, the basic interests, as applied in estate law, should be given great proportional weight (Buchanan & Brock, 1990). For example, if Aunt Mabel told her friend Susan that she would never want to be kept alive on a machine, but never mentioned this to her nieces or nephews, that would be considered weak oral evidence of Aunt Mabel's wishes. Proportional weight is then given to the basic or best interests of Aunt Mabel when advocating continuation or initiation of life-sustaining measures. Likewise, in cases where the advance directive or evidence of the known wishes of the patient is strong, the basic interest of the incompetent patient is given less proportional weight. For example, if Aunt Mabel had executed a detailed advance medical directive then discussed this directive with her friend Susan, her doctor, and her nieces and nephews, then the proportional weight of the basic or best interests of Mabel would be small (Buchanan & Brock, 1990).

This "variable weight" version of decision making does not allow for clear separation between substituted judgment and the best interests standard, which occurs presently (Buchanan & Brock, 1990). In clinical practice a combination of these standards is often the best way to arrive at a choice that preserves the autonomy and human dignity of the incapacitated patient.

Best Interests Standard

This standard falls at the far end of the continuum described by Meisel, with the subjective standard on the directly opposed end advocating for autonomous self-determination of the patient. The best interests standard advocates for the welfare of the incapacitated patient (Meisel, 1989). In cases where the patient has executed no advance directive, has never discussed his/her wishes concerning medical therapies, or has never been competent, the recommended standard is best interests.

Use of this standard for guidance in medical choice is not only about what the physician believes to be in the medical best interest of the patient. It also considers what the surrogate believes would be most beneficial to the patient (President's Commission, 1983). This measure of choice requires attention to the risks, collateral effects, and degree of success of the recommended therapy, and attempts to ascertain whether the therapy would relieve suffering and restore functioning. The quality of life following the therapy and the extent to which life can be sustained are also factors (President's Commission, 1983). The impact on the family is given some minor consideration. Measurement of competence for making informed choices in the medical setting is often tied to the result rather than the decision-making process. The inaccurate association of choice with competence sometimes leads to erroneous assumptions of patient incompetence. The only way to assure that the focus is on the process of deciding rather than on which decision is made is through universal standards of competency measurement. To date these are nonexistent. Various authors have designed tools but they usually focus on a single type of medical decision such as the use of an advance medical directive, like the tool discussed by Janofsky, McCarthy, and Folstein (1992). Bean, Nishisato, Rector, and Glancy specifically discuss electroconvulsive therapy (Grisso & Appelbaum, 1998). The clearest tool developed to date is by Appelbaum, Grisso, Frank, O'Donnell, and Kupfer (1999). The MacArthur Competency Assessment tool (MacCAT-T) rates all the factors for competency assessment. In the book *Assessing Competence to Consent to Treat: A Guide for Physicians and Other Health Professionals* (1998), Grisso and Appelbaum outline how to utilize this tool and provide a copy of the guide. The MacCAT-T or the shorter form developed by Chaitin is most useful. This shorter form may be found at the end of this book (see Appendix A). It is in the process of being sampled and tested, and neither its effectiveness nor reliability is well known at this time.

To return to the case of David, there is no question that knowing how to care for David is problematic. However, during deliberation of how to proceed, it is necessary to formulate the treatment plan that best assures preservation of his self-determination and human dignity.

David's Case: Outcome #2

When David was alone the doctor asked, "If your heart were to stop or if you had trouble breathing, how far would you like us to go?" David's response was, "Do everything, I need to live." He requested to be reconsidered for surgery. The attending physician returned later with the surgeon, who explained that surgery was far too risky and that he was no longer a candidate for such risky surgery.

A referral to the palliative care service was made. A palliative care consultant met with David. Later, a family meeting was set up with the attending physician, David, and his sister. A social worker was present to provide support to the patient and his family. Plans were made to provide for a comfortable death.

MEDICAL RESEARCH

In 2000, close to 19 million individuals participated in clinical trials in the United States. Each of them was required to give informed consent, but there is no actual test to ensure that they understood what was being asked of them. People may have different reasons for volunteering for clinical medical trials and may not entirely understand the risks and benefits. Some may enter trials as a last hope for a cure, or relief from suffering. Some may do so knowing it will not help their own situation, but they believe it might help someone in the future who faces a similar situation. Some enter because their physician, whom they trust implicitly, recommends it (Guyer, 2000). The motivations and decisions grow more complicated when families or surrogates are approached to give informed consent on behalf of an incapacitated family member. How can they decide whether to enroll their incapacitated mother or father at the end stage of an illness in a clinical trial?

Social workers who work in academic settings, teaching hospitals, or health facilities with university linkages need to know about medical research being conducted within the facility or on their particular medical unit. All medical research, particularly if it's federally funded, must be reviewed and approved by the Institutional Review Board of the facility. Each has standards that need to be followed for the protection of human subjects. By the time subjects are approached to volunteer, this step should have been completed and documentation should appear in the informed consent procedures and documents that volunteers review and sign. The researcher, or a designee, should fully explain the purpose of the study, procedures, risks, and benefits of participation.

Social workers may be asked into these conversations. As in any other treatment and decision-making discussion, the social worker needs to be familiar with the study protocols and be able to answer questions that will inevitably come from patients and families after the researcher leaves the room. The social worker can facilitate, through a family/team conference, the introduction of the medical research and explain what is involved.

Guyer (2000) suggested the following set of questions as a checklist for volunteers in medical research, which may also serve as a useful tool for social workers to ensure that individuals and families have the information needed to make a fully informed decision about participation.

What is the purpose of the study? What are the risks? Might there be benefits?

What is the phase of the trial: safety testing, efficacy testing, or comparison of drugs?

Are the drugs approved (known to be effective), or investigational or experimental (just being tested)?

Is this pure research or does the trial include therapies?

If this trial includes therapies, is one option a placebo?

Who is the appropriate volunteer? Do I fit this profile?

What is the reputation of the researcher? What ties does the researcher have to the sponsor?

Who is getting paid for my participation: me, the researcher, others?

If something goes wrong, who will treat me? Who will pay for my medical care?

Who will have access to the data and my medical records? Where are these data stored? How secure are they? Can the researcher or others use these data in future studies that are unrelated to this one?

Who is sponsoring the trial: the federal government, a pharmaceutical or biotechnology company, a medical center, someone else?

Is there a chance that the trial will be stopped early if the test material is effective? Would I then receive the test material no matter what group I started in?

Who do I contact with questions and concerns? (p. 25)

If an individual lacks the capacity to make a decision about participation in a clinical trial, the social worker's role is to assist the family to decide on behalf of the patient. The social worker can help the family work through their questions, essentially using the same hierarchy of decision making as for other medical treatments.

Did the individual, in a written advance directive, express a desire to be involved in medical research?

Has there been a discussion of this issue in advance of the individual's incapacity?

Use substituted judgment. What would the individual have wanted to do in this situation if able to make this decision?

What is in the best interest of the individual?

Social workers can play an essential role in facilitating medical research by helping patients and families to understand the purpose of studies and the value of their participation. Part of the responsibility of social workers as professionals is to assist in furthering knowledge in the field.

UNDERSTANDING THE EMOTIONAL EXPERIENCE

David's complex case clearly outlines some of the social, psychological, and emotional factors often present when confronting end-of-life choices. Critical illness and death increase the anxiety experienced by the patient, family and friends; it also increases the anxiety of the healthcare team. These professionals connect on a human level with their patients and experience stress and fear as a result of that empathy (Bowen, 1985). How to cope with and disseminate anxiety is seen in the cut-off, triangulation, and expression of self-differentiation, which are evidenced by all participants as the illness level increases. Heated discussions on the futility of care, allocation of resources, and whether to withhold or withdraw life-sustaining therapies can lead to judgmental sentences like, "How can she keep doing this to her brother?" This is not a reflection of an enlightened level of moral understanding, but the result of the stress and hopelessness that cases such as David's would evoke in any of us. The way individuals respond to such a high anxiety level will depend on the coping history of each individual and family grouping as they encounter critical illness and death.

Bowen (1985) eloquently describes the importance of understanding the stress reaction and relationship dynamics. This can enhance communication among the key players, in the bed and at the bedside. He describes three closed communication systems that surround the dying process. One is present within the healthcare team. Despite the fact that the healthcare providers have the key information, how the facts are disclosed too frequently adds to anxiety around illness and death. This can lead to emotional and practical cut-off at a time when openness and connectedness are most crucial. Proper disclosure of information will depend on the level of anxiety experienced by team members in regard to the dying patient, as well as their conceptual and personal experiences of illness and death.

Neither medical schools nor nursing schools adequately discuss the American view of death and reactions to death, nor do they encourage future professionals to explore their personal history of illness and death. Physicians are taught to identify a disease process and construct a treatment plan. Nurses are taught to participate in its execution. When an illness is deemed terminal, confusion arises as to how to proceed, because no one has received training on coping with the impact of the finality of this common and emotionally laden event. The result can be emotional cut-off, which is detrimental to open communication among all concerned (Bowen, 1985).

One demilitarized zone described by Bowen is the family, who sits sequestered in a small unfamiliar room, waiting for the prognosis and searching for facts. Each member experiences a different response to the illness and the anticipation of death. These reactive responses are rarely explored at this crucial time despite the insight that could be gained. Failure to acknowledge the natural stress dance that takes place within the family frequently leads to skewed interpretations and judgmental labeling of people and their relationships. Normal, multigenerational survival responses present themselves within any family. Too often, observers label these dynamics rather than attempting to understand the reasons for the emotions. In some situations the family may demonstrate a high level of anxiety at the bedside that contradicts the learned illness response of the nurse or physician (Bowen, 1985). This dichotomy can result in an inaccurate identification labeling the family as being in denial or unrealistic.

A third closed communication system also exists in the patient. A self-differentiated patient might be able to move within or even past the two closed systems described above in a low-reactive manner, though any one person in this environment can act as a trigger to increase anxiety. True self-differentiation in this complicated emotional maze is as rare as the presence of purely self-determined medical decision making. Interestingly, most patients instinctively understand the nature and severity of their illness and may even know that their death is approaching but react to the anxiety of healthcare providers or their families in ways that thwart their own ability to fully express their needs.

Despite their internal understanding of their illness, patients often sit silently, compressed by multitudes of fears and feelings about their critical illness and impending death. Sadly, they may wait for an opportunity to speak and not get it. At a time when a clear and open partnership between the autonomous patient and the healthcare provider is so essential, open talk is squelched by the anxiety in the other two rings of this three-ring circus. The emotional stress experienced by the dying patient is forgotten when empathy is critical to achievement of the American view of the good death.

COMMUNICATION AT THE END OF LIFE

Communication between patient and doctor, or the doctor and the family, has been the topic of many papers in the last decade. There are several reasons for this increased interest, not the least of which is the information that came out of the SUPPORT study (1995), which stated that communication between physicians and patients and their families was inadequate and ineffective.

This theme has continued to arise in studies conducted since SUPPORT. For example, Golin, Wenger, Liu, Dawson, Teno, Desbiens, et al. (2000) noted that "Communication about resuscitation preferences occurred infrequently [even] after hospital admission for a serious illness, even among patients wishing to forgo resuscitation" (p. S55). In a study conducted by Azoulay, Chevret, Leleu, Pochard, Barboteu, Adrie, et al. (2000), effective communication between physician and families in the ICU was viewed as a critical component to quality of care. They concluded that "Patient information is frequently not communicated effectively to family members by ICU physicians" (p. 3044). The ability to increase comprehension by family members was considered by this team to be so vital that they constructed a prospective study to discover which factors were associated with poor comprehension of the true status of ICU patients. They found that 54% of families, friends, or identified surrogates lacked real understanding of the patient's diagnosis, prognosis, or treatment, with prognosis most likely to be poorly comprehended and diagnosis the best understood.

Comprehension of diagnosis and prognosis was most likely to be poorly understood if the patient was in a coma or had experienced acute respiratory failure. High levels of anxiety were experienced by family members who were unable to speak with their loved one in a coma or on mechanical ventilation. Family members, friends, or surrogates of younger patients, cancer patients, and those with cultural differences from the ICU staff experienced even less ability to comprehend the diagnosis, prognosis, and treatment plan. The nature of the ties between the representative for the patient and the patient influenced comprehension of the information given in the ICU, with spouses more likely to have a good understanding. The authors of this study believed this correlation was due to the likelihood that the spouse had experienced the patient's illness prior to hospitalization in the ICU. Other factors were the amount of time the physician spent with the family, both delivering information and listening (Azoulay et al., 2000).

Three factors listed by family members of ICU patients as more important than the clinical skills of the ICU staff are frequent communication, continuity of care, and accessibility to their loved one, with communication taking top priority (Hickey, 1990; Molter, 1979). Unfortunately, when researchers reviewed the quality of the communication between the physician and the individuals representing the patient, they found it lacking. One study noted that physicians spend 75% of the meeting time talking and focus little effort on listening. These physicians even believe that they have done a fine job during the family meeting, though they have little training in effective communication and no training in negotiation (Tulsky, Chesney, & Lo, 1996). According to Curtis, Patrick, Shannon, Treece, Engelberg, and Rubenfeld (2001), the data suggested "that the quality of family-physician and patient-physician communication about end-of-life care is poor and is unlikely to improve under our current system of medical school and residency training" (p. 26).

Most efforts aimed at increasing communication have focused on specific topics like delivering bad news or writing advance medical directives. The process of informed consent during a terminal or life-limiting illness has not been examined in detail in the literature. Wenrich, Curtis, Shannon, Carline, Ambrozy, and Ramsey (2001) conducted a study to find out which physician skills were needed most by patients facing the end of their life, and which skills family members and healthcare professionals desired. Good communication was the highest priority for patients, family members, and healthcare workers.

In that study, good communication was discussed as having two components. The first was basic skills such as good listening and an ability to encourage questioning throughout the process. The second was conversation style specific to care at the end of life. This focused on delivering bad news in a sensitive way, being open to talking about dying, and timing, or being able to sense when patients are ready for this conversation. Other factors this study noted as important to effective communication were being straightforward and honest, and the ability to present information in an understandable fashion. These are skills that cross over both communication components.

Another interesting point made by these authors was that most physicians view breaking bad news as a one-time event and experience increased anxiety related to the continuing need to converse sensitively with dying patients and their families. In another study completed by Baile, Glober, Lenzi, Beale, and Kudelka (1999), nearly 50% of the oncologists interviewed rated their ability to break bad news as poor to fair. One can only imagine the anxiety they experienced when asked to continue to discuss the situation with dying patients and their families after they felt their first attempt at delivering bad news was not up to par. This anxiety often leads to emotional distancing. The patient and family may view this self-protective distancing as insensitivity and abandonment (Bowen, 1985).

The key to effective medical-ethical decision making is a low-judgment or neutral understanding of relationships among people and to recognize the depth of feeling induced by illness and death. This will result in the optimal, low-reactive communication necessary to discuss death. Open, low-reactive communication is required for autonomous medical decision making, or self-determination is not possible. Neutral communication is achieved by searching for ways to remove the emotional full-metal jacket donned during closed communication (Bowen, 1985). Wenrich et al. (2001) suggested that a good beginning is to assure that information is laid out in an organized, straightforward manner using language that is understood. One key is listening with interest, especially through asking open-ended questions. This method of communication is seen as a sign of concern. The family meeting or conference is the most-utilized mechanism through which physicians have such communication.

The Family Conference

According to Curtis et al. (2001), the biggest mistake clinicians make in the family meeting is lack of preparation. They suggest that preparing for an ICU family conference should be as thorough as for any ICU task, such as placement of a central access line to administer medication.

The purpose of a family conference is to provide professional caregivers with the opportunity to meet the family, inform them of the patient's condition and treatment plan, answer questions, and include the patient's surrogates in the decision-making process. There is no empirical literature comparing different methods of conducting family meetings. In fact, there are few descriptive studies of family meetings (Chaitin & Arnold, 2003; Curtis et al., 2001). Thus, much of what follows is a summary of expert recommendations, many based on family counseling literature and studies of giving bad news and discussing end-of-life care. The following information on how to conduct a family meeting is taken in part from an article written for *UpToDate* by Chaitin and Arnold (2003).

When is a meeting appropriate? A formal family meeting may be of value in the following situations:

> when a patient is first admitted to the ICU
> when there is a change in the patient's medical status
> when conflict is present among family members, between the patient and the family, or between the family and the providers
> when the healthcare team believes that the goals of care should be transitioned to palliative care
> when the family requests a meeting or the providers believe a meeting would be helpful

Less formal meetings with individual family members can occur more frequently to ensure that the family is kept informed about the patient's condition (Forrow, Arnold, & Parker, 1993).

Who should come? If a previously competent patient expressed prior wishes that certain people not be included, those wishes should be honored. In the absence of such restrictions, the meeting generally should be open to all family members. Invitations to some family members but not others in situations of conflict will be viewed as taking sides and will decrease the ability of providers to serve as impartial patient advocates. Having all family members hear the same information decreases misunderstandings. At the very least, the legal decision-maker, if there is one, and all family members who have visited or called should be offered the opportunity to attend. Family members should also be asked if they would like any friends or religious counselors to be present at the meeting.

Invite all relevant healthcare providers to the family meeting. Both the primary care physician and the ICU attending physician should, ideally, be present. In the literature, there is a consensus that it is best for the primary care doctor to be the bearer of bad news unless the specialist has a prior relationship with the patient (Fischer, Tulsky, & Arnold, 2000). It is unclear whether this applies in the ICU, where the ICU attending is involved in the day-to-day care of the patient and typically has more expertise with the patient's illness. However, there are data indicating that involving a primary care physician who knows the family and the patient does increase family satisfaction (Pochard, Azoulay, Chevret, Lemaire, Hubert, Canoui, et al., 2001). The nurse caring for the patient should always be invited to the meeting; given the time that nurses spend at the bedside, they will frequently have established a close relationship with the family. The nurse can also reinforce information to the family between meetings.

A social worker may be a valuable addition. He or she can help negotiate issues of family dynamics and individual coping mechanisms. Discussions between providers and the social worker prior to the meeting may help providers better understand the family relationships and beliefs (Bowen, 1985). Social workers may in fact be asked to coordinate such meetings.

Meeting before the family meeting. Family conferences bring together a number of different healthcare providers. It is important for providers to be on the same page, as conflicting data can confuse families and leave family members feeling that the professionals are not communicating with each other. One study found that the perception of conflicting information was an independent predictor of family dissatisfaction (Chaitin & Arnold, 2003; Pochard et al., 2001).

Thus, it may be useful for the healthcare team to meet and come to agreement on the major medical facts, the prognosis, and possible treatment plans. Data collected by the social worker, chaplain, or nurse regarding how the family perceives information, their coping mechanisms, and any specific communication styles can be discussed at this time.

This does not mean that the providers must always agree on the facts or what should be done for the patient. Uncertainty is present in many circumstances, but particularly in ICU care. Uncertainty and differences of opinion can and should be honestly described to the family by the team, particularly when they need to be involved as surrogate decision-makers.

Clinicians need to consider their own emotional reactions to the patient and the family prior to the family meeting. Data suggest that physicians' unacknowledged fears of loss and death serve as a barrier to emotional engagement with patients facing death (Kvale, Berg,

Groff, & Lange, 1999). Self-awareness may help caregivers avoid projecting their own feelings on families. A team discussion prior to meeting with the family may be helpful.

A facilitator should be chosen. Continuity of care is important for family satisfaction (Johnson, Wilson, Cavanaugh, Bryden, Gudmundson, & Moodley, 1998). For this reason, it is a good idea to attempt to have the same person serve as facilitator if there is more than one family meeting. No studies have compared physician facilitators with other healthcare providers, but usually the primary care physician or the ICU attending serves this role.

Where should the meeting be held? A comfortable, private room with tissues available is best. Seating should be arranged to allow all family members to "sit in the front row." An effort should also be made to spread providers throughout the space rather than seating providers and family on opposite sides. Providers should sit down during the conference, as this creates the impression that one has time to talk and listen.

Understanding the family. Family meetings follow many of the same rules as doctor-patient interactions (Fischer et al., 2000; Lipkin, Putnam, & Lazare, 1995). Providers should avoid jargon and explain the patient's condition and medical treatments in a simple, straightforward manner. The use of tools such as leaflets or videos can be an effective way to present information. One study found that families given an informational brochure upon the patient's admission to the ICU were more likely to understand the prognosis than those who had not received such information (Chaitin & Arnold, 2003; Azoulay et al., 2002). Audiotaping the meeting and giving the family the tape to listen to at home may also be useful (Butow, Dunn, Tattersall, & Jones, 1994; Tattersall, Butow, Griffin, & Dunn, 1994).

Family conferences are different from a one-on-one conversation between doctors and patients. First, the group dynamics must be addressed. Second, families are not groups of unrelated individuals; they are social structures with their own rules of interaction and decision making.

Much can be learned about the family system by talking to a social worker or primary care physician who knows the family. Paying careful attention during the conference will also yield clues about how the family interacts and the roles that particular members play. The social worker should attend to issues such as seating, interfamily communication, and handling emotions:

> Note whether there are consistent patterns to where family members sit relative to each other, as this could reflect old grudges. The person who sits closest to the physician may be the informal family spokesperson. If there are not enough seats, observe how the family negotiates who stands and who sits.

> Observe whether the family members talk about themselves, whether the conversation is respectful, who is involved, whether questions focus on a single topic, and who keeps talking when there are interruptions.

> Note how the family responds when a family member becomes emotional. Observe whether the reaction is empathic or dismissive of the emotions.

While insight into a family's dynamics can help the healthcare team understand reactions, it is crucial that providers not try to "correct" what they feel are dysfunctional dynamics. Providers should stay neutral in any family disputes. These dynamics predate the patient's illness and reflect lifelong patterns. While these interactions may seem dysfunctional to the healthcare team, they may serve useful functions within the family system, though these may not be immediately apparent to those outside of the system (Bowen, 1985). It is unlikely that a physician, meeting the family for the first time in a stressful situation, can influence these patterns of behavior. Attempts to do so, such as trying to encourage angry sisters to make up or asking family members to discuss their guilt about moving away from home, are likely to be viewed as intrusive. The family did not request counseling. In the case of disputes it is reasonable to say something like, "I can see that you all have some disagreements on a number of issues. I wonder if you could put these aside for now, so that we can focus on what is going on with your mother."

Starting a meeting. Introduce all of the providers and family members. Include name, position, role, and level of involvement in the patient's care. This is particularly important in teaching hospitals, where it is hard to distinguish between medical students, fellows, and attendings on the basis of dress or age. Knowing physicians' roles correlates with family satisfaction (Pochard et al., 2001).

After making sure that everyone is comfortably seated and that all the relevant family members are there, clarify the meeting's goals. The facilitator might say, on the first hospital day, "I wanted to spend some time talking with all of you about how your dad is doing. I also wanted to make sure that you all understood what we are doing for him and what we will be watching for over the next couple of days. Are there other things that you want to discuss here?"

Sharing clinical information. Prior to explaining the patient's condition, ask family members what they already know. Understanding the family's level of knowledge, emotional state, and degree of education allows for more efficient discussions. Sample questions to start this conversation include:

> What have the other doctors told you is going on with your father?
> What do you think is going on?
> To make sure we are on the same page, can you tell me your understanding of this disease?

Describing the clinical situation. The next step is to tell the family the assessment of the situation. This will include diagnostic, prognostic, and therapeutic information. Facts help to reduce the family's uncertainty about what is happening (and is likely to happen), increase their ability to act as the patient's surrogates in making decisions, and strengthen providers' relationship with the family (Cassell, 1985). To accomplish this, information must not only be conveyed, it must be understood. Experts recommend using vocabulary at a ninth-grade level with as little jargon as possible, and making modifications based on the family's understanding and communication style. Given that everyone is under stress, the ability to digest large chunks of information at one time is diminished. A rule of thumb is not to give more than three pieces of information without pausing to check comprehension. Pictures often help.

Multiple short meetings over time may be better than one long meeting. At the first meeting, it is enough to provide an idea of what is going on with the patient and the plans for therapeutic interventions. The next meeting may focus on progress since the last meeting and on prognosis. In a following meeting, if things are going badly, one might raise the future possibility of transitioning to palliative care.

Detailed pathophysiologic information is unlikely to increase a family's understanding of the clinical situation. Long, detailed discussions regarding urine output, ventilator settings, and pressors may confuse the listeners or lead to a situation where they focus on these details to the exclusion of the bigger picture. Some discussion of medical details, however, may help prove the medical team's competency.

Discussing prognosis. This can be difficult in the ICU because of uncertainty and the rapidity with which the clinical situation can change. These issues are best dealt with by being open. Any discussion of uncertainty needs to accomplish three tasks:

> Explain that uncertainty exists.
> Delineate the factors that will help decrease the uncertainty.
> Give an estimate of when more will be known about the prognosis.

One might say, "Your father is very sick. As we discussed, we are doing everything we can to help his body recover from the infection. Unfortunately, this is not always enough. The next 48 hours are going to be really important regarding how he does. The kinds of things we are looking for are whether his blood pressure gets better, how his kidneys are doing, and whether he wakes up."

It may be helpful to discuss best- and worst-case scenarios. A phrase that may help the family look at both sides is "hoping for the best and preparing for the worst" (Back, Arnold, & Hopfinger, 2003). The phrase emphasizes that providers understand the family's (and their own) hope that the patient will survive the hospitalization, while planting the seed that the patient may not. To ascertain fears and concerns, it may be helpful to ask if anyone has thought about what might happen if the patient does not improve. This conversation may lead to discussion of when it may become appropriate to change treatment to less aggressive care or to palliative care.

The speed with which a patient's status can change in the ICU can be hard for families to comprehend: "But he was doing so well just this morning." Taking a moment at the end of the first meeting to consider possible outcomes and normalize common reactions may help. An example might be:

> I have tried to describe to you what is likely to happen in the ICU. Unfortunately, when people are really sick, like your mom, things can change very rapidly. Your time here may well feel like a roller coaster. That is normal. It is why we try not to get too caught up in each and every lab test but try to look and see how your mom is doing overall. We will try to point out to you when the changes are something to worry about or when they are just bumps in the road that do not change her prognosis. We will contact you if there is a change in her status.

The literature stresses the importance of maintaining hope while remaining truthful. Caregivers can do this in a number of ways. First, while providing prognostic information, one must acknowledge its limitations. Second, even if one believes that family goals are unrealistic, providers should acknowledge them and express their sorrow that they are unlikely to be fulfilled. "Wish" statements (e.g., "I wish I could tell you that your mom is going to pull through") are a powerful way to do this. Finally, providers can gently inquire about other goals. For most families, the initial hope is that the patient will recover and return to his/her previous baseline. If this is not possible, families must be given time to understand and grieve the loss. Chaplains or other religious counselors may be helpful in this process. The family can then turn to discussing what the patient's new goals might be. This might mean staying alive until all the family can get to town, living until a fiftieth wedding anniversary, or dying in a dignified, peaceful manner.

Describing the therapeutic plan. It is critical to describe what is going to be done to improve the patient's situation. Precise medical details are only important insofar as they convince the family of the competence of the ICU team. It is more important that the family understands what the therapy means for the patient: "A tube needs to be placed in a large blood vessel to give your father blood," or "He is going on the kidney machine today to help out his kidneys, which are not working." Common complications can be mentioned, with an offer to answer any other questions the family might have.

Discussion should focus on treatment goals rather than treatments in isolation. People do not "want" CPR or intubation; they want to continue living with a certain quality of life. Ascertain what the family believes the patient's goals are, rather than asking them to choose specific treatments. Providers have technical expertise about the most efficacious way to achieve the patient's goals. Physicians should make recommendations about specific treatments that achieve the patient's goals. For instance, explicitly discuss what will be done to keep the patient comfortable and what trade-offs may exist between interventions that improve comfort and those that may improve prognosis.

Families are reassured by knowing a large team is caring for the patient and that the patient is receiving multiple therapies. Explaining all of the therapies being undertaken is a way to reinforce the seriousness of the situation. Paradoxically, it is even more important to stress the team's efforts when the subject becomes end-of-life care. Families of critically ill patients often worry about "giving up" too early. Emphasizing the efforts that were taken may reassure them that the healthcare team is trying all reasonable interventions.

Discussing end-of-life topics. Placing end-of-life conversations within the general framework of family conferences may make them less jarring; it is important for the family to hear what the doctors are thinking throughout the course of the illness. Waiting to raise the notion of palliative care until "there is nothing more to be done" may seem cold or disheartening. The family meeting allows providers to understand the patient's goals of therapy and determine whether ICU care is likely to achieve them. Furthermore, it creates an opportunity to foreshadow end-of-life discussions, allowing family to psychologically prepare themselves for bad news.

When ICU interventions are unlikely to accomplish the patient's goals, it is appropriate to raise the issue of transitioning to palliative care. Factors to consider are the patient's premorbid quality of life, the likelihood of survival, the likelihood of returning the patient to an acceptable post-ICU quality of life, and the pain and suffering that may result from ICU interventions (Tomlinson, Howe, Notman, & Ross-miller, 1990). Many of the principles for talking to families about end-of-life topics are similar to those used for talking to individual patients about these issues (Buchanan & Brock, 1990; Quill, 2000). Too often, these conversations occur later in the patient's illness than may be appropriate. DNR orders, for example, are typically written three days before death (Chaitin & Arnold, 2003).

Talking to surrogates about end-of-life issues raises unique concerns. First, and most importantly, physicians need to stress the ethical principle underlying surrogate decision making: What would the patient want if he or she could speak? Anecdotal evidence suggests that surrogates often feel as if they are being asked unfairly to make life-and-death decisions for their loved one. Don't ask, "What do you think we should do next?" Instead say, "If your dad were sitting here and could hear what we have said about his condition, what would he say?" Or, "What do you think your mom's opinion on this would be?" Specific questions such as, "Have you ever talked to your mom about what her wishes would be if she became critically ill?" may be helpful. Empirical data suggest that this way of wording the question results in the family member being better able to predict what the patient would want (Tomlinson et al., 1990).

Of course, surrogates may find these questions difficult. A common response is, "My dad would never have wanted to be like this, but I can't tell you to stop." This answer gives the providers two important pieces of information. First, one learns the ethically appropriate treatment plan that would be consistent with the patient's goals. Second, the answer emphasizes that family members feel they are being asked to make a life-and-death decision, which makes them uncomfortable. Providers can respond by stressing the appropriate surrogate role, and empathizing with the sadness: "I would never ask you to make the decision to stop. That is a horrible thing to ask a son to think about doing for his father. What I needed you to do was to tell me what your dad would have said, so that I could suggest to you the best way to respect his goals and values. And you have done that."

Attention to family dynamics is key. Typically, families make end-of-life decisions based on consensus, even if there is a durable power of attorney. After the patient dies, the legally appointed decision maker still needs to live and get along with the rest of the family. Thus, all opinions must be voiced and discussed during meetings. It also may be helpful to leave the room and let family members talk on their own, as they may not wish to disagree in front of a stranger (Chaitin & Arnold, 2003).

It is important to ensure that decisions to forgo a particular treatment are not viewed as equivalent to withdrawing care. Abandonment is a critical issue for dying patients and their families. Families need to know that the patient will receive appropriate, competent care, regardless of the stage of the illness. The following are phrases that might help in discussing end-of-life issues:

If your father were sitting here at the table, what would he say?

Sometimes what you want is different from what your mother would want. I really respect your ability to focus on her wishes.

I do not want you to feel like you are making medical decisions—that is my job. You can help greatly by telling me what your dad would have wanted if he could be here.

The goal of all this planning is so that you can stand as a family and have no regrets, no matter what happens.

I want you to be able to look back on this six months from now and be sure you did what your mom wanted.

Your father went to some trouble to make sure we knew his views regarding this form of treatment. We need to respect this decision like we would anything else he told us to do.

There are no more life-and-death decisions to be made, just type-of-death decisions.

How are you doing? What can we do for you?

Family emotions. Families may react to these difficult conversations in a number of ways. Psychophysiologic responses can include the fight-or-flight response, leading some individuals to the need to get up and walk around. Others have a parasympathetic response and become quiet, numb, and withdrawn. One may see a variety of emotional reactions to impending death, including sadness, anger, grief, guilt, fear, and anxiety.

All these reactions are normal. Launching into a biomedical discussion or providing false reassurance will convey that providers are uncomfortable with emotions. Supportive reactions involve active listening and letting family members know that caregivers are present and can deal with strong emotions. Knowing that someone understands what they are going through is psychotherapeutic (Soelle, 1975).

Conflict. Conflicts between families and healthcare providers regarding end-of-life decisions are common. In one study, over one third of doctors or nurses reported conflicts with families, of which 63% involved decision making at the end of life (Breen, Abernethy, Abbott, & Tulsky, 2001). In a study of family members from the same institution, 46% reported conflict with providers, most commonly over communication (Chaitin & Arnold, 2003; Abbott, Sago, Breen, Abernethy, & Tulsky, 2001). When conflicts occur, physicians may feel that their competence or judgment are not trusted and either redouble their effort to convince the family they are wrong or begin to question the family's competence or intentions. Families may feel isolated, misunderstood, or abandoned, and either feel pressured to give up or doubt the healthcare team's commitment to the patient's well-being. What should be a cooperative effort to achieve treatment goals turns into an exercise in frustration and distress.

Two points are worth emphasizing. First, families may need time to come to grips with end-of-life decisions. They are not usually familiar with the course of life-limiting illnesses. Early in the illness, they may even have been told to remain hopeful, or that the patient was being sent to the ICU because that was where he was most likely to get better. Allowing a family a day to think about new information may be enough for them to acknowledge their loved one's terminal condition. Second, having a family member in the ICU is always stressful and this may interfere with clearheaded decision making. One way to build a good relationship is to acknowledge the stress and offer to help.

Many families live far from the hospital, for example, and it is helpful if the social worker can arrange for closer accommodations or less expensive parking.

Wrap up. Prior to concluding the family meeting, the major issues should be summarized. If the discussion focused on news, summarize the major changes. Providing a written summary may add to knowledge and understanding of what was emphasized at the meeting. Another option is to ask those present to summarize the conversation. This allows providers to make sure that the family has heard the major points.

If the discussion focused on transitioning to palliative care, the summary should focus both on consensus decisions and areas of disagreement. There should be a discussion of what will happen next.

Always ask if there are questions. According to data on information acquisition, it is common for the family to forget the topics discussed at the meeting.

Finally, clinicians must ensure that there is an adequate follow-up plan, including:

> a family spokesperson for less formal, frequent conversations who can then communicate with other family members, particularly important in large families
>
> a way for the family to contact providers if questions or issues arise
>
> a clear plan for the next family meeting, whether an appointed time or based on certain criteria or change of status

Continuity is important during follow-up meetings. If such a meeting cannot occur, interested parties should be given an explanation so they do not feel abandoned (Chaitin & Arnold, 2003).

Summary. When a loved one is sick, it is understandable that friends and family will want to meet with providers regarding best care. Family members are often the chosen surrogates for discussing the patient's values and goals and negotiating treatment plans. This requires meeting on a regular basis. Structured meetings that attend to facts and possibilities and the resulting emotions improve the decision-making process and family satisfaction. It is not unusual for cultural norms, ethnic background, education level, or religious faith to have an impact on how choices are made at the end of life, for each of these factors plays a role in how individuals live their lives (see chapter 2).

Chapter Conclusion

The essential aspects of end-of-life decision making can be evaluated and made possible by the clinical social worker. Some of these factors are: clear and effective communication, autonomous decision making, holistic care based on the value system of the patient, understanding of the value structure of the patient, and facilitating successful family meetings. These skills alone do not make the clinician an expert. However, when sensitivity and awareness are combined with the contributions of other members of the interdisciplinary team, the autonomy and human dignity of patients can hopefully be preserved.

Chapter Six

ETHICS OF ORGAN DONATION

Four decades of medical scientific growth meshed medicine with technical expansion and discovery, permanently merging science with medicine, and medicine with technology and industry. The result has been an orchestration of mystery and magic. The general public has watched as death was seemingly averted by sustaining respiration indefinitely through the use of technology. It became possible in the 1960s to transplant organs from a cadaver to a human body so individuals who previously would have succumbed to renal failure or other organ failure were given renewed life through someone else's death.

The ability to sustain respiration and heartbeat brought about the series of quandaries discussed in this book. The power to transplant organs is accompanied by its own ethical dilemmas, which require specific attention beyond the issues outlined in previous chapters. Any healthcare professional must understand the range of ethical issues surrounding organ transplantation, not the least of which is how to define death. Other dilemmas include determination of who shall receive the few available organs, and how to respect the dignity of the dying donor while fighting to preserve the life of the potential recipient.

This chapter explores the brief history of organ donation and describes some of the issues. First, how do we go about defining death in the twentieth century? Second, depending on how death is defined, the way that organs are obtained is analyzed, with specific attention to nonheartbeating organs. Each section examines the role of the profession in preserving human dignity for the donor, the recipient, and their families.

CHANGING DEFINITION OF DEATH

Organs can be obtained in several ways. Donors from other species are referred to as *xenograft*. Donors within our species are referred to as *allograft*. Allograft organs can come from a live donor or a cadaver. Before initiating the process with a cadaver, the donor must be legally dead. Death can be declared in several ways.

Cardiopulmonary Death

The cessation of either the cardiac system or the pulmonary system will cause the cessation of the other. Death occurs when there is an irreversible cessation of cardiopulmonary function. Organ donation completed after the cessation of cardiac functioning is referred to as nonheartbeating. The majority of donations from nonliving donors are completed using nonheartbeating organs, and are largely unsuccessful due to nonviability (DeVita, Snyder, & Grenvik, 1993; Youngner, Arnold, & Schapiro, 1999). For transplantation to be successful, the organ must be viable; therefore, the ischemic time, the time when cellular destruction can occur, must be kept to a minimum. The largest factor contributing to warm ischemia time is lack of oxygen and nutritional flow to the viable organ (DeVita et al., 1993). Early transplant efforts failed mainly due to organ injury as a result of ischemic time. Successful organ transplantation is a race to beat the clock.

Up until 1960, the accepted definition of death was the irreversible cessation of respiration and cardiac functioning. When a person's heart stops beating, circulation to vital organs ceases and warm ischemia begins, potentially rendering organs nonviable for successful transplantation (DeVita et al., 1993; Caplan & Coelho, 1998). Several changes have been made to enhance the progress of transplantation. According to DeVita, Snyder and Grenvik (1993, p. 116), they are: improved mechanisms to match tissues of the recipient and donor to assure similarity in immune markers; improved supportive care for recipients, such as dialysis, so that life can be temporarily sustained; development of immunosuppressive therapy, which serves to block identification and rejection of invader-donated organs; improved organ viability through better preservation techniques; and improved surgical implantation techniques.

As kidney transplants were becoming more successful, use of related donors was losing favor in the transplant community due to the risk it places upon living donors. In addition, liver and heart transplants were being attempted without great success. These organs could not be given by living donors so new sources of heart beating donors were sought to increase overall success of the procedure (Munson, 2002; DeVita et al., 1993; Caplan & Coelho, 1998).

Brain Death

Once respiration and heart function could be sustained with the assistance of technology, the understanding of when death occurs became deeply confusing. As recently as 1989, a detailed study by Youngner, Landefeld, Coulton, Juknialis, and Leary explored the views and opinions of 195 physicians and nurses who were likely to be involved in the process of organ donation and demonstrated considerable confusion and discomfort regarding how death is defined. Only 35% of the respondents were able to correctly identify the legal and medical criteria for defining death. More than half of respondents were unable to "use a coherent concept of death consistently" (p. 2205). Youngner and his colleagues explain this confusion as a "lack of clarity about why brain-dead patients are dead" combined with a general sense of "discomfort" with the whole process of organ procurement and recovery (pp. 2205–2206; 2209–2210).

In 1968, the Ad Hoc Harvard Medical School Committee created a report that endeavored to define brain death. The report defined it as a lack of function at the cerebral, brain stem, and often the spinal level, and included irreversible coma among the criteria. Those in a persistent vegetative state (PVS) do not meet the old brain-death criteria, nor are they likely to meet cardiopulmonary criteria at the initial time of coma, thereby leaving PVS patients in limbo between the usual definition of life and the customary definition of death.

The Harvard Ad Hoc Committee report, combined with legal cases such as Karen Ann Quinlan's (see chapters 1 and 2), led to physician concerns about the burdens placed on patients and their families to sustain brain-dead patients through resuscitative methods and other technology. The development of the brain death criteria was progressive during the 1970s and led to the Uniform Death Act, proposed in 1981 by the President's Commission for the Study of Ethical Problems in Medicine and Biomedicine and Behavior Research (Fox & Swazey, 1992, pp. 60–63).

Much debate ensued over the proper death criteria for those with significant neurological impairment, especially from those who believed inappropriate legislation could cause discrimination against the handicapped. Their argument was that severe neurological injury was always followed by death, but the injury itself was *not* death (DeVita et al., 1993). In an effort to carefully develop clear standards around devastating neurological impairment, there emerged the Uniform Determination of Death Act (UDDA) in the early 1980s, which was approved by several prestigious organizations, including the American Medical Association, the American Academy of Neurology, and the American Bar Association. The act read: "An individual who has sustained either (1) irreversible cessation of circulatory and respiratory functions or (2) irreversible cessation of all functions of the entire brain, including the brain stem, is dead" (Devettere, 2000). Despite the establishment of this criterion, determination of brain death was not widely accepted socially. Because of this continued controversy it was stipulated that the neurologically impaired person (who met brain death criteria) should be declared dead prior to removal of the respirator, thereby avoiding prosecution for causing death via such removal (DeVita et al., 1993).

Organ donation via brain death. The establishment of brain death as a criterion for death did increase the donor pool for organ donation, but by no means provided enough organs for the over 30,000 patients awaiting transplantation. Despite endless efforts to clearly define death, there remains debate because some patients still had demonstrated cerebral electrical activity on EEG and endocrine studies, enough scientific evidence that "not all functions of the entire brain had ceased" (Caplan & Coelho, 1998, pp. 19–20). Some have theorized that once higher brain function ceases, significant aspects of life such as cognition, reason, personality, and capacity for intellectual interaction are gone, so the person in all human respects is dead. These individuals believe that a higher brain death protocol should be established.

There continues to be a question as to whether a permanently unconscious person stripped of all personality traits and ability to interact with the environment is to be considered alive or dead. Though some may believe these individuals might be better off dead, they are not, strictly speaking, biologically dead but rather devoid of those aspects that define life by more than biology (Caplan & Coelho 1998).

In an effort to increase the number of organs available for donation, there was a resurgence of interest in the use of nonheartbeating donors. But this practice was stopped due to poor survival rates and because some questioned the ethics of this practice (DeVita et al., 1993). However, with establishment of new brain death guidelines, there were more requests from families and surrogate decision-makers to remove life-sustaining technology. If this support were discontinued in the operating room, ischemia time would be reduced and the patient's organs could be utilized to sustain the life of others. Interest in nonheartbeating donations was renewed, which brought its own set of ethical dilemmas.

Higher-brain death. One solution for individuals diagnosed as persistently vegetative is that the definition of death be extended. According to Caplan and Coelho (1998, pp. 30–31), "The standard of higher-brain death would include: patients who fulfill the cardiorespiratory definition of death; those who fulfill current criteria of brain death; those rendered permanently unconscious; and anencephalic infants." The striation of neurological death criteria creates the potential to increase the donor pool and decrease the use of high-cost medical technology to sustain the lives of vegetative patients.

The ethical quandaries that accompany this definition of higher-brain death are considerable. For example, some questions might be: Are we more than just functional brains? Who should be allowed to determine the relative worth of humans? Should cost of care and the need for organs be a higher priority than the care of brain-dead individuals? When is it permissible to withdraw life support from a persistently vegetative patient if it is for the benefit of society?

Nonheartbeating organ donation (NHBOD). It soon became apparent that the need for organs far exceeded their availability. In the early 1990s, the University of Pittsburgh Medical Center attempted to establish criteria by which patients' families could consent to organ donation via nonheartbeating criteria after they had discussed the removal of life-sustaining interventions.

> A 48-year-old woman was physically devastated from multiple sclerosis. She communicated using a letter board and by mouthing words. The patient had carefully considered how she wanted to die and had

discussed this with her family. Part of her request was that her organs be donated following her death. The patient had a strong and loving family and was cared for by her three sisters, who supported her request.

When discussion took place regarding how organs were normally donated using brain death criteria, it was her suggestion that her ventilator be removed in the operating room; once she was declared dead her wish was that her organs be procured shortly thereafter. Endless hours of effort went into planning this process so that the patient would be comfortable and her family could spend time with her, as well as making sure this request was ethical and legal. An ethics consultant spent considerable time with the patient and family and all confirmed that the subject of donation had been raised by the patient herself.

The removal of the ventilator took about twenty minutes and remarkably the patient continued to breathe for several hours, rendering her organs nonviable. Her family was very distressed because they wanted their sister's life and death to have meaning, and believed meaning could be achieved through her unselfish donation so that others could live. This case and several others led the institution to pursue careful establishment of criteria by which patients like this could choose to donate organs via nonheartbeating criteria (DeVita et al., 1993, p. 134).

UPMC policy. The University of Pittsburgh Medical Center— Presbyterian and Montefiore University hospitals' ethics committee met to discuss dilemmas faced by personnel who worked on cases where organ donation was to follow the elective removal of life-sustaining technology. In some cases, individuals questioned if the institution was actively seeking their death for donation, while others felt it was reasonable to grant full freedom for patients or their surrogates to discontinue life-sustaining interventions and opt for organ donation following their death.

It is evident that there can be no ambiguity to the process of declaring death in the operating room. To preserve human dignity until death, the patient must be cared for by a team whose focus is patient care and not organ donation, with a clear priority being the physiological, psychological, and spiritual needs of the patient and family. Efforts must be taken to separate care for the patient from the procurement of organs. A mechanism for determination of death has to be established, which clearly outlines how the cardiopulmonary standards for death have been met before procurement of organs occurs.

To avoid conflict of interest in the formation of the nonheart-beating organ donation policy, members of the transplant service of UPMC and members of the Organ Procurement Organization were barred from attendance at these meetings. There was considerable concern that establishment of an ethical policy would be controversial. In Japan, for example, procurement of organs from a still-alive, brain-dead patient resulted in such outcry that organ donation following confirmation of brain death is still not common practice in that country (Caplan & Coelho, 1998).

The resulting UPMC policy was established after many hours of work over several years, with more than 100 people participating in the developmental process. Prior to use, the policy was reviewed by multiple outside experts in the field. The final UPMC policy focused on autonomy of the patient and the role of surrogates in responding to wishes regarding life-sustaining technology. Once a decision was made to withdraw technological support, then and only then was the subject of organ donation approached.

Within the UPMC policy, the determination-of-death standards were modeled on the historic definition of death, which is the loss of cardiopulmonary functioning. This removes, in some cases, the long wait associated with determination of brain death. "The delay in waiting for progression to brain death determination to legitimize donation not only consumes expensive resources, but is demoralizing for both family and staff, and is associated furthermore with secondary organ dysfunction and emerging evidence of graft dysfunction due to immunological activation of the donor organ" (Bell, 2003). For organs to be viable for transplant, blood circulation must remain intact and the time between death, retrieval, and transplantation must be short. Some scholars state that organs like the liver are no longer viable after a lapse of 15 minutes from time of death. If organs can be retrieved from the body immediately after death has been declared, they have a higher likelihood of remaining viable. It is speculated by Bell that the wait for a severely brain-injured individual to progress to brain death increases family suffering and increases the likelihood of a patient becoming persistently vegetative.

Under University of Pittsburgh guidelines, the patient, the family, or a surrogate is asked to grant consent to donate organs only after the decision has been made to withdraw life-sustaining intervention. An ICU attending physician is with the patient in the operating room and pronounces the patient dead by cardiovascular criteria prior to the start of organ retrieval. The initiation of nonheartbeating donation protocol does not begin at most UPMC hospitals until an evaluation is completed by a medical ethicist. The purpose of this evaluation is to assure that informed consent has occurred and that there is strict adherence to detailed hospital policy. This policy serves to separate the needs of donor from those of the potential recipient, while respecting the needs of all involved in the case.

UPMC policy states that donated organs are removed in the operating room only after an ICU physician has declared the patient dead using historically established cardiopulmonary criteria for death in conjunction with measurement of electrical activity per placement of a femoral artery catheter. Only when cardiopulmonary functioning ceases for between two to five minutes (depending on the criteria of the institution) is the patient pronounced dead. After the pronouncement of death, the organs can be immediately removed.

This procedure is supported by the Institute of Medicine but it is highly controversial (Devettere, 2000). The aspect of nonheartbeating donation of greatest ethical concern and debate is the time period before death is declared. Some believe the UPMC policy of two minutes of cardiovascular death is too short a period of time to be certain that death has occurred. The details and outcome of this debate are far too complex for this chapter but well worth the effort of intellectual inquiry.

Several authors have stated that once no heartbeat is present for five minutes then death can be pronounced, claiming that it's possible there could be some recoverable function if CPR were started at the two-minute point. Realistically, the decision to withdraw life-sustaining intervention has been made prior to gaining consent for NHBOD, so the question of use of CPR is merely intellectual. Despite this fact, the question of how much time must lapse before death can be declared in an NHBOD patient is strongly debated. One argument is that if the family is at the bedside following the removal of treatment it is cruel to ask them to tolerate ten minutes of "asystole, apnea, and unresponsiveness before the patient could be considered dead and it is not the normal practice to request that the family wait this length of time for the declaration of death. It would therefore appear somewhat illogical to impose different criteria for cardiovascular deaths were applied dependent on whether organ retrieval was countenanced" (Bell, 2003, p. 178). Despite this logic there remains concern that death could be declared prematurely, rejecting the dead donor rule, which is required prior to donation.

The ethical issues with NHBOD received national attention with the April 13, 1997, *60 Minutes* report "Not Quite Dead," when the case of Pamela James was the lead story.

> Pamela James was a 33-year-old woman who was shot in the head by an intruder who broke into her Ohio home in 1987. She was the mother of two small children. She was taken to the emergency room of the local hospital and subsequently transferred to St. Vincent Hospital in Toledo, where she was pronounced dead. Her liver, kidneys, heart, skin, and bones were recovered by a transplant team shortly after the pronouncement of death.
>
> David Williams, the attorney defending her assailant, reviewed the medical records and was stunned to discover that "the time of death listed by the coroner was virtually to the minute coincidental with the time the transplant team removed her heart" (Munson, 2002). Mr. Williams employed a neuropathologist to review the brain of Pamela James. He determined that her brain injury was "lower-grade" and one from which she might potentially have recovered. In Mr. Williams's opinion, Pamela James was "managed [medically] for the purpose of harvest, rather than managed as a neurological patient" and consequently she "was never given a chance to survive" (Munson, 2002, pp. 172–174).

The *60 Minutes* broadcast featured two individuals associated with the Cleveland clinic who had contacted the attorney general of Ohio, Carmen Marino, regarding concerns that physicians were killing patients for their organs. The report mentioned the alleged provision of massive doses of potentially harmful drugs solely to make patients' organs available for transplantation.

The investigation by Carmen Marino resulted in no evidence of legal wrongdoing by the Cleveland clinic. Despite this finding, the clinic was instructed that the district attorney's office would review the NHBOD protocol.

This whole process, especially the "Not Quite Dead" broadcast by Mike Wallace, outraged the transplant community. The Pamela James case did present several ethical concerns: Was Ms. James's family properly informed of her prognosis? If so, had they instructed the hospital to remove her from life-sustaining technology? Did they then consent to organ donation? Did Ms. James have an advance medical directive? Had the physicians completed the brain death protocol on Ms. James? If Ms. James was a nonheartbeating organ donor, how long did they wait after the heart stopped before procuring organs? All of these questions are legitimate, however, the transplant community felt that the *60 Minutes* presentation was biased and misleading; the whole thrust of the story was to claim that "aggressive" transplant surgeons were searching for ways to procure organs from patients who were not dead (Munson, 2002, pp. 173–176). This program caused a national public outcry that was a big setback to consent for organ donation.

Yet the *60 Minutes* program did bring to the surface the importance of three ethical principles that have served to structure the format of organ donation in America: Patients must be declared legally dead before donation (the dead donor rule). People may be allowed to die under "certain circumstances; they must never be actively killed" (Arnold & Youngner, 1993, p. 263). Informed consent must be obtained prior to the retrieval of organs.

Chapter Conclusion

Despite all efforts to determine the actual moment when someone is dead, especially after the body has been artificially sustained on life support, there remains no real clear demarcation line. Ronald Munson eloquently sums up this quandary when he states, "Human beings, unlike some of their machines, aren't equipped with a light that blinks off when they cease functioning" (Munson, 2002, p. 179). Our humanness has been debated by philosophers and theologians, who have delineated multitudes of factors that separate human beings from the rest of nature. Some believe it is the possession of free will and a soul that separates humans from animals. So how do we determine the exact time when the soul departs the body and leaves it dead? These are unanswerable questions, though the mystery of death has been pondered since the beginning of human reason.

Despite the unsolvable dilemma, two realities exist. One is that some individuals feel that if they are ever rendered permanently comatose, or reach a point where they can no longer interact with their environment, they would prefer not to be kept artificially alive; they'd rather have all technology withdrawn and be permitted to die. The other reality is that there is a great shortage of transplantable organs, and over 30,000 very ill people on donor lists. Individuals with incurable diseases or those in PVS who, would wish to be removed from life-sustaining therapies could potentially provide enormous help to ease the suffering of those who wait for organ transplants. Nonheartbeating organ donation is a potential solution to their suffering. Institutions that work with NHBOD have safety mechanisms in place to protect the dignity of donor patients while they remain alive, to make sure that death is not prematurely declared and that organ procurement does not take place until the patient has been declared dead by a physician who is not part of the transplant team. To be able to give life to someone else even as death claims you is the nature of modern medical miracles and must be handled with deep respect for both the dying and the living.

Chapter Seven

ETHICAL ANALYSIS AND RESOLUTION OF ETHICAL PROBLEMS IN HEALTH CARE

The potential for ethical quandaries is present in every clinical encounter that occurs between the patient and provider (Jonsen, Siegler, & Winslade, 1998). Clinical social workers who work with healthcare professionals need to be familiar with the processes through which ethical problems are resolved, in healthcare settings in general and in their healthcare center specifically. Healthcare professionals, patients, and families frequently obtain recommendations from ethics committees and/or consultants regarding how to resolve difficult ethical problems as they occur. Quite often, these quandaries are related to end-of-life decision making.

ETHICS COMMITTEES

Ethics committees are a primary hospital resource for resolution of ethical dilemmas. One of the main goals of the committee is to assist in the resolution of conflict and increase communication between parties. Communicational difficulty is documented as the primary issue of concern expressed by the families of patients who are facing end-of-life issues (Azoulay, Pochard, Chevret, Jourdain, Bornstain, Wernet, et al., 2002). For decades, issues related to lack of communication or miscommunication have been the topics of numerous articles in medical and ethical journals.

There is no data on how many ethical problems are resolved through better communication among patient, family, and team members at any juncture in providing care. Only the most difficult ethical problems and situations are normally referred to ethics committees or consultants for review and assistance.

Emergence of Ethics Committees

The early beginnings of ethics committees in health care can be traced to the discovery of chronic hemodialysis (for kidney failure) in 1962. Until this procedure became widely available, not everyone who needed hemodialysis was able to obtain it. Patient selection committees were formed to establish criteria to decide who would receive the procedure. This was the medical profession's first impetus toward looking at its own values with respect to delivery of medical treatment (Jonsen, 1993).

Another development that led to the formation of ethics committee also occurred in the 1960s. An article by Dr. Henry Beecher published in the *New England Journal of Medicine* (1968) exposed many unethical research studies that were being performed at that time and in past decades. The most famous of these was the Tuskegee study that looked at the effects of syphilis on African-American men and withheld treatment during the course of the research. This attention to unethical practices in medical research resulted in the creation of a national commission to review all federally funded research to ensure that ethical standards were met (Jonsen, 1993).

Another important event in the development of ethics committees was the first heart transplant, performed by Dr. Christiaan Barnard in 1967, which drew a strong public reaction around the issues of organ donation and determining brain death (Wilson-Ross, 1986). In 1976, the first legal case involving life support received much attention. The case of Karen Ann Quinlan was the first of its kind to review the ethical questions connected with the use and withdrawal of life-sustaining medical therapy. The judge deciding this case suggested that hospitals develop a mechanism by which to solve ethical dilemmas, in an effort to keep complex choices at the bedside and out of the courtroom. Between 1975 and 1986 larger healthcare institutions developed ethics committees. These "prognosis committees" served to confirm medical diagnoses rather than to deliberate on ethical issues. As an outgrowth, however, many hospitals began to develop policies regarding

Do-Not-Resuscitate orders, living wills, and hospice care for the terminally ill (Jonsen, 1993). However, many institutions still had not developed a formal method to address the issues. In 1986, the Joint Commission on Accreditation of Healthcare Organizations (JCAHO) standards required that all healthcare organizations have some method of analyzing and resolving ethical problems that arise within the organization. The JCAHO standards helped push remaining hospitals to develop mechanisms with which to deal with ethical quandaries.

Abortion selection committees (prior to *Roe v. Wade*) and the medical-moral committees that existed in Catholic hospitals to ensure that treatment was consistent with Catholic beliefs were other forerunners of ethics committees (Wilson-Ross, Glaser, Rasinski-Gregory, Gibson, & Bayley, 1993). Still, few hospitals formed ethics committees prior to the early 1980s. Several legal cases involving infants and deliberation of their prospective quality of life brought the focus back onto ethical concerns. The Department of Health and Human Services stepped in to devise the Infant Doe regulations in 1983 and to encourage the formation of Infant Care Review Committees (ICRCs) to develop and monitor institutional policies for managing certain diagnoses. The ICRCs were also to review cases seeking to withhold life-sustaining treatment (Cranford & Doudera, 1984).

More recent public attention focused upon the first right-to-die case heard by the U.S. Supreme Court. The 1990 Nancy Cruzan case involved a request by the family that her feeding tube be withdrawn, in accordance with her spoken wishes made prior to the car accident that put her in a persistent vegetative state. This request was taken as far as the Missouri Supreme Court, where it was denied then sent to the U.S. Supreme Court. During this review, the nation waited for direction on how to deal with these complex questions. The Supreme Court supported all that had been decided to date, namely:

> A competent patient had the right to refuse any and all medical therapies, even if such a refusal could result in death.
>
> Incompetent patients could retain and exercise this right though the use of a surrogate; frequently family serves this role.
>
> All medical therapies are considered to be the same under the law, including artificial feedings and ventilator support.

Following the Supreme Court review of the Nancy Cruzan case, the Patient Self-Determination Act was passed. This act required that all hospitals that provided care to Medicare and Medicaid patients ask patients if they had executed a power of attorney for health care or a living will. The institution had to place a copy of any executed documents in the patient's health record; if no such document existed, the institution had to provide information on how to execute such a document. Finally, all institutions were required to give patients a summary of the hospital's policies relating to withdrawal and withholding of life-sustaining treatment (see chapter 4 for more on advance directives).

In the past fifteen years, formation of ethics committees in healthcare facilities has occurred rapidly. Technological advances in medicine signal the need to evaluate the prolonging of life versus quality of life. Although there is no federal mandate for healthcare facilities to utilize ethics committees, JCAHO requires in its accreditation standards that healthcare organizations have a process in place for addressing ethical problems.

Definition and Functions of Ethics Committees

Ethics committees are defined as "multidisciplinary groups of healthcare professionals within a healthcare institution that has [have] been specifically established to address the ethical dilemmas that occur within that institution" (Cranford & Doudera, 1984). Membership on ethics committees varies; however, they are generally comprised of physicians, nurses, clergy, social workers, attorneys, administrators, and lay members (Wilson-Ross, 1986). In a 1989 study, 60% of hospitals had ethics committees and a social worker was a member on 76% of them (Skinner, 1991). In 1995, a statewide (PA) study documented the substantial growth in the formation and use of ethics committees and revealed that 88% of hospitals had ethics committees and social workers were members of about three-quarters of them (Csikai, 1997).

As can be seen through the issues that led to development of ethics committees, the primary purpose is protection of patients' rights and interests (Hoffman, 1993). Common dilemmas discussed in hospital ethics committees are related to patients' wishes regarding medical treatment (with advance directives or without), conflicts about recommended courses of treatment, resource allocation, and matters of policy for the institution. Typically, ethics committees perform three functions: education, policy development and review, and case consultation and review (Wilson-Ross, 1986). The educational function involves enhancing the knowledge and awareness of committee members and other hospital staff of current bioethical issues so that they may engage in thoughtful multidisciplinary discussions. This goal is potentially achieved through many avenues such as in-services, conferences, pertinent reading materials, and discussion. In policy development, ethics committees focus on, for example, generating institutional policies regarding how decisions are to be made for incapacitated patients, DNR orders, and forgoing life-sustaining treatment. The committee may also be charged with overseeing the implementation of these policies. In case consultation and review, ethics committees serve as a forum for discussion of ethical and social concerns and make recommendations on individual cases. Case review should ensure that the voices of all interested parties are heard and that the recommended solution is appropriate (Cranford & Doudera, 1984).

An ethics consultation service will analyze and recommend courses of action to resolve ethical problems that arise in the institution. This may be a multidisciplinary consultation team or an individual consultant who reports back to the committee at large. Development of ethical guidelines in specific areas of medical practice is essential.

A critical role for the ethics committee is to educate committee members and other hospital staff about aspects of clinical ethics that may occur in daily practice. Ethics committees can also promote opportunities for ethical thought and discussion of contentious issues that occur away from the institutional setting, as in nursing homes or hospice agencies. Other advantages are practical and include reducing litigation by diffusing conflicts between providers and patients and their families. On an organizational level, ethics committees can explore and illuminate the values and practices of the moral community by which the institution wishes to be known.

Concerns about the use of ethics committees include infringement on the doctor-patient relationship, potential for undermining patients' autonomy because of competing institutional and individual interests, and that the committee itself adds an additional level of bureaucracy in an environment already heavy with it (Gillon, 1997).

In an era of accountability, ethics committees should establish a clear mission and vision, and their activities should be in line with the institution's mission statement. Operating procedures and methods to evaluate the processes and outcomes produced by committee work must also be established, to validate the committee's existence to institutional leaders. It has been recommended that the committee be established under the senior operations officer who will oversee operations and provide a budget and clinical staff support. The committee should establish relationships with other key committees and administrative areas within the institution to remain viable.

Role of Ethics Committees in Alternative Health Settings

The number of ethical issues encountered when care is provided in the home is likely to be on the rise due to an increasing focus on transferring healthcare to the community. This managed care focus pushes care from the hospital into the home or nursing facility. Even when patients and families have accepted hospice services or skilled nursing care, ethical issues may still surface during the course of the illness and care.

Hospices and skilled nursing facilities may face organizational issues, like access to services among diverse economic and racial backgrounds and conflict between individual rights and state regulations (Byock, 1994). For example, nursing facilities are legally obligated to provide adequate nutrition and hydration to their patients, yet an individual has the right to refuse artificial feeding. A site-based ethics committee would be charged with clarifying the obligation to state regulations and serving the rights of the patient. Ethics committees in hospice settings provide excellent forums for healthcare professionals to discuss difficult cases, educate staff and the community, and formulate agency policy that can minimize the occurrence of ethical dilemmas.

Since ethics committees are recent phenomena first implemented in hospitals, much of the research and literature has centered on hospital ethics committees and consultation teams. Little is known about the extent to which such committees are being utilized in community-based organizations like home health, long-term care, or hospice.

As the hospice movement continues to gain strength in numbers of agencies, patients, and types of terminal illnesses, ethical dilemmas will proportionally increase in number and complexity. A decision to accept hospice services does not preclude the occurrence of ethical issues regarding end-of-life care. In fact, because care at the end of life can be emotionally charged, ethical considerations will be central, unlike in areas of medical care where these issues arise less frequently. The kinds of issues that hospice personnel are facing include: the definition of euthanasia and the question of assisted suicide; differential access and unequal utilization of hospital services among diverse cultures and socioeconomic groups; and the limitations on palliative care practice. For example, there are obstacles to the effective use of narcotics at the end of life, which come from lack of understanding of the elements of physiological addiction and dependence and the proper mechanisms by which pain can be managed.

Healthcare personnel who work with patients outside the hospital environment face the difficulty of having to define when medical care becomes futile in conjunction with the economics of healthcare cost effectiveness (Byock, 1994). These issues are no less ethically problematic because they occur beyond the walls of the hospital and, and they must be analyzed with the same degree of deliberation utilized within the hospital.

An interdisciplinary ethics committee can be an avenue for examination of issues and enhancement of hospice services. Fife (1997), in an anecdotal review of the role of ethics committees in hospice programs, suggested that about 10% of non-hospital-based hospices utilize ethics committees. The ethics committee employed by one large hospice corporation was described as interdisciplinary, with representation from all members of the hospice team, including physicians, nurses, social workers, clergy, administrators, volunteers, and home health aides. Community members concerned with hospice issues comprise about one-fourth of the committee. The committee's functions resemble those of hospital ethics committees and include education, policy review, case review and, in some cases, research.

Hospice ethics committees may take different forms. Individual hospices may create their own committee or several small hospices may form a joint committee, enabling them to discuss community issues as well. Hospital-based hospice services may have their own committees or have access to and/or a representative on the hospital ethics committee. Among possible challenges in forming hospice ethics committees are staff turnover, a need for systematic training, and the cost of employing an ethics consultant or other hired staff to do the training (Fife, 1997).

ETHICS CONSULTATION

Eighty-one percent of American hospitals have an ethics consultation service of some kind in place, despite the fact that consultation is still the most controversial function performed by ethics committees (Moreno, 2003). The controversy surrounding the development of a formal consultation service within a hospital environment comes from a mistaken belief that doctors, nurses, and other skilled professionals should inherently understand the difference between right and wrong; determination of the "right thing to do" should be innate to professional training. If this statement were accurate, then all cases would be resolved without conflict or disagreement; however, there are no formal medical school programs that include aspects of negotiation, communication, and conflict resolution.

Prior to the 1970s, issues of conflict in medicine were resolved by social workers, patient representatives, administrators, or attorneys. The increase in technological care and confusion as to when death has occurred, combined with ever-changing ethical conflict, has necessitated delegating resolution of ethical problems to individuals with academic training in ethical theory (Aulisio, Arnold, & Youngner, 2003). For consultants to possess minimal competency, they must possess a minimal understanding of ethical theory. Hoffman (1993) surveyed 466 ethics consultants to inquire about their knowledge and education. Of those who responded, 30% had received zero formal education in the field of bioethics. One would expect that a consultant would have at least some level of formal education in theoretical constructs delineating how individuals make decisions under stress. They should also know common etiologies for miscommunication and conflict resolution techniques (Aulisio et al., 2003).

The role of the ethics consultant is conceptualized as one of facilitator rather than moral authoritarian. The facilitator's role is "to work with the patient, family, and healthcare provider to facilitate a decision that is consistent with their values" (Arnold & Wilson-Silver, 2003).The core functions are to gather data, enhance communication, identify areas of ethical discomfort, and then clarify the goals of all participants (Casarett, Daskal, & Lantos, 1998).The intended purpose of an ethics consultation is "an effort on the part of those caring for a patient to discover what their obligations to the patient require and how these obligations can best be satisfied" (Freedman, in Baylis, 2000). Determination of these obligations is accomplished through the identification, analysis, and recommendation of potential solutions in problematic situations that contain ethical, value-laden issues so that patient care (process and outcome) may be improved (Jurchak, 2000; Aulisio, Arnold, & Youngner, 1998).Typical issues for an ethics consultant might include: beginning-of-life decisions, end-of-life decisions, refusal of care, and issues related to organ donation and transplantation (Aulisio et al.).

Some have debated that this service was already in place through the work of the ethics committee.While a committee approach may be appropriate in long-term care settings, in the acute hospital setting an individual or small-team approach is the preferred mechanism for case consultation. Problems in using committees for case consultation include: difficulty in gathering enough committee members for a meeting quickly; members may not be interested or qualified; and "groupthink" can sabotage ethical resolution of complex case issues.

More importantly, the process calls for the involvement of the patient, family, and other providers to give personal accounts of the situation, which in a committee situation can be impersonal and potentially persecutory. If an individual or small-team approach is used, accessing the larger committee for review after the situation is resolved is advantageous for evaluation purposes, and new policy may be formulated from issues that may have been raised during the individual consultation.A committee's greatest strength is the fact that it is normally multidisciplinary, thus, not every member needs in-depth knowledge of every aspect of an ethical problem. Ethics consultants should be members of the ethics committee; however, not every member needs to be, nor should, serve as a consultant No matter how the consultant's role is defined, successful completion of the task requires an inordinate degree of communication skills combined with a varied knowledge base.

Skills and Knowledge Required by Ethics Consultants

The training or education necessary to conduct ethics consultation has received much attention recently. The American Society of Bioethics and Humanities (ASBH) issued a report entitled "Core Competencies for Health Care Ethics Consultation" in 1998. The report was developed by a task force compromised of 21 scholars from a variety of disciplines, including medicine, nursing, law, philosophy, and religious studies. The ASBH report described the needed competencies in terms of core skills and knowledge. All of the following information is taken from this report.

Three categories of skills were identified: ethical assessment skills, process skills, and interpersonal skills. These categories were further defined in terms of basic skills (ability to use in common cases) and advanced skills (ability to use in complex cases) (Aulisio et al., 2003).

Ethical assessment skills. These are needed to identify the underlying uncertainty or conflict that is causing the need for case consultation. To resolve complex conflicts, ethics consultants should possess multiple abilities and skills:

> Ability to discern and gather relevant data, including clinical and psychosocial information
> Ability to assess the social and interpersonal dynamics, and ask questions such as, What role does religion play? or, Are there any cultural or ethnic issues in this case?
> Ability to distinguish the ethical dimensions from overlapping medical, legal, or psychiatric issues
> Ability to identify the assumptions that parties bring to this case, such as unvoiced agendas, quality-of-life desires and ego trips
> Ability to identify the relevant values of the parties involved

The consultant must be able to evaluate the relevant data, which may include:

> Knowledge of bioethics; the law; institutional policies, practices, and guidelines; professional codes; and religious teachings

Concepts such as confidentiality, privacy, informed consent, best interests, and related rules of law

How to critically evaluate and apply relevant aspects of bioethics, the law, hospital policy, guidelines, and professional codes to the case in question

To effectively evaluate and apply relevant knowledge, the consultant must know how to:

Bring up moral considerations to help analyze the case under review

Identify and justify a range of morally acceptable options, along with their consequences

Evaluate evidence and arguments for and against different options

Recognize and acknowledge personal limitations and possible conflicts of interest between personal moral views and the objective role of consultant, including acceptance of group consensus even if the consultant disagrees personally

To gain the basic skills for ethics consultation requires training and experience in identification and analysis of ethical issues, which can be obtained through readings, seminars, and bioethics case presentations as well as in-service training conducted at the institution where the consultant is employed (Aulisio et al., 2003, pp. 165–204).

Process skills. According to the ASBH report, process skills focus on resolution of value uncertainty or conflict as it emerges. These include the ability to conduct formal and informal meetings, as well as the following individual abilities:

Ability to identify key decision-makers and involved parties and include them in all pertinent discussions

Ability to set ground rules for formal meetings, such as the length, who should participate, and the purpose and structure of the meeting

Ability to express and stay within the limits of the consultant's role during the meeting and not become overemotional or attached to a certain outcome

Ability to create an atmosphere of trust that respects privacy and confidentiality and allows parties to feel free to express their concerns

The consultant must be able to build a moral consensus around the issues of concern in the case in question. To do this requires:

The ability to help individuals to critically analyze the values underlying their assumptions and decisions, and the possible consequences of these decisions

The ability to negotiate between competing moral views

The ability to engage in creative problem solving

Processing skills include the ability to utilize institutional structures and resources to facilitate implementation of whatever becomes the chosen option. The consultant must also be able to document the interactions and elicit feedback from appropriate people to complete the consultation.

Interpersonal Skills. These skills are seen as critical to every aspect of ethics consultation:

The ability to listen well and to communicate interest, respect, support, and empathy to all of the involved parties

The ability to educate all parties regarding the ethical dimensions of the case

The ability to elicit the moral views of those involved

The ability to represent the views of the involved parties to others on the case

The ability to enable everyone to communicate effectively and to be heard by others

The ability to recognize and attend to potential barriers to communication

Process skills and interpersonal skills are acquired and perfected through experience alone. The ability to set up a formal meeting is one thing, but facilitating the meeting is of primary value. Basic process and interpersonal skills should be supplemented with interactive and experience-based educational opportunities. In-service practice can be gained, for example, through role-play of a case consultation. These skills can also be learned in short intense courses that focus on interpersonal communication, psychology, sociology, education, and human aspects of social work. Interpersonal communication and processing a complex consultation form the basis of social work education. Acquisition of advanced interpersonal and process skills develops over time and with experience in practice and actual ethics consultations. Advanced skills are critical to be able to handle more complex situations, such as resolving conflict among angry, confused, or difficult family members or patients. These skills are taught in master's degree programs in ethics or doctoral programs in healthcare ethics.

THE CONSULTATION PROCESS

The ASBH task force also identified character traits and personal qualities that contribute to successful case consultation: tolerance, patience, compassion, honesty, forthrightness self-knowledge, courage, prudence, humility, and integrity. Along with identifying basic and advanced core knowledge and skills, the ASBH report goes further and specifies which are needed by at least one committee member, by every member of the consultation team or ethics committee, or that at least one member should be able to access.

Several models for the consultation process have been described in the literature. The approach recommended in the ASBH report is the *ethics facilitation approach*. This involves "identifying and analyzing the nature of the value uncertainty and facilitating the building of consensus" (Aulisio et al., 1998, p. 6). The process begins by collecting data from all parties involved (use of interpersonal skills), clarifying relevant concepts (use of knowledge of bioethics and facilitation), clarifying normative issues (use of knowledge of society and institutional beliefs and policies), and identifying a range of morally acceptable options. To build consensus, consultants may be charged with the responsibility of ensuring that each party's voice is heard. The consultant may also be asked to assist individuals to clarify their own values, facilitate building a moral understanding of the situation, and identify options for resolution within the prevailing context.

To begin, a request for consultation must be made. A primary question is, Who should have access to ethics consultation services? This should be decided as a matter of institutional policy, along with what rights individuals have during the process. All stakeholders should have open access to the process, including patients, families and surrogates, healthcare providers, and administrators. Patients should be notified when a consultation is requested and for what reason; patients should be informed of the nature of the process that will take place, and who is invited to participate. The patient should then be informed of the recommendations of the consultation team/committee. Ethics consultations should be documented in the patient record or in another type of permanent record, with the method of documentation clearly outlined as a matter of policy. Finally, a mechanism for retrospective case review should be specified, for accountability and quality improvement (Aulisio et al., 1998).

CLINICAL ETHICS

Committees and consultations often rely on the rules of clinical ethics to examine ethical problems that occur in healthcare practice. Clinical ethics as a discipline attempts to understand and reduce human suffering in the clinical (medical) setting. The knowledge and methods used in this discipline come from many fields, including clinical medicine and bioethics, biomedical and social sciences, health policy, philosophy, humanities, law, theology, and population and information sciences (Roberts, 2001). The goal of clinical ethics is "to improve the quality of patient care by identifying, analyzing, and attempting to resolve the ethical problems that arise in practice" (Singer, Pellegrino, & Siegler, 2001, p. 1). The focus is thus on interactions that occur, for example, between the practitioner and patient and between health/social policy and healthcare delivery systems. It is "inherently relational, informed by clinical experience, conceptual analysis, and empirical evidence" (Roberts, 2001, p. 8).

According to Fletcher, Miller, and Spencer (1997), those engaged in clinical ethics "must interact professionally and, at times, intimately with clinicians and patients in their world and know their language, practices, and beliefs" (p. 7). Clinical ethics is seen as a practical endeavor that provides a structured approach to the analysis and resolution of ethical problems in clinical practice. Such an approach helps to identify the aspects of care that have potential for causing ethical problems. According to Jonsen, Siegler, and Winslade (1998), four major areas must be considered in every case: medical indications, patient preferences, quality of life, and contextual features.

Medical indications include diagnosis, current treatment, and the purpose and goals of medical interventions. Patient preferences are ethically relevant to consider as they are based on the patient's own values and personal evaluation of what the potential benefits and burdens are in the situation. Other issues include whether the patient has sufficient information, can understand and comprehend the consequences of a proposed treatment plan, and whether the patient's response is voluntary. Since the purpose of medical intervention is to improve quality of life, the extent to which this occurs must be assessed. The difficulty in making such a subjective judgment should be recognized, but not be avoided.

Lastly, the context for the dilemma inevitably comes into play, things like family and other social arrangements, institutional policy, and financial considerations. Examination of these four areas will help to organize data for discussion of the case, whether in a formal ethics committee or by a consultation team. Reviewing the issues of a case in this manner can move the process along to resolution so that the healthcare team does not become mired in debate about one area or another instead of looking at the situation as a whole. This may change the recommendations and outcomes.

The following outline by Jonsen, Siegler, and Winslade (1998) was proposed as a guide to information that should be obtained in order to analyze a case situation.

Medical Indications

What is the medical problem? history? diagnosis? prognosis?
Is the problem acute? chronic?
What are the goals of treatment? critical? emergent? reversible?
What is the likelihood of success?
What is the plan in case of therapeutic failure?
In sum, how can this patient benefit from medical and nursing care, and how can harm be avoided?

Patient Preferences

What has the patient expressed about preferences for treatment?

Has patient been informed of the benefits and risks, understood, and given consent?

Is patient mentally capable and legally competent? Is there evidence of incapacity?

Has patient expressed prior preferences, for example, an advance directive or living will?

If incapacitated, who is an appropriate surrogate? Is surrogate using appropriate standards?

Is patient unwilling or unable to cooperate with medical treatment? If so, why?

In sum, is patient's right to choose being respected to the extent possible under ethics and law?

Quality of Life

What are the prospects, with or without treatment, for a return to patient's normal life?

Are there biases that might prejudice provider's evaluation of patient's quality of life?

What physical, mental, and social deficits is patient likely to experience if treatment succeeds?

Is patient's present or future condition such that continued life might be judged undesirable?

Any plan or rationale to forgo treatment?

Any plans for comfort and palliative care?

It should be noted that quality-of-life statements and references do not apply in all cultures and in all faiths. For example, in Orthodox Judaism every second of life holds the same meaning as every other second of life. Therefore, an observant Jew would not consider the quality of the life, only the living of life from one second to the next.

Contextual Features

Are there family issues that might influence treatment decisions?

Are there provider (physicians and nurses) issues that might influence treatment decisions?
Are there financial and economic factors?
Are there religious, cultural factors?
Is there any justification to breach confidentiality?
Are there problems of allocation of resources?
What are the legal implications of treatment decisions?
Is clinical research or teaching involved?
Is there any provider or institutional conflict of interest?

Another approach in clinical ethics is the "case method of moral problem solving" (Miller, Fletcher, & Fins, 1997). This method includes the task of assessment, and also provides direction for resolution beyond gathering and organization of data and assessment of the problem. Carefully considering the details of a case within a context of a collaborative effort, including inquiry, negotiation, and making decisions about what action is appropriate in morally problematic cases is referred to as clinical pragmatism. The following outline was suggested by Miller, Fletcher, and Fins (1997, p. 24) to determine a diagnosis of the ethical problems and to propose a potential solution.

Moral Diagnosis

Examine how the moral problems in this case are being framed by the participants. Determine whether this framing should be reconsidered or replaced by an alternative understanding.

Identify and rank the range of relevant moral considerations.

Identify any relevant institutional policies pertaining to the case.

Consider ethical standards and guidelines, drawing on consensus statements of commissions or interdisciplinary or specialty groups.

Consider similar cases and discussions in the literature that might shed light on the analysis and resolution of moral problems in the case.

Identify the morally acceptable options for resolving the moral problems posed by the case.

Goal Setting, Decision Making, and Implementation

Consider or reconsider and negotiate the goals of treatment and care for the patient.

Consider ideas (hypotheses) for possible interventions to meet the needs of the patient and resolve moral problems.

Deliberate merits of alternative options for resolving the moral problems.

Endeavor to resolve conflicts.

Assess whether ethics consultation is necessary or desirable:

> Is there persistent conflict between clinicians and patients or surrogates or among clinicians themselves regarding how to resolve the moral problems posed by the case?

> Would ethics advice help in understanding or providing guidance on moral issues presented by the case?

Negotiate acceptable plan of action.

If negotiation, including ethics consultation, fails to achieve satisfactory resolution, consider judicial review.

Implement plan of action.

Evaluation

Current evaluation

Is the plan of action working? If not, why not?

Do the observed results of implementing the plan indicate the need for a modification of the plan?

Have conditions changed in a way that suggests the need to rethink the plan?

Are interactions between clinicians and the patient or surrogate helping to meet the needs of the patient, to respect the patient as a person, and to serve the goals of the plan of care?

Have relevant interests, institutional factors, and normative considerations been adequately addressed in planning for the care of the patient?

Retrospective review

What opportunities for resolving the moral problems were missed?

How did the care received by the patient match up to standards of good practice?

What factors contributed to a less than optimal resolution of the problems posed by the case?

Was the process of problem solving satisfactory in this case?

What might have been done to improve the care of the patient?

Are there desirable changes in institutional policy, feasible changes in the clinical environment, or educational interventions that might help to prevent or resolve moral problems posed by similar cases?

ETHICAL DECISION MAKING IN SOCIAL WORK

A growing body of literature can be found regarding ethical decision making in social work (Congress, 1999; Loewenberg, Dolgoff, & Harrington, 2000; Mattison, 2000; Reamer, 1995). Two primary models of processes to be followed when ethical problems arise in social work practice have been put forth. In particular, the Reamer model (1995, pp. 64–65) closely resembles the process of clinical ethics, especially in that it takes a practical approach to reaching resolutions in challenging cases.

Reamer's Model

Identify the ethical issues, including the social work values and duties that conflict.

Identify the individuals, groups, and organizations that are likely to be affected by the ethical decision.

Tentatively identify all possible courses of action and the participants involved in each, along with the possible benefits and risks for each.

Thoroughly examine the reasons in favor of and opposed to each possible course of action, considering relevant:

> ethical theories, principles, and guidelines
> codes of ethics and legal principles
> social work practice theory and principles

personal values (including religious, cultural, and ethnic values and political ideology), particularly those that conflict with one's own

Consult with colleagues and appropriate experts (such as agency staff, supervisor's agency administrators, attorneys, and ethics scholars).
Make the decision and document the decision-making process.
Monitor, evaluate, and document the decision.

In addition, Loewenberg, Dolgoff, and Harrington (2000) proposed a general decision-making model similar to Reamer's but also discussed more specific guidelines pertaining to the priority of ethical principles when one is dealing with problematic cases. After determining that the NASW Code of Ethics does not address the specific problem or that code rules conflict, their conception of an "ethical principles screen" is to be used. The principles are in order of priority: protection of life; equality and inequality; autonomy and freedom; least harm; quality of life; privacy and confidentiality; truthfulness and full disclosure. The use of this screen interfaces well in discussion of bioethical problems in health care. Still, social workers need to be knowledgeable about bioethical and other medical principles and theories used by those in the medical setting, particularly in ethics committees, to be able to contribute fully to the deliberations.

ETHICS COMMITTEES AND CONSULTANTS AND THE SOCIAL WORK ROLE

Social workers are integral to all aspects of the healthcare system. Most hospital systems employ social workers, although in recent years there has been a trend toward cutting social workers in favor of discharge planners. Social workers are also employed in alternative health settings, such as home health, hospital, and community clinics. Medicare guidelines for hospice require that social workers must be a fundamental part of the interdisciplinary team approach in caring for terminally ill individuals. Social workers form relationships with patients and families and work to maximize quality of life and resolve ethical issues.

While hospitals and organizations affiliated with hospital systems have responded to meet the JCAHO accreditation standard that mandates a method of resolution of ethical problems, the standard does not specify who should be on committees or be consulted. The emphasis on multidisciplinary ethics committees seems to recognize the importance of a holistic perspective. Social workers' involvement on these committees is a good fit, as the profession's foundation rests on consideration of a holistic view of people in their environment. Because ethics committee processes recognize the value of a holistic perspective in decision making, many authors have called for the participation of social workers on formal ethics committees (Abramson & Black, 1985; Csikai & Sales, 1998; Foster, Sharp, Scesny, McLellan, & Cotman, 1993; Furlong, 1986; Gelman, 1986; Reamer, 1995; Silverman, 1992).

The social work role on hospital and hospice ethics committees has received a small amount of research attention (Csikai, 2004; Csikai, 2002; Csikai & Sales, 1998; Csikai, 1997; Skinner, 1991). In a 1995 study, social workers were found to be members of 75% of the committees (Csikai, 1997). However, considering the three main functions of ethics committees—education, policy development and review, and case consultation and review—social work involvement was moderate. Social workers report that they would like to have a greater role. The chairs of ethics committees (a majority of whom were physicians) were also surveyed. The chairs indicated that they had expected social workers to be more involved, especially in educational activities. In spite of this, social work respondents reported a fairly high level of satisfaction with their roles on the committees. This was positively correlated with the amount of involvement they had with various activities of the committees (Csikai, 1997). Findings suggest that social workers have an opportunity for even greater involvement, especially in education, an area unclaimed by other professionals (Csikai & Sales, 1998).

It has been suggested that social workers could make a significant contribution to the activities of ethics committees, whose purpose is the protection of patients' rights (Hoffman, 1993). The values embraced by social work are respect for self-determination, affirmation of the uniqueness of individuals, affirmation of the worth and dignity of individuals, and confidentiality. These values are central to the profession and congruent with those of ethics committees as well (Csikai & Sales, 1998; Csikai, 1997).

Regarding hospice ethics committees, a 1999 study (using similar methods as the above study) found that social work representation on hospice ethics committees was only about 53%, but that such committees were only present in 23% of the hospices studied (n = 182). Overall, 73% of social workers had access to an ethics committee of some type, for example, through a hospital system (Csikai, 2002). Similar findings were seen in terms of amount of involvement and expectations for involvement in the various committee activities among the social workers and chairs of the hospice ethics committees. However, the ordering of expectations for individual committee activities differed. The chairs expected that social workers should almost always be involved in facilitating discussion of cases during committee deliberations while social workers expected much less of this activity. Also, chairs expected greater involvement in presentation of information at seminars. In the policy area, chairs thought that advocating for social justice was most important, whereas social workers indicated that promoting self-determination in agency policy was the highest expectation. Also, as with hospital ethics committees, education is an area of responsibility where social workers were expected to take on a greater role, and provide leadership for the agency and community.

OPPORTUNITIES FOR SOCIAL WORKERS

In reviewing the approach, skills, and knowledge recommended by ASBH for ethics committee members, one can see several social work parallels.

First, in the approach to resolution of cases, the process itself mirrors the problem-solving method used as a hallmark of the social work profession. Through engagement, data collection and assessment, intervention, evaluation, termination, and follow-up, social workers are able to approach cases in a thorough and balanced manner. Also, encouragement of family and healthcare professionals in the end-of-life decision-making process is a matter of routine for social workers. Educational background and training in group processes, such as in consensus building, (also recommended by ASBH), are strengths.

In policy matters, social workers can bring much to the table in terms of formulation and review of policies to ensure that they meet the patients' and families' needs and respect diversity regarding age, culture, religion, socioeconomic level, and spiritual affiliation. Providing education is integral to assist in resolving issues through the problem-solving process, with the goal of improving quality of life. Skill in education is easily transferable to larger systems, such as the hospital, hospice agency, and the community. Education of staff members and the community about ethical issues, including planning seminars or conferences on hospice ethics and issues of death and dying, is an area where social workers can have a direct impact.

Social workers must be able to demonstrate their knowledge and skills in practice situations and advocate for themselves to increase involvement on ethics committees. The nature of ethics committees is multidisciplinary, so a social work member serves as a representative of the profession, as the physician represents the medical profession, the nurse the nursing professions, and so on. Values and perspectives from the various professions are shared in relation to the particular ethical problem under consideration. Social workers who are not standing members of ethics committees need to know how to access these forums in their facility to discuss ethical problems encountered in their practice. They may attend meetings regarding a specific case and serve as advocates for the patient and family as needed to resolve the problem.

Another role for social workers is facilitating discussion of particularly difficult or emerging issues in bioethics, such as physician-assisted suicide. Such forums for multidisciplinary discussion are useful to acknowledge the range of views on the issues so that they may be dealt with in an open manner. Many health professionals are asked by their patients to discuss assisted suicide, but few are willing to discuss it with others since it is illegal in all but one state.

When there are no ethics committees in the facility, social workers are ideal professionals to initiate formation. They can gather those who are interested and qualified, arrange education on purpose and access for new members, staff, and community, and be part of evaluating effectiveness. Particularly as chairs of ethics committees and case consultation teams, social workers can employ their knowledge of group processes to ensure participation from everyone.

Chapter Conclusion

While formal ethics committees or case consultation teams may not be present in all healthcare settings, some method of resolution will be in place. Social workers must be aware of the processes that are generally followed and contribute their expertise appropriately. They must engage in continuing education as healthcare practices continually change. Social workers need to keep extending their training in order to be included in growth areas such as on-site ethics consultation, formation of on-site palliative care programs, and development of ethics and communication services at extended care facilities. Based on their current knowledge base and sound interpersonal skills, with additional advanced training, social workers are the natural choice to be ethics consultants or serve as part of a palliative care team.

Chapter Eight

CONFIDENTIALITY, PRIVACY, TRUTH TELLING, AND MEDICAL ERROR

Trust provides the basis of all intimate relationships, and it is essential in the formation of all professional relationships. For example, truthful and detailed information is required if a physician is going to properly diagnosis an illness, but in order for patients to feel comfortable with the provision of detailed information, they must first trust that the data provided will be kept confidential. People who are ill, particularly those facing the end of life, are especially vulnerable.

The responsibility for creating safety with the vulnerable patient lies with the professional: the clinical social worker, physician, nurse, psychologist, medical ethicist, and others. The best way to establish safety is to assure that personal and private information remains private. Most professions have a strict set of guidelines within their codes of ethics that dictate how and when information can be relayed and to whom such information can be given. Hospital policies and regulations, Joint Commission on Accreditation of Healthcare Organizations (JCAHO) guidelines, and federal regulations also dictate how private patient information can be shared. All of these standards and guidelines are beneficial at the time of the establishment of trust, and they are essential to the development and sustenance of a professional relationship. At the same time, they may be confusing. On occasion, these guidelines and regulations inhibit the provision of information at times when families are desperate to know things that the healthcare provider is forbidden to tell.

The goal of this chapter is to first clarify why we keep information private and under what circumstances we are permitted to provide information to others. Second, this chapter will explore the nature of truth telling in the hospital environment. Third, within each section the regulations that guide the keeping of secrets in the professional environment will be discussed, as well as when and why laws or circumstances may require that the professional break a confidence. Finally, this chapter will touch upon medical error and the responsibility of the hospital and the institution to report and discuss such errors openly. Information on the federal Health Insurance Portability and Accountability Act (HIPAA) of 1996, which regulates the kinds of information that can be revealed within healthcare institutions and to whom this information can be revealed, is also presented.

THE SECRETS WE KEEP

As humans enter into relationships, the degree to which one member shares personal information with another defines the intimacy of that relationship. Intimate relationships are rooted in loyalty and the keeping of a confidence is the test. There are often boundaries on what type and under what circumstances information is shared. When boundaries are not in place, providing intimate data may feel inappropriate or embarrassing. Recall the last time someone sat next to you on an airplane or a bus and told you his/her life story, complete with way too much personal information. Such a breach of intimacy rules can make the listener uncomfortable. This discomfort stems from the fact that there was no shared understanding between the speaker and the listener as to the boundaries of the relationship prior to the sharing of this intimate data. Normally, as relationships get emotionally closer the degree of intimacy increases on both sides. This works for relationships between friends and lovers as well as with relationships between professionals and their patients or clients. What is required of a close friend or lover differs from the degree of confidentiality that must exist between a doctor and a patient. For example, if I become aware that my best friend's husband may be abusing prescription medication I might try to speak with him about his dependence and see if I can help. However, if a patient tells her doctor of her concern that her husband may be abusing prescription medication, the physician cannot call the patient's husband to discuss this issue, even if the husband is his patient. The husband would have to come to the physician, requesting help. The friend, however, based upon the intimacy of the relationship, can risk the breach of confidence that the professional cannot, legally and ethically. This professional relationship could not survive without such a contingency in place (Bok, 1983).

BLENDING OF PRIVACY, CONFIDENTIALITY, AND AUTONOMY

Numerous reasons exist for why professionals keep secrets, not the least of which is to generate an atmosphere of trust. Professional relationships are formulated and maintained upon trust. In the medical field, confidentiality of medical information has been part of medical practice since its inception as a profession. The Hippocratic Oath states, in part: "Whatever, in connection with my profession, or not in connection with it, I may see or hear in the lives of men, which ought not to be spoken abroad I will not divulge as reckoning that all should be kept secret" (quoted in Britton, 1975, p. 34). This trust allows patients to share the personal information that doctors require to diagnose and treat illness. Clinical social workers cannot obtain the data required for a clinical psychosocial assessment nor could psychological intervention continue without a trusting relationship between the patient and the clinician. For example, if I went to my doctor to discuss my concerns with sleeplessness and divulged the details of a case that had been keeping me up all night, he would be bound to keep the case details confidential as well as the fact that I suffer from insomnia.

Privacy is connected closely with the concept of autonomy and self-determination. As stated in chapter 3, preservation of autonomy is one of the primary principles of the informed consent statute. Legally, a variety of constitutional rights involve aspects of autonomy and privacy, such as abortion rights, rights to contraception and procreation, issues related to shock treatments, rights against psychosurgery, and issues related to behavioral therapy and surrounding the provision and withdrawal of life-sustaining therapies (Shapiro & Spece, 1981). The sense of privacy discussed within the law refers to a "zone of privacy." This zone of privacy is about the process surrounding the keeping of secrets. According to U.S. Supreme Court Justice Blackman, the zone of privacy consists of "personal rights that can be deemed fundamental, that is implicit in the concept of ordered liberty" (Shapiro & Spence, 1981, p. 56). The right to confidentiality between doctor and patient stems from an unspoken contract, whereas the right of privacy is said to be constitutionally based.

The preservation and expression of autonomy is dependent upon confidentiality. The capacity to participate in the informed consent process relies on the patient's ability to assimilate and provide information. The provision of information depends on the trust and loyalty generated within the medical profession, which is formulated upon the ability of the profession to keep such data confidential. Within medical decision making, two factors are required to support autonomous choice: "One is the ability to keep private information private and the other is the independence to make certain kind of important decisions" (Shapiro & Spece, 1981, p. 56).

CONFIDENTIALITY DEFINED

According to Bok (1983), confidentiality refers to "the boundaries surrounding shared secrets and the process of guarding these boundaries" (p. 25). Confidential information can be quite intimate in nature or may not be intimate at all. The information may seem trivial in substance and might even seem false, nonetheless, it must be kept private—except under certain defined circumstances. These circumstances include the threat of danger to self or others, the provision of medical information to designated surrogates in a situation where a patient is believed to be incapable of participating in the informed consent process (see chapter 3), insurance companies, and the reporting of child abuse, elder abuse, gunshot wounds, and car accidents, as dictated by state and federal law. The sharing of medical information to family members, surrogates, or friends is guided by federal HIPAA standards (discussed later in this chapter).

Even if the patient does not directly request that shared information be kept secret, the moral, ethical, and legal responsibility of most professionals is to keep such data private. The obligation to keep patient information confidential is part of an unspoken contract between patient and doctor (Bok, 1983). However, maintaining a level of confidentiality is not a simple process.

HOW SECURE IS THE PATIENT RECORD?

Medical records contain personal data, which, in some cases, if revealed, could prove personally devastating. Embarrassment and humiliation can lead to damage to self-esteem; loss of employment; loss of social, educational, and financial opportunities; and even lead to discrimination and infringement upon legal rights (Cleaver, 1985). Despite the harm that would come from a breach of confidence of the medical record, legal concern about protection of such information is fairly new. "The privacy interest recognized in medical records is in its infancy" (Schuchman, 1982). Years ago, a breach in confidence was at the discretion of the family or town doctor. Currently, however, with the advent of third-party payment, the increased presence of government participation in medical care, and the advent of automated record keeping, there is an increase in the amount, type, and accessibility of medical data available on any one individual (Cleaver, 1985).

The technology of record keeping has changed greatly over the years. More patient data is automated and it is now possible for thousands of people to have access to one patient record. Most medical offices and some hospitals keep totally automated medical records. In addition, medical records are not only sought by those in health care or associated with health care. Private medical information may be sought by law enforcement, public health officials, occupational and health researchers, third-party payers, and employers (Cleaver, 1985). It is the ease of access combined with the increased number of people who want access that has created a new level of fear in the general public. There is a sense that such data is at risk of being accessed by any individual with the skills to break or hack into a computer system that contains confidential patient information.

Of additional concern is the requirement that healthcare employees obtain medical care and treatment within the hospital system through which they are employed. Another worry is companies who hire a company physician to care for employees who are ill or injured in the workplace; it is not always clear to the employee where the loyalties of the "company doc" lie. For example, if I am hospitalized in the hospital where I am employed, who can access my medical record? How much information on my condition does human resources have a right to access? Can my boss review my automated record to find out when I will be discharged and when I will be able to return to work? What prevents a breach of confidence from occurring?

Most hospitals and physician offices have safety mechanisms in place to prevent outsiders from accessing data contained within the automated patient record and have hired companies to create a fire wall to prevent unauthorized access. Hospitals have started to create strict policies that prohibit unauthorized access to patient records, especially employee records. These hospitals have code-tracking devices that alert the information systems departments if unauthorized access occurs. Breach of the confidentiality policy can result in a formal penalty up to dismissal from one's job.

Privacy Protection of the Medical Record

The constitutional and common law reference to a right to privacy usually refers to the right to be free to be left alone and free to control one's personal information (*Katz v. United States*, 1967; *Roe v. Wade*, 1973; *Griswold v. Connecticut*, 1965; *In Re: Karen Ann Quinlan*, 1996). This request for creation of a tort right of privacy was first recognized in a *Harvard Law Review* article by Warren and Brandeis published in 1890. This article discussed how the advance of civilization had eroded the privacy of the individual, thereby making privacy much more essential. It was speculated that the invasion of privacy led to mental pain and distress and called for protection from this inflicted injury.

Over time, various health law cases referred to a constitutional right to be left alone (*Olmstead v. United States*, 1928) and a general constitutional right to privacy (*Griswold v. Connecticut*, 1965). In 1970 the U.S. Supreme Court first examined privacy issues related to the medical record.

In *Whalen v. Roe* (1968), the U.S. Supreme Court reviewed the constitutionality of a New York statute that required that all prescriptions for dangerous drugs be filed with the State Health Department. The file contained the name, address, and age of all patients prescribed these drugs, along with the name of the physician who wrote the prescription, the dose and name of the drug, and the pharmacy filling the prescription (Cleaver, 1985). The appellate court contended that this statute violated the patient's right to avoid disclosure of personal matters and that it impeded individual decision making. The Supreme Court disagreed. Similarly, in the case of *Planned Parenthood of Missouri v. Danforth* (1966), the court decided that the recording laws did not violate a woman's right to have an abortion. Both cases, *Whalen* and *Planned Parenthood*, acknowledged a privacy interest in medical records (Cleaver, 1985).

The common law efforts at protection have succeeded but are considered by Cleaver (1985) and others to be inadequate. "Common law protections for sensitive medical information include actions for invasion of privacy, defamation, breach of confidence, breach of statutory duty, breach of fiduciary duty, breach of contract, and tortuous interference with a contractual relationship" (p. 176). The focus of these actions seems to be upon the disclosure of the information and not upon the safety of the medical record itself.

Federal Freedom of Information Act (FOIA) and Privacy Act of 1974

The purpose of the FOIA was to allow public access to federal records. The act is based upon the premise that a truly informed public is essential to a democratic form of government. However, the FOIA was not prepared for how this act would affect medical records held by the government. To counteract the disclosure encouraged by the FOIA, the government enacted the Privacy Act of 1974, which states, "The right to privacy was personal and fundamental" (Cleaver, 1985). The Privacy Act is aimed at promoting governmental respect for the privacy of its citizens. The Privacy Act had several requirements within it, all aimed at protecting disclosed information and giving individuals limited control over their medical records that are held by the government (Cleaver, 1985).

State-Held Open Records and Privacy Statutes

Several states have enacted open records and privacy statutes with privacy protections. These protections relate to records held by a state agency or a state-funded entity and pertain to the "collection, maintenance, use and disclosure of personal information" (Cleaver, 1985, pp. 176-177). The state laws are not applicable to federal agencies and differ greatly in the type and extent of the protection noted in federal statutes.

Health Insurance Portability and Accountability Act (HIPAA) and Patient Privacy

A major piece of federal legislation, the Health Insurance Portability and Accountability Act (HIPAA), and Patient Privacy (1996) focused upon three direct areas related to patient care: insurance portability, administrative simplification, and privacy and security. Healthcare employees undergo training programs in order to learn how to abide by HIPAA standards. Lack of compliance can result in governmental fines up to $250,000, imprisonment, and disciplinary action, up to and including termination of employment. Deadlines for compliance with the privacy requirements were in April, 2003.

Under the privacy and security section of this legislation, healthcare providers must use certain methods in an effort to assure that a patient's "protected health information" remains private and secure. Institutions and all healthcare employees are required to provide patient medical information on a need-to-know basis only to individuals, institutions, or organizations that use this information to provide treatment, obtain payment, or perform related healthcare operations. This restriction applies to all information—verbal, written, or electronically stored—and consists of the patient's general information: name, medical record number, Social Security number, address, and date of birth. The restriction also applies to health information such as diagnosis, medical history, treatments, and medications.

Strict rules are in place to govern the release of protected health information (PHI) when this information is not being used for treatment, payment, or healthcare operations. The established rules vary depending upon the degree of sensitivity of the requested information. If PHI is to be released it is only, in most circumstances, after a patient has signed an authorization giving consent. A valid authorization to release PHI must contain the following:

> Patient's full name at the time the treatment was rendered
> Identification information (date of birth, Social Security number, medical record number)
> How the released information is to be used

Name of facility where PHI was created

Name of the person, company, or agency to whom the information is to be released

Dates of treatment

The exact type of information to be released, specified on the document, for example, behavioral health, HIV

Date and signature of the patient or legal representative

In addition, institutions are required to post in the public areas and to hand out public notices that outline how patients' health information may be used or disclosed. Patients are to be notified of their rights under HIPAA and whom to contact if they feel their privacy rights have been violated. Patients have a right to receive an accounting of the date of the disclosure of their medical information, the name of the entity or person who received the PHI data, a brief description of the PHI disclosed, and the reason for the disclosure.

The HIPAA standards also contain guidelines for purchasing, the use of protected health information in marketing, the use of protected health information in fundraising, and the use and disclosure of protected health information for research purposes pursuant to HIPAA privacy rules.

Physician-Patient Privilege

The relationship of trust developed between a doctor and patient is referred to as physician-patient privilege. Legal reference to this relationship only pertains to the protection of the patient medical record from disclosure during the discovery phase; it does not pertain to any other areas. The privilege is in place to protect the patient but does not protect the physician or the medical institution where the care was provided (Cleaver, 1985). The patient can choose to waive the privilege, otherwise waiver is implied in situations where the patient is bringing a personal injury action. However, this type of waiver only applies to the part of the record pertaining to the injury alone. The privilege is "further limited by statutory and common law exceptions which have been created where important public interests are at stake and where the intrusion of patient privacy interests would be minor" (Cleaver, 1985, pp. 177–178).

WHO CAN ACCESS THE PATIENT RECORD

Determining who can gain access to a patient's medical record is resolved through a series of questions (Cleaver, 1985):

What is the purpose for which the medical records are being requested?
What are the laws governing the request and the parties?
Who is the subject of this record?
What is the status of the party seeking access to this medical record?
What degree of confidentiality would remain if the request for access were granted?

Purposes for Released Medical Records

Public health. The privacy interests of the individual patient can be diminished for the sake of public health, public epidemiological interests, and for occupational health research. The open records statutes of various states call for a balancing of individual private interests with the interests of the public's need to know (Cleaver, 1985).

Reporting laws. Many states require the reporting of "venereal diseases, child abuse, elder abuse, injuries caused by deadly weapons, fetal deaths, and abortions, as well as prescriptions given for dangerous drugs" (Cleaver, 1985, p. 178)." Social workers must be particularly careful in reporting suspected child abuse and elder abuse, for it is a requirement of most states and has direct impact on the maintenance of a state license to practice social work.

Duty to warn: The Tarasoff case. The duty to warn comes from the case of *Tarasoff v. Regents of the University of California* (1976). In this case, Prosenjit Poddar was a graduate student at the University of California who had dated a woman named Tatiana Tarasoff. She broke off this relationship and Poddar sought psychotherapy at the university clinic. He confided to his psychologist that he intended to kill an unnamed woman when she returned from a trip.

The psychologist could identify this woman as Tarasoff and he notified the campus police that Mr. Poddar was dangerous and that he should be committed for observation and treatment in a psychiatric hospital. Poddar was detained but released by the local police, who saw him as rational. Poddar broke off his relationship with his therapist and two months later he killed Tatiana Tarasoff. The Tarasoff family brought suit against the psychologist, his supervisor, the campus police, and the University of California for failing to warn them of the peril their daughter was in, and also for failing to detain Poddar for treatment. The suit was at first dismissed but then the California Supreme Court reversed this dismissal, stating that:

> regardless of the therapist's unsuccessful attempt to confine Poddar, since they knew he was at large and dangerous, their failure to warn Tatiana or others likely to apprise her of the danger constituted a breach of the therapist's duty to exercise reasonable care to protect Tatiana (Roth & Meisel, 1977, p. 509).

Physicians, psychiatrists, therapists, social workers, and all concerned have a duty to conduct a detailed assessment of the dangerousness of a particular patient, and they have a duty to warn. The assessment of dangerousness should include: the patient's behavior, affect, somatic functioning, interpersonal relationships, and cognition, or the acronym *BASIC*. (Oppenheimer & Swanson, 1990).

When assessing a patient's behavior, the therapist should complete a detailed violence history, including how recently these actions occurred, as well as the severity and frequency of violent actions. The therapist should discover if the patient has been arrested or convicted of violent behavior. Was the patient ever hospitalized for "dangerous" behavior? Has the patient reported being in an altercation at work, school, or in bars? Was the patient a victim of child abuse? Did the patient witness spousal abuse as a child? Has the patient participated in abusive behavior toward a spouse and child? Does the patient have a history of poor impulse control? If the answer to a majority of these questions is yes, Oppenheimer and Swanson (1990) speculate that past behavior is the best predictor of a patient's future behavior. They recommend that the therapist gain insight into the patient's current circumstances, being particularly aware of answers to the following questions: Is the patient's present situation similar in any way to a past situation when the patient became violent? Has the patient made a specific threat against an identifiable victim? Although a verbal threat alone is not sufficient cause to warn an intended victim, these authors suggest that the therapist should ascertain how the patient intends to implement the plan. This should include an assessment of the lethality, and the detail, coherency, and organization of the plan, suggesting that a highly lethal, well-organized plan to harm another person increases the likelihood of danger.

In the assessment of affect, Oppenheimer and Swanson (1990) recommend that the therapist assess if the patient is angry, sad, or labile. They suggest that, "if the patient seems angry, the therapist should assess if the anger is over-controlled or under-controlled; over-controlled anger can be more dangerous than anger that is easily expressed" (p. 182). The therapist should assess if the anger is generalized or directed toward an individual, or both. Anger directed toward an individual by a generally angry person increases the likelihood that violence will occur.

In the assessment of somatic expression, Oppenheimer and Swanson (1990) state that this refers to the general physical functioning and health of the patient. Somatic symptoms are said to provide an index of the patient's stress level, which can have detrimental effects on health. The deterioration of health is not the sole predictor of violence but when combined with the disinhibiting effect of alcohol or drugs, an increased propensity toward violence is possible.

In the assessment of the patient's interpersonal relationships, the therapist should review how connected the patient is with others. Is the patient emotionally connected with family, friends, or coworkers? Is the patient in frequent contact with others? It is believed that low levels of social support and the presence of social isolation often increase the likelihood that violence is possible, especially if the person to whom the patient has directed anger has been a main support person. Feelings of isolation and loneliness can predicate acting out, as can a history of using violence in the past to resolve conflict.

In the assessment of the cognitive expression of the patient, Oppenheimer and Swanson (1990) recommend that the therapist gain a detailed history of the patient's homicidal ideation and fantasies. The therapist should investigate if the patient anticipates any adverse consequences for actions. If so, does this anticipation reduce the intensity of affect? Further, is the patient able to separate the fantasy of desiring to harm another person from the actual behavior? In the assessment of the patient, does the patient report having hallucinations, delusions, or paranoid ideations? Oppenheimer and Swanson speculate that the "presence of a psychotic thought process increases the likelihood of violence" and therefore the assessment of such is crucial (p. 182).

If the patient is assessed as being at risk for performing violence toward another, then the therapist must come up with a plan to involuntarily commit the patient if the patient will not agree to voluntarily seek psychiatric treatment. The therapist may choose to notify the police, utilize social or environmental manipulation "to reduce lethality," or use conjoint therapy with the patient and the intended victim.

No matter what plan the therapist decides is optimal, warning the victim must be part of any plan, even when such a warning will violate the trust between the patient and the doctor or therapist. Roth and Meisel (1977) suggest that the therapist inform the patient of the limits of confidentiality by stating what the therapist is obligated to do and thereby gain permission to contact the intended victim. It is essential that social workers, physicians, psychologists, and counselors make every effort to inform the intended victim while maintaining the trusting relationship between themselves and the patient. However, if there is a choice between maintaining the relationship and warning the intended victim, the therapist must issue the warning. The ruling in the Tarasoff case is frequently cited in social work literature and texts as evidence that confidentiality is not the only rule for social workers to heed.

Consumer health organizations. Under the FOIA, consumer health organizations may research government-funded medical providers and are permitted to publish their findings in order to advance consumer knowledge of available medical care (Cleaver, 1985).

Law enforcement purposes. In situations where the disclosure of information is necessary for public purposes, medical records can be subpoenaed for use in administrative or grand jury investigations.

These cases may apply to situations of Medicaid and Medicare fraud, employee health and safety, medical misconduct, and/or nonpayment of taxes (Cleaver, 1985).

Medical records can also be sought in civil actions. These records are necessary in actions related to personal injury, insurance policy disputes, and issues related to malpractice, divorce, and when wills are contested. However, in cases such as these, discovery can be opposed by statutes that make such information privileged (Cleaver, 1985).

The use of medical records in criminal cases can be varied. The defendant or the prosecution can offer the record in evidence. Records may be used in presenting considerations or they can be used to impeach the credibility of a witness. Conflict exists as to whether or not a witness can be impeached by his/her own medical record. According to Cleaver (1985), "victims' medical records are admissible if relevant to an element of the crime. The defendant's own records may be admitted if it is important to consider the state of his/her health or mind at the time of the alleged crime" (p. 168).

Third-party payers. Insurance companies, the government, and employers have a legitimate need to see health information under certain circumstances. Most people do not object to information being provided to insurance companies, unless they refuse to pay the claim or the way they obtained or shared medical information is questioned. Insurance companies only have the right to part of the medical record and it is the responsibility of the physician to go through the medical office record and to surrender only pertinent information (Cleaver, 1985; Holloman, Edwards, & Matson, 1994). Anytime private medical information is provided to a third party, there are potential consequences. For example, if this information were to get into the hands of the employer or a life-insurance salesman, the patient could be denied life insurance or could lose his/her job or be denied a promotion (Garrett, Baillie, & Garrett, 1993).

Patient Viewpoint on When Confidentiality Can Be Breached

Sankar, Moran, Merz, and Jones (2003) reviewed 122 articles that reported research with patients regarding confidentiality and they found the following: First, patients were "confused about basic ethical, legal, and practical limits on medical confidentiality. Second, patients' confidentiality concerns were often more local and specific than the concerns that policies and new federal regulations address. Third, patients prefer that medical information be used exclusively for treatment and, finally, patients will delay or forego treatment, or alter stories about symptoms and onset of illness, to be sure those details never emerge publicly" (pp. 665–666).

Patients' opinions vary by population as to when confidentiality can be broken, which information can be provided, and who is an allowed recipient (Sankar et al., 2003). For example, adolescents permitted breaches of confidentiality based upon the severity of the problem, such as with sexual abuse or suicide attempts, and required information was delivered to the appropriate parties in these situations. Female victims of domestic abuse stated that confidentiality could be breached only in situations where the woman "wanted relief from the burden of disclosure" (Rodriguez, Craig, Mooney, & Bauer, 1998, pp. 339–340).

Patients are not generally aware of the specific laws protecting medical information. However, they expect that their medical information will be kept confidential. In several studies, patients accepted that information would be shared among doctors, but they rejected the release of information to employers, family members, and third-party payers (Ginsburg, Menapace, & Slap, 1997; McGuire, Toal, & Blau, 1985; Schmid, Appelbaum, Roth, & Lidz, 1983; Kinzie, Holmes, & Arent, 1985; Lorge, 1989; Merz, Spina, & Sankar, 1999; VandeCreek, Miars, & Herzog, 1987; Trippitelli, Jamison, Folstein, Bartko, & DePaulo, 1998).

Interestingly, patients expressed concern that nurses and medical students had full access to their medical records. Some indicated that they did not want office staff to have access at all (Sankar et al., 2003). Patients wanted only limited access of records by certain members of the healthcare teams, and even more limited access to certain family members. Many patients did not anticipate that their cases would be presented at large conferences, or shared with the spouses of their physician or discussed at parties (Weiss, 1982). The concern of this patient population was that their private medical information would find its way into their intimate social circle and cause some patients to forgo treatment or change medical information to avoid this type of disclosure. Statutes and laws were aimed at preventing this very concern; patients would avoid treatment if confidentiality could not be assured. The current protective practices do not seem to go far enough to assure that the trusting relationship sought at the beginning of the medical profession can be attained. Trust remains one of the primary factors necessary in the building and maintaining of the relationship between doctor and patient, and indeed, among all helping professionals.

TRUTH TELLING

Who has a right to it and when should truth be told? Healthcare ethics is fraught with dilemmas like the conflict that occurs when you are faced with two competing principles. For example, one may believe that every effort should be made not to lie to a patient while following the principle of maleficence, which states that a physician should do no harm. However, sometimes physicians have to lie to avoid harming their patient. Lying can be defined as a "falsehood in those circumstances in which the other has a reasonable expectation of the truth" (Bok, 1983, p. 14). There is no absolute right to the truth because circumstances change with each case. This makes the choice to provide or withhold the truth confusing at best. For example, Mrs. Pallocette is an 89-year-old woman who has been diagnosed with metastatic breast cancer, with metastases to her spine, liver, lungs, and femurs. She has a history of depression and anxiety, especially since the death of her eldest son Joe, who died of lung cancer. She was born outside of Palermo, Italy, and her family is not in the habit of openly discussing illness. Mrs. Pallocette's daughter Rita requested that her mother not be told of her diagnosis. She fears that her mother will "have a breakdown" if she is told of her diagnosis because "they would have never discussed her illness in the old country." In this case, the provision of the truth could prove harmful to this patient.

Ethically, each case requires that the physician or health care professional ask the following questions (Garret, Baillie, & Garret, 1993, p. 106):

Who is requesting the information?
Where is the conversation taking place?
What is the role or position of the communicators?
What is the nature of the truth involved in the exchange of information?

In the case of Mrs. Pallocette, the daughter is requesting that the whole truth not be told to her mother. She is having this conversation in a private conference room close to her mother's room. Rita is the power of attorney for her mother. The nature of the truth is the withholding of her full diagnosis to keep the patient from further emotional trauma and to follow how her culture and family would have dealt with such a diagnosis. It would be ethically appropriate to follow this request, at least for the time being. The doctor may accept this initial request, with the contingency that if Mrs. Pallocette asks direct questions related to her diagnosis he will answer them, or he may suggest that they both meet with Rita's mother to assess which questions to answer in relation to her illness. As can be seen by this case, each situation presents its own unique features requiring careful consideration.

MEDICAL ERROR

In medicine, mistakes are unfortunately common. Because physicians are human, mistakes are expected and at times even understandable (Wu, Cavanaugh, McPhee, Lo, & Micco, 1997). However, despite the fact that errors occur and are expected, patients and their families are rarely informed of these errors. One study completed by Wu, Folkman, McPhee, and Lo in 1991 demonstrated that medical residents reported informing their attending physicians about serious mistakes only half of the time, and told families of these mistakes less than a quarter of the time.

The AMA code of ethics requires that a physician report an "accident, injury, or bad result stemming from his/her treatment." Frequently, it is assumed that this means that the physician should tell the department director or supervisor. The American College of Physicians Ethics Manual (1992) states that physicians should disclose to patients information related to a procedural error or errors in judgment made in the course of providing treatment. In consideration of this requirement, the logical question is; Why are errors discussed with patients and families so infrequently? Some state that the single most significant obstacle to reporting medical error is fear of malpractice litigation (Baylis, 1997; Liang, 1999; Martin, Wilson, Fiebelman, Gurley, & Miller, 1991; Wu et al., 1997; Leape, 1994). Ironically, "however, several studies have indicated that open communication, honesty, and disclosure of mistakes to patients will actually decrease the likelihood of a lawsuit" (May & Aulisio, 2001). Communication issues were cited as the primary reason for lawsuits in 80% of the cases, according to one study (Avery, 1985). However, fears do not change overnight, nor do physicians suddenly learn how to communicate more effectively because they wish to disclose an error to a patient or their family.

A mistake is defined as a "commission or an omission with potentially negative consequences for the patient that would have been judged wrong by skilled and knowledgeable peers at the time it occurred, independent of whether there are any negative consequences" (Wu et al., 1997, p. 770). Errors can be system based because they occur on a systems level. In this form of error, the mistake occurs from flaws in the system where medicine is practiced. In situations where such errors occur, the system is so inherently flawed that it sets the individual up to make mistakes. When a system error occurs, the responsibility for its occurrence is shared by a series of individuals, not just one.

Conversely, individual errors occur as a direct result of deficiencies "in the physician's own knowledge, skill, or attentiveness" (Wu et al., 1997). In cases of individual error, the physician is solely responsible.

Ethically, individuals have a right to know when a medical mistake occurs because it is logical and appropriate and is a matter of respect (Finkelstein, Wu, Holtzman, & Smith, 1997). A recent report published by the Institute of Medicine, *To Err Is Human*, stated that "most errors and safety issues go undetected and unreported, both externally and within health care organizations" (Kohn, Corrigan, & Donaldson, 1999). How patients and families are informed of medical error is outlined within hospital policy or institutional policy. The JCAHO has strict guidelines in each institution regarding the reporting of medical errors, as do most state departments of health. It is imperative that the clinical social worker become aware of these policies, guidelines, and standards.

SOCIAL WORK STANDARDS FOR PRIVACY AND CONFIDENTIALITY

Standard 1.07(a) of the NASW Code of Ethics (1996) states that "Social workers should respect clients' right to privacy. Social workers should not solicit private information from clients unless it is essential to providing services or conducting social work evaluation research. Once private information is shared, standards of confidentiality apply." (Reamer, 1998, p. 56).

Social workers can disclose confidential information with the consent of the client or other person legally authorized to do so [Standard 1.07(b), NASW Code of Ethics, 1996]. As previously stated, there are exceptions to this standard. Local, state, and/or federal regulations may require disclosure of confidential information that pertains to a number of sources such as: protection of third parties from harm [Standard 1.07(c)]; mandatory reporting of suspected child or elder abuse and neglect; assessment, treatment, or referral of clients for substance abuse issues; coordination of services with other agencies involved with the client; service delivery within the agency that serves clients (with other staff members); deceased clients; news media; peer supervision and consultation; minors' parents or guardians; or law enforcement. Social workers must clarify when consent is and is not necessary for such disclosures (Reamer, 1998).

Additionally, social workers should inform clients whenever possible that they are going to disclose information and should reveal the possible consequences of the disclosure. When social workers enter into the helping relationship, a discussion of what confidentiality means and what the limitations are to the clients' rights to confidentiality is necessary. The social worker must inform clients of circumstances that may cause disclosure to become necessary, as in the disclosure of abuse or intent to harm another person [Standard 1.07(e), NASW Code of Ethics, 1996]. Even in these cases, unless the social worker believes there will be further harm, the client should be informed that the disclosure is to take place and why.

In the medical setting, ensuring privacy and confidentiality of client's information is often difficult, for the reasons enumerated earlier in this chapter. Social workers have a particular responsibility, however, to make every effort to protect information that patients share as well as information that is to be shared with patients and families. For example, Jack Smith, 80 years old, is transported to the emergency department of a large urban trauma center for treatment after he fell from a ladder while cleaning the gutters on his house. Mr. Smith's wife rides with paramedics during the transport. They arrive at the emergency department and Mr. Smith is immediately taken into the trauma room for treatment. Mrs. Smith is greeted by the social worker, who escorts Mrs. Smith, who is tearful and visibly shaken, to a private family room. They discuss the circumstances of the injury and Mr. Smith's medical history and the social worker quickly assesses the couple's psychosocial-spiritual history while they await the outcome of the initial medical assessment.

Particularly since the diagnosis is unknown, privacy for this family is essential. Mr. Smith's daughter and son-in-law arrive shortly after the physician and nurse have told the wife that he has suffered a severe spinal cord injury at C2 level and has been placed on a ventilator to assist him to breathe. The physician also stated that because of the severity of the injury, the likelihood that Mr. Smith will regain consciousness and be able to breathe on his own without ventilatory support is very small. The family is left to discuss with the social worker what Mr. Smith's wishes for treatment would be in this situation. Such an intimate and difficult discussion calls for the utmost privacy and confidentiality. As other family members begin to arrive, Mrs. Smith is asked who she would like to be with her in the "family room" for discussion and disclosure of confidential information about the end-of-life decisions to be made.

While this level of privacy may be possible in some circumstances and is certainly ideal, most of the time it is difficult to ensure. Considering that most hospital rooms are semi-private, often the patient's roommates may be present during discussion of diagnosis, prognosis, and treatment options. The social worker may be able to arrange family meetings with the physician and other healthcare professionals when the roommate is out of the room for physical therapy, for example. If the patient can physically leave the room, the social worker's office or other private office or conference room may be used. At the very least, the patient and family should be asked whether they are comfortable discussing personal information with the roommate present.

The home setting is much more intimate and privacy may afford the patient and family better control. In this setting, the professionals are the outsiders and patients and families feel most comfortable—on their own turf. However, as many health professionals enter the home, privacy may diminish there as well. Consider the daughter caring for her mother, who is dying from pancreatic cancer. A hospice nurse visits twice a week and a nurse's aide visits every other day to bathe the patient. This patient and family are giving up precious privacy to allow professionals to assist with care. The social worker can examine the arrangements for care and discuss how to schedule visits to maximize privacy. Perhaps afternoon visits for bathing will be best, as the daughter feels she is able to spend more quality time with her mother in the mornings.

Social Workers and HIPAA

The HIPAA medical privacy regulations apply to all healthcare professionals, including social workers working in healthcare facilities. Social workers should make themselves aware of these regulations and of the way their facility records compliance with the law. The NASW Code of Ethics (1996) places a higher standard on social workers than HIPAA regulations to maintain confidentiality of client records. According to the HIPAA Privacy Rule, social workers may disclose patient information without patient consent for a number of purposes. For example, this disclosure may occur if there is a court order. However, if a court orders disclosure of patient information and the social worker believes this will cause harm to the patient, then a request should be made that the court withdraw the order or limit the information that is to be disclosed [Standard 1.07(j), NASW Code of Ethics]. If a subpoena is issued, special procedures under the HIPAA Privacy Rule apply; it is noted that this is inconsistent with the NASW

Code of Ethics, unless the patient has consent to the disclosure or is court ordered, or meets other mandatory disclosure requirements (i.e., state laws). In addition, if the state law is more protective of patient privacy than the HIPAA Privacy Rule, then the stricter standard is to be followed. If a social worker should receive a subpoena or have other questions about what is legally required, he or she should seek legal counsel to be sure of the correct action. Hospitals and most healthcare facilities have legal counsel on staff that can be consulted in these matters.

Chapter Conclusion

A trusting relationship with healthcare professionals is essential to good medical care. In these relationships we trust that personal information will be kept confidential. Patients expect to be told the truth regarding their illness and treatment options. These signs of respect can go far in transforming impersonal healthcare facilities or agencies into caring institutions. The vulnerability of people who are ill, and particularly those facing death, must be protected. End-of-life decision making requires that patients and families be extended, as much as possible, privacy, confidentiality, and truth telling, even in the face of medical error.

The concept of privacy and confidentiality is familiar to social workers and to most other professionals through their codes of ethics. The NASW Code of Ethics (1996) holds social workers to strict professional standards of ethical conduct regarding confidentiality; in some cases they are expected to uphold higher standards than state or federal laws (HIPAA) may require. Social workers are skilled in the essential components of helping relationships and should assist other professionals to recognize when these relationships are not working effectively. Social workers can instruct and model ways to provide adequate assurance of privacy and confidentiality to meet the needs of patients and families when they are most vulnerable.

REFERENCES

Preface

Hoffman, D. E. (1993). Evaluating ethics committees: A view from the outside. *Milbank Quarterly, 71*(4), 677-705.

Howell, J. H., & Sale, W. F. (1995). *Life choices: A Hastings Center introduction to bioethics.* Washington, DC: Georgetown University Press.

Jonsen, A. R., Siegler, M., & Winslade, W. J. (1998). *Clinical ethics* (4th ed.). New York: McGraw Hill.

National Association of Social Workers. (2004). *Standards for social work practice in palliative and end of life care.* Retrieved August 25, 2005, from http://www.naswdc.org/practice/bereavement/standards/default.asp

Chapter 1

Beauchamp, T. L. (1994). The 'four-principles' approach. In R. Gillon (Ed.), *Principles of health care ethics* (pp. 1-12). New York: John Wiley & Sons, Ltd.

Beauchamp, T. L., & Childress, J. F. (1994). *Principles of biomedical ethics* (4th ed.). New York: Oxford University Press.

Beauchamp, T. L., & Childress, J. F. (2001). *Principles of biomedical ethics* (5th ed.). New York: Oxford University Press.

Berg, J. W., Appelbaum, P. S., Lidz, C. W., & Parker, L. S. (2001). *Informed consent: Legal theory and clinical practice* (2nd ed.). New York: Oxford University Press.

Bouvia v. County of Riverside (1983).

Csikai, E. L. (1999). Hospital social workers: Attitudes toward euthanasia and assisted suicide. *Social Work in Health Care, 30*(1), 51-73.

Cummings, S. M., & Cockerham, C. (1997). Ethical dilemmas in discharge planning for patients with Alzheimers disease. *Health & Social Work, 22*(2), 101-108.

Devettere, R. J. (2000). *Practical decision making in health care ethics: Cases and concepts* (2nd ed.). Washington, DC: Georgetown University Press.

Dubeuil, 629 So.2d 957, 962-63 (Fla. 1992).

Dworkin, G. (1971). Paternalism. In R. A. Wasserstrom (Ed.), *Morality and the law* (pp. 107-126). Belmont, CA: Wadsworth Publishing.

Foster, L. W., Sharp, J., Scesny, A., McLellan, L., & Cotman, K. (1993). Bioethics: Social work's response and training needs. *Social Work in Health Care, 19*(1), 15-39.

Garrett, T. M., Baillie, H. W., & Garrett, R. M. (1993). *Health care ethics: Principles and problems* (2nd ed.). Englewood Cliffs, NJ: Prentice Hall.

In re Quinlan. (1976). 355 A.2d 647 (NJ).

Joffe, S., Manocchia, M., Weeks, J. C., & Cleary, P. D. (2003, April). What do patients value in their hospital care? An empirical perspective on autonomy centred bioethics. *Journal of Medical Ethics, 29*(2), 103–108.

Kelly, D. F. (1991). *Critical care ethics: Treatment decisions in American hospitals.* Kansas City, MO: Sheed & Ward.

Lo, B. (2000). *Resolving ethical dilemmas* (2nd ed.). New York: Lippincott, Williams and Wilkins.

Macklin, R. (1987). *Mortal choices: Bioethics in today's world.* New York: Pantheon Books.

Matter of Baby K, 16 F.3d 590 (1994).

Meisel, A. (1989). *The right to die: The law of end-of-life decisionmaking.* New York: Wiley Law Publications, John Wiley & Sons.

Munson, R. (1988). *Intervention and reflection: Basic issues in medical ethics* (3rd ed.). Belmont, CA: Wadsworth Publishing.

Pellegrino, E. D. (1991). Informal judgments of competence and incompetence. In M. A. G. Cutter & E. E. Shelp (Eds.). *Competency: A study of informal competency determinations in primary care* (pp. 29–45). Dordrecht, Holland: Kluwer Academic Pubishers.

Pellegrino, E. D. (1993). The metamorphosis of medical ethics: A 30-year retrospective. *Journal of the American Medical Association, 269*(9), 1158–1162.

Pellegrino, E. D., & Thomasma, D. C. (1987). The conflict between autonomy and beneficence in medical ethics: Proposal for a resolution. *Journal of Contemporary Health Law and Policy, 3*(23), 23–46.

Pence, G. E. (1995). *Classic cases in medical ethics.* New York: McGraw Hill.

Quill, T. E., Dresser, R., & Brock, D. W. (1997). The rule of double effect—A critique of its role in end-of-life decision making. *New England Journal of Medicine, 337*(24), 1168–1771.

Reamer, F. G. (1998). *Ethical standards in social work.* Washington, DC: NASW Press.

Sulmasy, D. P., & Pellegrino, E. (1999). The rule of double effect: Clearing up the double talk. *Archives of Internal Medicine, 159*, 545–550.

Chapter 2

Abbott, K. H., Sago, J. G., Breen, C. M., Abernethy, A. P., & Tulsky, J. A. (2001). Families looking back: One year after discussion of withdrawal or withholding of life-sustaining support. *Critical Care Medicine, 29*, 197.

American Society of Nephrology and Renal Physicians Association. (2002). *Clinical practice guideline on shared decision-making in the appropriate initiation of and withdrawal from dialysis.* Washington, DC: Author.

Arnold, R., Youngner, J. S., Schapiro, R., & Spicer, C. M. (Eds.). (1995). *Procuring organs for transplant: The debate over nonheartbeating cadaver protocols*. Baltimore, MD: John Hopkins University Press.

Asch, D. A. (1996). The role of critical care nurses in euthanasia and assisted suicide. *New England Journal of Medicine, 334*(21), 1374-1379.

Ashley, B., & O'Rourke, K. (1997). *Health care ethics: A theological analysis* (4th ed.). Washington, DC: Georgetown University Press.

Azoulay, E., Chevret, S., Leleu, G., Pochard, F., Barboteu, M., Adrie, C., et al. (2000). Half the families of intensive care unit patients experience inadequate communication with physicians. *Critical Care Medicine, 28*(8), 3044-3049.

Bachman, J. G., Alcser, K. H., Doukas, D. J., Lichtenstein, R. I., Corning, A. D., & Brody, H. (1996). Attitudes of Washington physicians and public toward legalizing physician-assisted suicide and euthanasia in Washington. *New England Journal of Medicine, 334*, 303-330.

Back, A. L., Wallace, J. I., Starks, H. E., & Pearlman, R. A. (1996, March 27). Physician-assisted suicide and euthanasia in Washington state: Patient requests and physician responses. *Journal of the American Medical Association, 275*(12), 919-925.

Beecher, H. K. (1968, June 27). Ethical problems created by the hopelessly unconscious patient. *New England Journal of Medicine, 278*(26), 1425-30.

Beer, J. E., & Stief, E. (1997). The mediator's handbook (3rd ed.). New Society Publishers.

Bleich, D. (1998). *Bioethical dilemmas: A Jewish perspective*. Hoboken, NJ: KTAV Publishing House.

Bowker, J. W. (Ed.). (1997). *The Oxford dictionary of world religions*. Oxford: Oxford University Press.

Brymer, C., Gangbar, E., O'Rourke, K., & Naglie, G. (1995). Age as determinant of cardiopulmonary resuscitation outcome in the coronary care unit. *Journal of the American Geriatric Society, 43*, 634-7.

Burns, J. P., Edwards, J., Johnson, J., Cassem, N. H., & Troug, R. D. (2003). Do-not-resuscitate order after 25 years. *Critical Care Medicine, 31*(5), 1544-1546.

Caralis, P. V., Davis, B., Wright, K., & Marcial, E. (1993). The influence of ethnicity and race on attitudes toward advance directives, life-prolonging treatments, and euthanasia. *Journal of Clinical Ethics, 4*(2), 155-163.

Chochinov, M. H. (2002). Dignity-conserving-care: A new model for palliative care. *Journal of the American Medical Association, 287*(17), 2253-2260.

Clarfield, A. M., Gordon, M., Markwell, H., & Alibhai, S. M. H. (2003, August). Ethical issues in end-of-life geriatric care: The approach of three monotheistic religions—Judaism, Catholicism, and Islam. *Journal of the American Geriatrics Society, 51*(8), 1149-1154.

Cohen, L. M., McCue, J. D., Germain, M., & Kjellstrand, C. M. (1995, January 9). Dialysis discontinuation: A 'good' death? *Archives of Internal Medicine, 155*(1), 42-47.

Cohen, S., Fihn, S. D., Boyko, E. J., Jonsen, A. R., & Wood, R.W. (1994). Attitudes toward assisted suicide and euthanasia among physicians in Washington state. *New England Journal of Medicine, 331*(2), 89-94.

Connery, J. S. (1980, October 11). Prolonging life: The duty and its limits. *Catholic Mind,* 43-57.

Crawley, L. M., Marshall, P. M., Lo, B., & Koenig, B. A. (2002). Strategies for culturally effective end-of-life care. *Annals of Internal Medicine, 136*(9), 674-679.

Crawley, L., Payne, R., Bolden, J., Payne, T., Washington, P., & Williams, S. (2000, November 15). Initiative to improve palliative and end-of-life care in the African American community palliative and end-of-life care in the African American community. *Journal of the American Medical Association, 284*(19), 2518-2521.

Cruzan v. Harmon, 760 sw 2d408 (Mo. 1988).

Csikai, E. L., & Bass, K. (2000). Health care social workers' views of ethical issues, practice, and policy in end-of-life care. *Social Work in Health Care, 32*(2), 1-22.

Csikai, E. L., & Sales, E. (1998). The emerging social work role on hospital ethics committees: Social workers' and chairs' perspectives. *Social Work, 43*(3), 233-242.

Curtis, J. R., Patrick, D., Shannon, S., Treece, P., Engelberg, R., & Rubenfeld, G. D. (2001). The family conference as a focus to improve communication about end-of-life care in the intensive care unit: Opportunities for improvement. *Critical Care Medicine, 29*(2), N26-N33.

Daaleman, T. P., & VandeCreek, L. (2000). Placing religion and spirituality in end-of-life care. *Journal of the American Medical Association, 284*(19), 2514-2517.

Dash, T., & Mailloux, L. (2001). Withdrawal from and withholding of dialysis. *UptoDate, 9*(3).

Devettere, R. J. (2000). *Practical decision making in health care ethics: Cases and concepts* (2nd ed.). Washington, DC: Georgetown University Press.

DeVita, M. A., Snyder, J. V., & Grenvik, A. (1993). History of organ donation by patients with cardiac death. *Kennedy Institute of Ethics Journal, 3,* 113-129.

D'Oronzio, J. C. (1997). Rappelling on the slippery slope: Negotiating public policy for physician-assisted death. *Cambridge Quarterly of Healthcare Ethics, 6*(1), 113-117.

Dubler, N. N., & Liebman, C. B. (2004). *Bioethics mediation: A guide to shaping shared solutions.* New York: United Hospital Fund.

REFERENCES

Emanuel, E. J. (1994). Euthanasia: Historical, ethical and empiric perspectives. *Archives of Internal Medicine, 154*(5), 1890-1901.

Galanti, G.A. (1991) *Caring for patients from different cultures.* Philadelphia, PA: University of Pennsylvania Press.

Goodlin, S. J., Zhong, Z., Lynn, J., Teno, J. M., Fago, J. P., Desbiens, N., et al. (1999). Factors associated with use of cardiopulmonary resuscitation in seriously ill hospitalized adults. *Journal of the American Medical Association, 282,* 2333-2339.

Goodman, K. W. (2001, March). Persistent legislative state: Law, education, and the well-intentioned healthcare ethics committee. *Healthcare Ethics Committee Forum, 13*(1), 32-40.

Hasan, R. (1994). The conception of context in text. In M. Gregory & P. Fries (Eds.), *Discourse in society: Functional perspectives.* Norwood, NJ: Ablex Publishing.

Hite, C., & Marshall, M. F. (1997). Death and dying. In J. C. Fletcher, P. A. Lombardo, M. F. Marshall, & F. G. Miller (Eds.), *Introduction to clinical ethics* (2nd ed., pp. 127-153). Frederick, MD: University Publishing Group.

Irish, D., & Lundquist, K. (1993). *Ethnic variations in death, dying and grief: Diversity in universality.* Philadelphia, PA: Francis and Taylor Group.

Johnson, C. J., & McGee, M. G. (1998). *How different religions view death and afterlife* (2nd ed.). Philadelphia, PA: Charles Press.

Jonsen, A. R., Siegler, M., & Winslade, W. J. (1998). *Clinical ethics* (4th ed.). New York: McGraw Hill.

Kalish, R. A., & Reynolds, D. K. (1981). *Death and ethnicity: A psychocultural study.* Farmingdale, NY: Baywood.

Kamisar, Y. (1993). Are laws against assisted suicide unconstitutional? *Hastings Center Report, 23*(3), 35.

Kelly, D. F. (1979). *The emergence of Roman Catholic medical ethics in North America.* New York: Edwin Mellen Press.

Kelly, D. F. (1991). *Critical care ethics: Treatment decision in American hospitals.* Kansas City, MO: Sheed and Ward.

Koenig, H. (1993). Legalizing physician-assisted suicide: Some thoughts and concerns. *Journal of Family Practice, 37*(2), 171-179.

Lee, M. A., Nelson, H. D., Tilden, V. P., Ganzini, L., Schmidt, T. A., & Tolle, S. W. (1996, February 1). Legalizing assisted suicide—Views of physicians in Oregon. *New England Journal of Medicine, 334*(5), 310-315.

Lo, B., Ruston, D., Kates, L., Arnold, R., Cohen, C., Faber-Langendoen, K., et al. (2002). Discussing religious and spiritual issues at the end of life. *Journal of the American Medical Association, 287,* 749-754.

Mauro, T. (1997, June 27). Assisted suicide ban upheld but states can enact new laws. *USA Today.*

Meisel, A. (1989). *The right to die: The law of end-of-life decisionmaking.* New York: Wiley Law Publications, John Wiley & Sons.

Meisel, A. (1995). *The right to die: The law of end-of-life decisionmaking* (2nd ed.). New York: Aspen Publishers.

Miller, F. G., & Brody, H. (1995). Professional integrity and physician-assisted death. *Hastings Center Report, 25*, 8-17.

Miller, F. G., Fins, J. J., & Snyder, L. (2000, March 21). Assisted suicide compared with refusal of treatment: A valid distinction? University of Pennsylvania Center for Bioethics Assisted Suicide Consensus Panel. *Annals of Internal Medicine, 132*(6), 470-475.

Murphy, D. I., Murray, A. M., & Robinson, B. E. (1989). Outcomes of cardiopulmonary resuscitation in the elderly. *Annals of Internal Medicine, 111*, 199-205.

Murphy, S. T., Palmer, J. M., Azen, S., Frank, G., Michel, V., & Blackhall, L. (1996). Ethnicity and advance care directives. *Journal of Law and Medical Ethics, 24*, 108-117.

National Association of Social Workers. (2004). *Standards for social work practice in palliative and end of life care*. Retrieved August 25, 2005, from http://www.naswdc.org/practice/bereavement/standards/default.asp

Oregon Department of Health Services. (2004). Sixth annual report on Oregon's Death with Dignity Act. Retrieved August 23, 2005, from http://egov.oregon.gov/DHS/ph/pas/docs/year6.pdf

Pellegrino, E. D. (2000). Decisions to withdraw life-sustaining treatment: A moral algorithm. *Journal of the American Medical Association, 283*(8), 1065-1067.

Pence, G. (1990). *Classic cases in medical ethics: Accounts of the cases that have shaped medical ethics, with philosophy, legal and historical backgrounds*. New York: McGraw Hill.

Pence, G. E. (1995). *Classic cases in medical ethics: Accounts of the cases that have shaped medical ethics, with philosophy, legal and historical backgrounds* (2nd ed.). New York: McGraw Hill.

President's Commission for the Study of Ethical Problems in Medicine and Biomedical and Behavioral Research. (1983). *Deciding to forgo life-sustaining treatment: Ethical, medical, and legal issues in treatment decisions*. Washington, DC: U.S. Government Printing Office.

Renard, J. (2001). *The handy religion answer book*. New York: Barnes & Noble.

Robinson, E., & Mylott, L. (2001). Cardiopulmonary resuscitation: Medical decision or patient/surrogate choice? *International Anesthesiology Clinic, 39*(3), 67-83.

Rosner, F. (1991). *Modern medicine and Jewish ethics* (2nd ed.). Hoboken, NJ: KTAV Publishing House.

Schneiderman, L. J., Jecker, N. S., & Jonsen, A. R. (1990). Medical futility: Its meaning and ethical implications. *Annals of Internal Medicine, 112*(12), 949-954.

Schneiderman, L. J., Jecker, N. S., Jonsen, A. R. (1996, October 15). Medical futility: Response to critiques. *Annals of Internal Medicine, 125*(8), 669–674.

Sjokvist, P., Berggren, L., Svantesson, M., & Nilstun T. (1999). Should the ventilator be withdrawn? Attitudes of the general public, nurses and physicians. *European Journal of Anesthesiology, 16*(8), 526–533.

Suchman, A. L., Markakis, K., Beckman, H. B., & Frankel, R. (1997, February 26). A model of empathic communication in the medical interview. *Journal of the American Medical Association, 277*(8), 678–682.

SUPPORT investigators. (1995). A controlled trial to improve care for seriously ill hospitalized patients: The study to understand prognoses and preferences for outcomes and risks of treatments. *Journal of the American Medical Association, 274*(20), 1591–1598.

Teno, J. M. (2003). Now is the time to embrace nursing homes as a place of care for dying persons. *Journal of Palliative Medicine, 6*, 293–296.

Thurman, R. (1998). Inner revolution: Life, liberty, and the pursuit of real happiness. New York: Riverhead Books.

Turner, L. (2001). Medical ethics in a multicultural society. *Journal of the Royal Society of Medicine, 94*(11), 592–594.

Youngner, S., Arnold, R. M., & Schapiro, R. (1999). *The definition of death: Contemporary controversies*. Baltimore, MD: Johns Hopkins University Press.

Chapter 3

American Medical Association, Council on Ethical and Judicial Affairs. (1998). Optimal use of orders not to intervene and advance directives. *Psychology, Public Policy, & Law, 4*(3), 668–675.

Azoulay, E., Chevret, S., Leleu G., Pochard, F., Barboteu, M., Adrie, C., et al. (2000). Half the families of intensive care unit patients experience inadequate communication with physicians. *Critical Care Medicine, 28*(8), 3044–3049.

Blacker, S., Cohen, I., & Sormanti, M. (2002, July). Presentation at project on death in America retreat. Lake Tahoe, CA.

Blackhall, L. J., Murphy, S. T., Frank, G., Michel, V., & Azen, S. (1995). Ethnicity and attitudes toward patient autonomy. *Journal of the American Medical Society, 274*(10), 820–825.

Cantor, J. (1998). Making advance directives meaningful. *Psychology, Public Policy, & Law, 4*(3), 629–652.

Caralis, P. V., Davis, B., Wright, K., & Marcial, E. (1993). The influence of ethnicity and race on attitudes toward advance directives, life-prolonging treatments, and euthanasia. *Journal of Clinical Ethics, 4*(2), 155–163.

Corr, C. (1998). Death in modern society. In D. Doyle, G. Hanks, & N. MacDonald, (Eds.), *Oxford textbook of palliative medicine* (pp. 31–39). Oxford: Oxford University Press.

Covinsky, K. E., Fuller, J. D., Yaffe, K., Johnston, C. B., Hamel, M. B., Lynn, J., et al. (2000). Communication and decision-making in seriously ill patients: Findings of the SUPPORT project. *Journal of the American Geriatrics Society, 48*, S187–S193.

Csikai, E. L. (1999). Euthanasia and assisted suicide: Issues for social work practice. *Journal of Gerontological Social Work, 31*(3/4), 49–63.

Csikai, E. L., & Bass, K. (2000). Health care social workers' views of ethical issues, practice, and policy in end-of-life care. *Social Work in Health Care, 32*(2), 1–22.

Csikai, E. L., & Sales, E. (1998). The emerging social work role on hospital ethics committees: Social workers—and chairs—perspectives. *Social Work, 43*(3), 233–242.

Culver, C. M. (1998). Advance directives. *Psychology, Public Policy, & Law, 4*(3), 676–687.

Dexter, P. R., Wolinsky, F. D., Gramelspacher, G. P., Zhou, W. H., Eckert, G. J., Waisburd, M., et al. (1998). Effectiveness of computer-generated reminders for increasing discussions about advance directives and completion of advance directive forms: A randomized, controlled trial. *Annals of Internal Medicine, 128*, 102–110.

Dhooper, S. S. (1997). *Social work in health care in the 21st century.* Thousand Oaks, CA: Sage Publications.

Dowdy, M. D., Robertson, C., & Bander, J. A. (1998). A study of proactive ethics consultation for critically and terminally ill patients with extended lengths of stay. *Critical Care Medicine, 26*(2), 252–259.

Fischer, G. S., Arnold, R. M., & Tulsky, J. A. (2000). Talking to the older adult about advance directives. *Clinics in Geriatric Medicine, 16*(2), 239–254.

Goodman, K. W. (1998). End-of-life algorithms. *Psychology, Public Policy, & Law, 4*(3), 719–727.

Goold, S. D., Williams, B., & Arnold, R. M. (2000). Conflicts regarding decisions to limit treatment: A differential diagnosis. *Journal of the American Medical Association, 283*(7), 909–914.

Halper, S. (1993). Teams and teamwork: Health care settings. *American Speech-Language Hearing Association, 35*, 34–48.

Hanson, P., Cornish, P., & Kayser, K. (1998). Family conferences as forums for decision making in hospital settings. *Social Work in Health Care, 27*(3), 57–74.

High, D. M. (1993). Why are elderly people not using advance directives? *Journal of Aging and Health, 5*(4), 497–515.

Johnston, S. C., Pfeifer, M. P., & McNutt, R. (1995). The discussion about advance directives. *Archives of Internal Medicine, 155*, 1025–1030.

Kolarik, R. C., Arnold, R. M., Fischer, G. S., & Tulsky, J. A. (2002). Objectives for advance care planning. *Journal of Palliative Medicine, 5*(5), 697–704.

La Puma, J., Orentlicher, D., & Moss, R. J. (1991). Advance directives on admission: Clinical implications and analysis of the Patient Self-Determination Act of 1990. *Journal of the American Medical Association, 266*, 402–405.

Levine, C., & Zuckerman, C. (1999). The trouble with families: Toward an ethic of accommodation. *Annals of Internal Medicine, 130,* 148-152.

Loewenberg, F. M., Dolgoff, R., & Harrington, D. (2000). *Ethical decisions for social work practice* (6th ed.). Itasca, IL: F. E. Peacock Publishers.

Mick, K. A., Medvene, L. J., & Strunk, J. H. (2003). Surrogate decision making at end of life: Sources of burden and relief. *Journal of Loss and Trauma, 8,* 149-167.

Morrison, R. S., Morrison, E. W., & Glickman, D. F. (1994). Physician reluctance to discuss advance directives: An empiric investigation of potential barriers. *Archives of Internal Medicine, 154,* 2311-2318.

National Association of Social Workers. (2004). *Standards for social work practice in palliative and end of life care.* Retrieved August 25, 2005, from http://www.naswdc.org/practice/bereavement/standards/default.asp

National Hospice Foundation. (1999, June 8). Press release: *Baby boomers fear talking to parents about death.*

President's Commission for the Study of Ethical Problems in Medicine and Biomedical and Behavioral Research. (1982). *Making health care decisions* (Vol. 1). Washington, DC: U.S. Government Printing Office.

Pulchalski, C. M., Zhong, Z., Jacobs, M. M., Fox, E., Lynn, J., Harrold, J., et al. (2000). Patients who want their family and physicians to make resuscitation decisions for them: Observations from SUPPORT and HELP. *Journal of the American Geriatrics Society, 48,* S84-S90.

Quill, T. E., Meier, D. E., Block, S. D., & Billings, J. A. (1998). The debate over physician-assisted suicide: Empirical data and convergent views. *Annals of Internal Medicine, 128*(7), 552-558.

Rich, B. A. (1998). Personhood, patienthood, and clinical practice: Reassessing advance directives. *Psychology, Public Policy, & Law, 4*(3), 610-628.

Roberts, A. R. (2000). An overview of crisis theory and crisis intervention. In A. Roberts (Ed.), *Crisis intervention handbook: Assessment, treatment, and research* (pp. 3-30). New York: Oxford University Press.

Schofield, R. F., & Amodeo, M. (1999). Interdisciplinary teams in health care and human service settings. *Health & Social Work, 24*(3), 210-219.

Schonwetter, R. S., Walker, R. M., Solomon, M., Indurkhya, A., & Robinson, B. E. (1996). Life values, resuscitation preferences, and the applicability of living wills in an older population. *Journal of the American Geriatrics Society, 44,* 954-858.

Shulman, N. M., & Shewbert, A. L. (2000). A model of crisis intervention in critical and intensive care units of general hospitals. In A.R. Roberts (Ed.), *Crisis intervention handbook: Assessment, treatment, and research* (pp. 412-429). New York: Oxford University Press.

Soskis, C. W., & Kerson, T. S. (1992). The Patient Self-Determination Act: Opportunity knocks again. *Social Work in Health Care, 16*(4), 1-8.

Sugarman, J., Powe, N. R., Brillantes, D. A., & Smith, M. K. (1993). The cost of ethics legislation: A look at the Patient Self-Determination Act. *Kennedy Institute of Ethics Journal, 3*(4), 387-399.

SUPPORT investigators. (1995). A controlled trial to improve care for seriously ill hospitalized patients: The study to understand prognoses and preferences for outcomes and risks of treatments. *Journal of the American Medical Association, 274*(20), 1591-1598.

Teno, J., Lynn, J., Connors, A. F., Wenger, N., Phillips, R., Alzola, C., et al. (1997). The illusion of end-of-life resource savings with advance directives. *Journal of the American Geriatrics Society, 45*, 513-518.

Teno, J. M., & Lynn, J. (1996). Putting advance-care planning into action. *Journal of Clinical Ethics, 7*(3), 205-213.

Teno, J. M., Nelson, H. L., & Lynn, J. (1994). Advance care planning: Priorities for ethical and empirical research. *Hastings Center Report, 24*(6), S32-S36.

Teno, J. M., Stevens, M., Spernak, S., & Lynn, J. (1998). Role of written advance directives in decision making. *Journal of the American Geriatrics Society, 13*, 439-446.

Ulrich, L. P. (1994). The Patient Self-Determination Act and cultural diversity. *Cambridge Quarterly of Healthcare Ethics, 3*(3), 410-413.

VandeCreek, L., & Frankowski, D. (1996). Barriers that predict resistance to completing a living will. *Death Studies, 20*, 73-82.

Chapter 4

Amar, D. F. (1994). The role of the hospice social worker in the nursing home setting. *American Journal of Hospice and Palliative Care, 11*(3), 18-23.

Baer, W. M., & Hanson, L. C. (2000, August). Families' perception of the added value of hospice in the nursing home. *Journal of the American Geriatrics Society, 48*(8), 879-882.

Bernabei, R., Gambassi, G., Lapane, K., Landi, F., Gatsonis, C., Dunlop, R., et al. (1998, June 17). Management of pain in elderly patients with cancer. *Journal of the American Medical Association, 279*(23), 1877-1882.

Brenner, P. R. (1997). Issues of access in a diverse society. *Hospice Journal, 12*(2), 9-16.

Brody, H. (1992). Teamwork and informed consent. *Journal of the American Board of Family Practitioners, 5*(2), 229-230.

Byock, I. (1994). Ethics from a hospice perspective. *American Journal of Hospice & Palliative Care, 11*(4), 9-11.

Cassell, E. J. (1991). *Nature of suffering and the goals of medicine.* New York: Oxford University Press.

Cowles, L. A. (2003). *Social work in the health field: A care perspective* (2nd ed.). New York: Haworth Press.

Csikai, E. L. (1999). Hospital social workers: Attitudes toward euthanasia and assisted suicide. *Social Work in Health Care, 30*(1), 51-73.

Csikai, E. L. (2004). The social work role in resolving ethical issues in hospice. *Health & Social Work, 29*(1), 67-76.

Cummings, S. M., & Cockerham, C. (1997). Ethical dilemmas in discharge planning for patients with Alzheimers disease. *Health & Social Work, 22*(2), 101-108.

Devettere, R. J. (2000). *Practical decision making in health care ethics: Cases and concepts* (2nd ed.). Washington, DC: Georgetown University Press.

Doyle, D., Hanks, G., & MacDonald, N. (1998). *Oxford textbook of palliative medicine*. Oxford: Oxford University Press.

Ferrell, B. R. (1998). The family. In D. Doyle, G. Hanks, & N. MacDonald (Eds.), *Oxford textbook of palliative medicine* (pp. 909-917). Oxford: Oxford University Press.

Fine, P. (2004). Hospice referral and care: Practical guidance for clinicians. Retrieved August 23, 2005, from http://www.medscape.com/viewprogram/3345_pnt

Hite, C., & Marshall, M. F. (1997). Death and dying. In J. C. Fletcher, P. A. Lombardo, M. F. Marshall, & F. G. Miller (Eds.), *Introduction to clinical ethics* (2nd ed., pp. 127-153). Frederick, MD: University Publishing Group.

Jennings, B., Ryndes, T., D'Onofrio, C., & Baily, M. A. (2003). Access to hospice care: Expanding boundaries, overcoming barriers. *Hastings Center Report Special Supplement, 33*(2), S3-S59.

Jones, B., Nackerud, L., & Boyle, D. (1997). Differential utilization of hospice services in nursing homes. *Hospice Journal, 12*(3), 41-56.

Kulys, R., & Davis, A. (1986). An analysis of social services in hospices. *Social Work, 31*, 448-456.

Lamers, W. M. Jr. (2002). Defining hospice and palliative care: Some further thoughts. *Journal of Pain & Palliative Care Pharmacotherapy, 16*(3), 65-71.

Lunney, J. R., Lynn, J., Foley, D. J., Lipson, S., & Buralnik, J. M. (2003). Patterns of functional decline at the end of life. *Journal of the American Medical Association, 289*(18), 2387-2392.

MacDonald, D. (1991). Hospice social work: A search for identity. *Health & Social Work, 16*(4), 274-280.

McCallin, A. (2001). Interdisciplinary practice—a matter of teamwork: An integrated literature review. *Journal of Clinical Nursing, 10*(4), 419-428.

Miller, F. G. (1997). A communitarian approach to physician-assisted death. *Cambridge Quarterly of Healthcare Ethics, 6*, 78-87.

Miller, S. C., Gozalo, P., & Mor, V. (2001). Hospice enrollment and hospitalization of dying nursing home patients. *American Journal of Medicine, 111*, 38-44.

Miller, S. C., & Mor, V. N. T. (2002). The role of hospice in the nursing home setting. *Journal of Palliative Medicine, 5*(2), 271-277.

Monroe, B. (1998). Social work in palliative care. In D. Doyle, G. Hanks, & N. MacDonald (Eds.), *Oxford textbook of palliative medicine* (pp. 867-882). Oxford: Oxford University Press.

National Hospice and Palliative Care Organization. (2004). *Hospice facts and figures*. Retrieved August 23, 2005, from http://www.nhpco.org/files/public/Hospice_Facts_110104.pdf

Quill, T. (1991a). Death and dignity: A case of individualized decision making. *New England Journal of Medicine, 324*, 691-694.

Quill, T. (1991b). Correspondence: Death and dignity: The case of Diane. *New England Journal of Medicine 325*, 658-660.

Reese, D. J., & Raymer, M. (2004). Relationships between social work involvement and hospice outcomes: Results of the National Hospice Social Work Survey. *Social Work, 49*(3), 415-422.

Reynolds, K., Henderson, M., Schulman, A., & Hanson, L. C. (2002). Needs of the dying in nursing homes. *Journal of Palliative Medicine, 5*(6), 895-901.

Sachs, G. A., Shega, J. W., & Cox-Hayley, D. (2004). Barriers to excellent end-of-life care for patients with dementia. *Journal of General Internal Medicine, 19*(10), 1057-1063.

Saunders, C. (1998). Foreword. In D. Doyle, G. Hanks, & N. MacDonald (Eds.), *Oxford textbook of palliative medicine* (pp. v-ix). Oxford: Oxford University Press.

Vachon, M. (1998). The emotional problems of the patient. In D. Doyle, G. Hanks, & N. MacDonald (Eds.), *Oxford textbook of palliative medicine* (pp. 883-907). Oxford: Oxford University Press.

Chapter 5

Abbott, K. H., Sago, J. G, Breen, C. M, Abernethy, A. P., & Tulsky, J. A. (2001). Families looking back: One year after discussion of withdrawal or withholding of life-sustaining support. *Critical Care Medicine, 29*, 197.

Appelbaum, P., Grisso, T., Frank, E., O'Donnell, S., & Kupfer, D. J. (1999). Competence of depressed patients for consent to research. *American Journal of Psychiatry, 156*, 1380-1384.

Azoulay, E., Chevret, S., Leleu G., Pochard, F., Barboteu, M., Adrie, C., et al. (2000). Half the families of intensive care unit patients experience inadequate communication with physicians. *Critical Care Medicine, 28*(8), 3044-3049.

Back, A., Arnold, R. M., & Hopfinger, T. Q. (2003). Hope for the best, and prepare for the worst. *Annals of Internal Medicine, 138*(5), 439-443.

Baile, W. F., Glober, G. A., Lenzi, R., Beale, E. A., & Kudelka, A. P. (1999). Discussing disease progression and end-of-life decisions. *Oncology, 13*, 1021-1038.

Barber v. Superior Court, 195, Cal. Rptr. 484 (Ct. App. 1983).

Beauchamp, T. L., & Childress, J. F. (1994). *Principles of biomedical ethics* (4th ed.). New York: Oxford University Press.

Berg, J. W., Appelbaum, P. S., & Grisso, T. (1996). Constructing competence: Formulating standards of legal competence to make medical decisions. *Rutgers Law Review, 48*, 345-396.

Bowen, M. (1985). *Family therapy in clinical practice*. New Jersey: Aronson Publications.

Boyle, P.J. (1995). Shaping priorities in genetic medicine. *Hastings Center Report, 25,* 52-58.

Breen, C. M., Abernethy, A. P., Abbott, K. H., & Tulsky, J. A. (2001). Conflicts associated with decisions to limit life-sustaining treatment in intensive care units. *Journal of General Internal Medicine, 16,* 283.

Buchanan, A. E., & Brock, D. W. (1990). *Deciding for others: The ethics of surrogate decision making.* New York: Cambridge University Press.

Butow, P. N., Dunn, S. M., Tattersall, M. H., & Jones, Q. J. (1994). Patient participation in the cancer consultation: Evaluation of a question prompt sheet. *Annals of Oncology, 5,* 199.

Canterbury v. Spence, 464 F. 2d 772 (DC Cir. 1972).

Cassell, E. J. (1985). *Talking with patients: The theory of doctor-patient communication and clinical technique.* Cambridge, MA: MIT Press.

Chaitin, E., & Arnold, R. M. (2003). Communication in the ICU: Holding a family meeting. [Electronic version]. *UptoDate, 11*(2).

Curtis, J. R., Patrick, D. L., Shannon, S. E., Treece, P. D., Engelberg, R. A., & Rubenfeld, G. D. (2001, February). The family conference as a focus to improve communication about end-of-life care in the intensive care unit: Opportunities for improvement. *Critical Care Medicine, 29*(2) Supplement, N26-N33.

Devettere, R. J. (2000). *Practical decision making in health care ethics: Cases and concepts* (2nd ed.). Washington, DC: Georgetown University Press.

Faden, R. R., & Beauchamp, T. L. (1986). *A history and theory of informed consent.* Oxford: Oxford University Press.

Fischer, G. S., Tulsky, J. A., & Arnold, R. M. (2000). Communicating poor prognosis. In R. Portenoy & E. Bruera (Eds.), *Topics in palliative care* (pp. 75-90). New York: Oxford University Press.

Forrow, L., Arnold, R. M., & Parker, L. S. (1993). Preventive ethics: Expanding the horizons of clinical ethics. *Journal of Clinical Ethics, 4,* 287.

Golin, C. E., Wenger, N. S., Liu, H., Dawson, N. V., Teno, J.M., Desbiens, N. A., et al. (2000). A prospective study of patient-physician communication about resuscitation. *Journal of the American Geriatrics Society, 48*(5), S52-60.

Grisso, T., & Appelbaum, P. (1998). *Assessing competence to consent to treatment: A guide for physicians and other health professionals.* New York: Oxford University Press.

Gutheil, T. C., & Appelbaum, P. S. (1983). Substituted judgment: Best interests in disguise. *Hastings Center Report, 13,* 8-11.

Guyer, R. L. (2000). Trials with errors—preserving the integrity of clinical trials. *Bioethics Forum, 16*(4), 23-30.

Hickey, M. (1990). What are the needs of families of critically ill patients? A review of the literature since 1976. *Heart Lung, 19,* 401.

Janofsky, J. S., McCarthy, R. J., & Folstein, M. F. (1992). The Hopkins competency assessment test: A brief method for evaluating patients' capacity to give informed consent. *Hospital Community Psychiatry, 43,* 132-135.

Johnson, D., Wilson, M., Cavanaugh, B., Bryden, C., Gudmundson, D., & Moodley, O. (1998). Measuring the ability to meet family needs in an intensive care unit. *Critical Care Medicine, 26,* 266.

Kuczewski, M. G. (1996). Reconceiving the family: The process of consent in medical decision making. *Hastings Center Report, 26*(2), 30–37.

Kvale, J., Berg, L., Groff, J. Y., & Lange, G. (1999). Factors associated with residents' attitudes toward dying patients. *Family Medicine, 31,* 691.

Lidz, C. W., Appelbaum, P. S., & Meisel, A. (1988). Two models of implementing informed consent. *Archives of Internal Medicine, 148,* 1385–1389.

Lipkin, M., Putnam, S., & Lazare, A. (1995). *The medical interview.* New York: Springer-Verlag.

Meisel, A. (1989). *The right to die: The law of end-of-life decisionmaking.* New York: Wiley Law Publications, John Wiley & Sons.

Molter, N. C. (1979). Needs of relatives of critically ill patients: A descriptive study. *Heart Lung, 8,* 332–339.

Natason v. Klein, 350 P2d 1093 (Kan. 1960).

Pellegrino, E. D. (1991). Informal judgments of competence and incompetence. In M. A. G. Cutter & E. E. Shelp (Eds.), *Competency: A study of informal competency determinations in primary care* (pp. 235–273). Dordrecht, Holland: Kluwer Academic Publishers.

Pochard, F., Azoulay, E., Chevret, S., Lemaire, F., Hubert, P., Canoui, P., et al. (2001). Symptoms of anxiety and depression in family members of intensive care unit patients: Ethical hypothesis regarding decision-making capacity. *Critical Care Medicine, 29,* 1893.

President's Commission for the Study of Ethical Problems in Medicine and Biomedical and Behavioral Research. (1983). *Making health care decisions: The ethical and legal implications of informed consent in the patient/practitioner relationship* (Vols. I–III). Washington, DC: U.S. Government Printing Office.

Quill, T. E. (2000). Perspectives on care at the close of life. Initiating end-of-life discussions with seriously ill patients: Addressing the "elephant in the room." *Journal of the American Medical Association, 284,* 2502.

Roth, L., & Meisel, A. (1977). Dangerousness, confidentiality, and the duty to warn. *American Journal of Psychiatry, 134*(5), 508–511.

Roth, L. R., Appelbaum, P. S., Sallee, R., Reynolds, C. F., Huber, G. (1982). The dilemma of denial in the assessment of competency to consent to treatment. *Journal of Psychiatry, 139,* 910–913.

Salgo v. Leland Stanford J. University Board of Trustees, 317 p.2d 170 (Cal. App. 1957).

Schaffner, K. F. (1991). Competency: A triaxial concept. In M. A. G. Cutter & E. E. Shelp (Eds.), *Competency: A study of informal competency determinations in primary care* (pp. 253–281). Dordrecht, Holland: Kluwer Academic Publishers.

Schloendorff v. Society of New York Hospitals, 105NE 92, (NY 1914).

Smith, D. H., & Pettegrew, L. S. (1986). Mutual persuasion as a model for doctor-patient communication. *Theoretical Medicine, 7*, 127-147.

Soelle, D. (1975). *Suffering*. Philadelphia, PA: Fortress Press.

Tattersall, M. H., Butow, P. N., Griffin, A. M., & Dunn, S. M. (1994). The take-home message: Patients prefer consultation audiotapes to summary letters. *Journal of Clinical Oncology, 5*, 199.

Tomlinson, T., Howe, K., Notman, M., & Rossmiller, D. (1990). An empirical study of proxy consent for elderly persons. *Gerontologist, 30*, 54.

Tulsky, J. A., Chesney, M. A., & Lo, B. (1996, June 24). See one, do one, teach one? House staff experience discussing do-not-resuscitate orders. *Archives of Internal Medicine, 156*(12), 1285-1289.

Wenrich, M. D., Curtis, J. R., Shannon, S. E., Carline, J. D., Ambrozy, D. M., & Ramsey, P. G. (2001). Communicating with dying patients within the spectrum of medical care from terminal diagnosis to death. *Archives of Internal Medicine, 161*, 868-874.

Chapter 6

Arnold, R. M., & Youngner, S. J. (1993). The dead donor rule: Should we stretch it, bend it, or abandon it? *Kennedy Institute of Ethics Journal, 3*(2), 263-278.

Bell, M. D. D. (2003). Nonheartbeating organ donation: Old procurement strategy—new ethical problems. *Journal of Medical Ethics, 29*(3), 176-181.

Caplan, A. L., & Coelho, D. (1998). *The ethics of organ transplants: The current debate*. New York: Prometheus Books.

DeVita, M. A., Snyder, J. V., Grenvik, A. (1993). History of organ donation by patients with cardiac death. *Kennedy Institute of Ethics Journal, 3*, 113-129.

Devettere, R. J. (2000). *Practical decision making in health care ethics: Cases and concepts* (2nd ed.). Washington, DC: Georgetown University Press.

Fox, R., & Swazey, J. P. (1992). *Spare parts: Organ replacement in American society*. Oxford: Oxford University Press.

Munson, R. (2002). *Raising the dead: Organ transplants, ethics and society*. New York: Oxford University Press.

Youngner, S., Arnold, R. M., & Schapiro, R. (1999). *The definition of death: Contemporary controversies*. Baltimore, MD: Johns Hopkins University Press.

Youngner, S., Landefeld, C. S., Coulton, C. J., Juknialis, B. W., & Leary, M. (1989). 'Brain death' and organ retrieval: A cross-sectional survey of knowledge and concepts among health professionals. *Journal of the American Medical Association, 261*, 2205-2210.

Chapter 7

Abramson, M., & Black, R. B. (1985). Extending the boundaries of life: Implications for practice. *Health & Social Work, 10*, 165-173.

American Society of Bioethics and Humanities. (1998). *Core competencies for healthcare ethics consultation*. Glenview, IL: Author.

Arnold, R. M., & Wilson-Silver, M. H. (2003). Techniques for training ethics consultants: Why traditional classroom methods are not enough. In M. P. Aulisio, R. M. Arnold, & S. Youngner (Eds.), *Ethics consultation: From theory to practice* (pp. 70–87). Baltimore, MD: Johns Hopkins University Press.

Aulisio, M. P., Arnold, R. M., & Youngner, S. J. (1998). Can there be educational and training standards for those conducting health care ethics consultation? In J. F. Mongagle & D. C. Thomasma (Eds.), *Health care ethics: Critical issues for the 21st century* (pp. 484–496). Gaithersburg, MD: Aspen Publishers.

Aulisio, M. P., Arnold, R. M., Youngner, S. J. (Eds.). (2003). *Ethics consultation: From theory to practice*. Baltimore, MD: Johns Hopkins University Press.

Azoulay, E., Pochard, F., Chevret, S., Jourdain, M., Bornstain, C., Wernet, A., et al. (2002). Impact of a family informational leaflet on effectiveness of information provided to family members of intensive care unit patients: A multicenter, prospective, randomized controlled trial. *American Journal of Respiratory and Critical Care Medicine, 165*, 438.

Baylis, F. (2000). *The roles and responsibilities of the ethics consultant*. Hagerstown, MD: University Publishing Group.

Beecher, H. K. (1968, June 27). Ethical problems created by the hopelessly unconscious patient. *New England Journal of Medicine, 278*(26), 1425–1430.

Byock, I. (1994). Ethics from a hospice perspective. *American Journal of Hospice & Palliative Care, 11*(4), 9–11.

Casarett, D., Daskal, F., & Lantos, J. (1998) The authority of the clinical ethicist. *Hastings Center Report, 28*, 6–12.

Congress, E. P. (1999). *Social work values and ethics: Identifying and resolving professional dilemmas*. Chicago: Wadsworth Publishing.

Cranford, R. E., & Doudera, A. E. (1984). The emergence of institutional ethics committees. *Law, Medicine, & Health Care, 12*(1), 13–20.

Csikai, E. L. (1997). Social workers' participation on hospital ethics committees: An assessment of involvement and satisfaction. *Arete, 22*(1), 1–13.

Csikai, E. L. (2002). The state of hospice ethics committees in hospice and the social work role. *Omega: The Journal of Death and Dying, 45*(3), 245–259.

Csikai, E. L. (2004). The social work role in resolving ethical issues in hospice. *Health & Social Work, 29*(1), 67–76.

Csikai, E. L., & Sales, E. (1998). The emerging social work role on hospital ethics committees: Social workers' and chairs' perspectives. *Social Work, 43*(3), 233–242.

Fife, R. B. (1997). The role of ethics committees in hospice programs. *Hospice Journal, 12*(2), 57–63.

Fletcher, J. C., Miller, F. G., & Spencer, E. M. (1997). Clinical ethics: History, content, and resources. In J. C. Fletcher, P. A. Lombardo, M. F. Marshall, & F. G. Miller (Eds.), *Introduction to clinical ethics* (2nd ed., pp. 3–20). Frederick, MD: University Publishing Group.

Foster, L. W., Sharp, J., Scesny, A., McLellan, L., & Cotman, K. (1993). Bioethics: Social work's response and training needs. *Social Work in Health Care, 19*(1), 15-39.

Furlong, R. M. (1986). The social worker's role on the institutional ethics committee. *Social Work in Health Care, 11*(4), 93-100.

Gelman, S. R. (1986). Life vs. death: The value of ethical uncertainty. *Health & Social Work, 11*(2), 118-125.

Gillon, R. (1997). Clinical ethics committees—pros and cons. *Journal of Medical Ethics, 23*, 203-204.

Hoffman, D. E. (1993). Evaluating ethics committees: A view from the outside. *Milbank Quarterly, 71*(4), 677-705.

Jonsen, A. R. (1993) The birth of bioethics. *Special Supplement, Hastings Center Report, 23*(6), S1.

Jonsen, A. R., Siegler, M., & Winslade, W. J. (1998). *Clinical ethics* (4th ed.). New York: McGraw Hill.

Jurchak, M. (2000) Report of a study to examine the process of ethics case consultation. *Journal of Clinical Ethics. 11*, 49-55.

Loewenberg, F. M., Dolgoff, R., & Harrington, D. (2000). *Ethical decisions for social work practice* (6th ed.). Itasca, IL: F. E. Peacock Publishers.

Mattison, M. (2000). Ethical decision making: The person in process. *Social Work, 45*(3) 201-212.

Miller, F. G., Fletcher, J. C., & Fins, J. J. (1997). Clinical pragmatism: A case method of moral problem solving. In J. C. Fletcher, P. A. Lombardo, M. F. Marshall, & F. G. Miller (Eds.), *Introduction to clinical ethics* (2nd ed., pp. 127-153). Frederick, MD: University Publishing Group.

Moreno, J. (2003). Can ethics consultation be saved? Ethics consultation and moral consensus in a democratic society. In M. P. Aulisio, R. M. Arnold, & S. Youngner (Eds.), *Ethics consultation: From theory to practice* (pp. 23-35). Baltimore, MD: Johns Hopkins University Press.

Reamer, F. G. (1995). *Social work values and ethics*. New York: Columbia University Press.

Roberts, L. W. (2001). Clinical ethics as a parent discipline. *BioMed Central Medical Ethics, 2*(1).

Silverman, E. (1992). Hospital bioethics: A beginning knowledge for the neonatal social worker. *Social Work, 37*(2), 150-154.

Singer, P. A., Pellegrino, E. D., & Siegler, M. (2001). Clinical ethics revisited. *BioMed Central Medical Ethics, 2*(1), 1-12.

Skinner, K., (1991). *A national survey of social workers on IECs: Patterns of participation and roles*. Unpublished doctoral dissertation, State University of New York at Albany.

Wilson-Ross, J. (1986). *Handbook for hospital ethics committees*. Chicago: American Hospital Publishing, Inc.

Wilson-Ross, J., Glaser, J. W., Rasinski-Gregory, D., Gibson, J., & Bayley, C. (1993). *Health care ethics committees: The next generation*. Chicago: American Hospital Publishing.

Chapter 8

American College of Physicians. (1992). American College of Physicians Ethics Manual (3rd ed.). *Annals of Internal Medicine, 117*, 947-960.

Avery, J. K. (1985). Lawyers tell what turns some patients litigious. *Medical Malpractice Review, 2*, 35-37.

Baylis, F. (1997). Errors in medicine: Nurturing truthfulness. *Journal of Clinical Ethics, 8*, 336-340.

Bok, S. (1983). *Secrets: On the ethics of concealment and revelation*. New York: Pantheon Books.

Britton, A. H. (1975). Rights to privacy in medical records. *Journal of Legal Medicine, 3*(7), 30-7.

Cleaver, C. (1985). Privacy rights in medical records. *Fordham Urban Law Journal, 13*, 165-204.

Finkelstein, D., Wu, A., Holtzman, N., & Smith, M., (1997). When a physician harms a patient by a medical error: Ethical, legal, and risk management considerations. *Journal of Clinical Ethics, 8*, 330-335.

Garrett, T., Baillie, H., & Garrett, R. (1993). *Health care ethics: Principles and problems* (3rd ed.). Englewood Cliffs, NJ: Prentice Hall.

Ginsburg, K. R., Menapace, A. S., & Slap, G. B. (1997, December). Factors affecting the decision to seek health care: The voice of adolescents. *Pediatrics, 100*(6), 922-930.

Griswold v. Connecticut, 381 U.S. 479, 484 (1965).

Holloman, W., Edwards, D., & Matson, C. (1994). Obligations of physicians to patients and third-party payers. *Journal of Clinical Ethics, 5*(2), 113-120.

In Re Quinlan, 70 NJ 10 (1976).

Katz v. United States, 389 U.S. 347, 350 (1967).

Kinzie, J. D., Holmes, J. L., & Arent, J. (1985). Patient's release of medical records: Involuntary uninformed consent? *Hospital Community Psychiatry, 36*, 843-847.

Kohn, L. T., Corrigan, J. M., & Donaldson, M. S. (Eds.). (1999). To err is human: Building a safer health system. *Committee on Quality of Health Care in America (Institute of Medicine)*. Washington, DC: National Academy Press.

Leape, L. L. (1994). Error in medicine. *Journal of the American Medical Association, 272*, 792-798.

Liang, B. A. (1999). Error in medicine: Legal impediments to U.S. reform. *Journal of Health Politics, Policy and Law, 24*, 25-38.

Lorge, R. E. (1989). How informed is patients' consent to release of medical information to insurance companies? *British Medical Journal, 298*, 1495-1596.

Martin, C. A., Wilson, J. F., Fiebelman, N. D., Gurley, D. N., & Miller, T. W. (1991). Physicians' psychologic reactions to malpractice litigation. *Southern Medical Journal, 84*, 1300-1304.

May, T., & Aulisio, M. (2001). Medical malpractice, mistake prevention, and compensation. *Kennedy Institute of Ethics Journal, 11*(2), 135-146.

McGuire, J. M., Toal, P., & Blau, B. (1985). The adult client's conception of confidentiality in the therapeutic relationship. *Professional Psychology: Research and Practice, 16*, 375-384.

Merz, J. F., Spina, B. J., & Sankar, P. (1999). Patient consent for release of sensitive information for their medical records: An exploratory study. *Behavioral Science & Law, 17*, 445-454.

Olmstead v. United States, 277 U.S. 438 (1928).

Oppenheimer, K., & Swanson, G. (1990). Duty to warn: When should confidentiality be breached? *Journal of Family Practice, 30*(2), 179-184.

Planned Parenthood of Missouri v. Danforth, 428 U.S. 52 (1976).

Reamer, F. G. (1998). *Ethical standards in social work.* Washington, DC: NASW Press.

Rodriguez, M. A., Craig, A. M., Mooney, D. R., & Bauer, H. M. (1998). Patient attitudes about mandatory reporting of domestic violence: Implications for health care professionals. *Western Journal of Medicine, 169*, 337-341.

Roe v. Wade, 410 U.S. 113, 152-153 (1973).

Roth, L., & Meisel, A. (1977). Dangerousness, confidentiality, and the duty to warn. *American Journal of Psychiatry, 134*(5), 508-511.

Sankar, P., Moran, S., Merz, J., & Jones, N. L. (2003). Patient perspectives on medical confidentiality. *Journal of General Internal Medicine, 18*(8), 659-669.

Schmid, D., Appelbaum, P. S., Roth, L. H., & Lidz, C. (1983). Confidentiality in psychiatry: A study of the patient's view. *Hospital Community Psychiatry, 34*, 353-355.

Schuchman, H. (1982). Confidentiality of health records. *Committee on Confidentiality of the American Psychiatric Association.*

Shapiro, M. H., & Spece, R. (1981). *Cases, materials and problems on bioethics and law.* St. Paul, MN: West Publishing Co.

Tarasoff v. Regents of University of California, 17 Cal.3d 425, 551 P.2d 334 (1976).

Trippitelli, C. L, Jamison, K. R, Folstein, M. F., Bartko, J. J., & DePaulo, J. R. (1998). Pilot study on patients' and spouses' attitudes toward potential genetic testing for bipolar disorder. *American Journal of Psychiatry, 155*, 899-904.

VandeCreek, L., Miars, R. D., & Herzog, C. E. (1987). Client anticipations and preferences for confidentiality of records. *Journal of Counseling Psychology, 34*, 62-67.

Weiss, B. D. (1982). Confidentiality expectations of patients, physicians, and medical students. *Journal of the American Medical Association, 247*, 2695-2697.

Whalen v. Roe, 429 U.S. 589 (1977).

Wu, A., Cavanaugh, T., McPhee, S., Lo, B., & Micco, G. (1997). To tell the truth: Ethical and practical issues in disclosing medical mistakes to patients, *Journal of General Internal Medicine, 12*, 770-775.

Wu, A. W., Folkman, S., McPhee, S. J., & Lo, B. (1991). Do house officers learn from their mistakes? *Journal of the American Medical Association, 265*, 2089-2094.

Appendix A

CHAITIN INFORMED CONSENT
CAPACITY TOOL

Patient's name: _____ Patient's number _____

Examiner's name: _____ Date: _____

Reason for consultation: _____

Medical Information

Admission Date: _____ Diagnosis: _____

History and physical (brief):

_____

_____

_____

Task in question (procedure requested or required):

_____

Goals of treatment or procedure (as outlined by MD):

_____

_____

Does the patient evidence understanding of the goals of treatment?
Yes _____ No _____

How is this evidenced?

_____

_____

Are there factors prohibiting this understanding? Yes _____ No _____

If yes, what are they?

_____

_____

Risks and benefits of this procedure (as outlined by MD):

_____

_____

Patient's explanation of this procedure, including the risks and benefits (in his or her own words):

_____

_____

Are these factors related to cultural issues or issues of religious faith?
Yes _____ No _____

Judgement Questions

If your apartment were on fire, what would you do?

_____

_____

How will you make sure there is food in your home?

_____

_____

If you were very sick and could not move well, how would you make
sure your needs were met?

_____

_____

Does the patient evidence fear of death? _____

fear of abandonment by family or medical
team? _____

fear of dependency? _____

Is the patient capable of rendering a <u>voluntary</u> choice, free from internal constraints (sedation, dementia, mental illness, or extreme fear)?
Yes _____ No _____

If yes, would patient benefit from assistance from social work?

Yes _____ No _____

or clergy? Yes _____ No _____

If no to above, what is the nature of these internal constraints?

_____

Is the patient capable of rendering a voluntary choice, free from external constraints (manipulation or coercion)? Yes _____ No _____
What steps can be taken to eliminate these external constraints?

_____

_____

Is the patient able to evidence a choice? Yes _____ No _____
If no, what is hampering the patient's ability to choose?
The patient is unable to render a choice _____
Why? _____
Has the patient has requested that another choose for him or her? ___
Why? _____
Whom has the patient indicated to choose for him or her? _____
If the patient is able to evidence a choice, upon what factors has the
patient based his or choice?

_____

_____

_____

Appendix B

NASW Standards for Social Work Practice in Palliative and End of Life Care

STANDARDS FOR PROFESSIONAL PRACTICE

Standard 1. Ethics and Values

The values, ethics, and standards of both the profession and contemporary bioethics shall guide social workers practicing in palliative and end of life care. The NASW Code of Ethics (NASW, 2000) is one of several essential guides to ethical decision making and practice.

Interpretation:

Social workers who practice in palliative and end of life care must be prepared for challenges that encompass evaluation of ethical dilemmas and value conflicts and consider questions related to religion, spirituality, and the meaning of life. To be an effective practitioner in this area, specialized training in palliative and end of life care is preferred.

The minimal knowledge base needed for work in this practice area includes an understanding of the following basic ethical principles:

- Justice: the duty to treat all fairly, distributing the risks and benefits equally
- Beneficence: the duty to do good, both for individuals and for all
- Nonmaleficence: the duty to cause no harm, both for individuals and for all
- Understanding/Tolerance: the duty to understand and to accept other viewpoints, if reason dictates that doing so is warranted
- Publicity: the duty to take actions based on ethical standards that must be known and recognized by all that are involved
- Respect for the person: the duty to honor others, their rights, and their responsibilities, as showing respect for others implies that we do not treat them as a mere means to our end
- Universality: the duty to take actions that hold for everyone, regardless of time, place, or people involved
- Veracity: the duty to tell the truth
- Autonomy: the duty to maximize the individual's right to make his or her own decisions

- Confidentiality: the duty to respect privacy of information and action
- Equality: the duty to view all people as moral equals
- Finality: the duty to take action that may override the demands of law, religion, and social customs

In addition, the social workers working in palliative and end of life care are expected to be familiar with the common and complex bioethical considerations and legal issues such as the right to refuse treatment; proxy decision-making; withdrawal or withholding of treatment, including termination of ventilator support and withdrawal of fluids and nutrition; and assisted suicide. End of life issues are recognized as controversial, because they reflect the varied value systems of different groups. Consequently, NASW does not take a position concerning the morality of end of life decisions, but affirms the right of the individual to determine the level of his or her care. Particular consideration should be given to special populations, such as people with mental illness, with developmental disability, individuals whose capacity or competence is questioned, children, and other groups who are vulnerable to coercion or who lack decisional capacity.

Standard 2. Knowledge

Social workers in palliative and end of life care shall demonstrate a working knowledge of the theoretical and biopsychosocial factors essential to effectively practice with clients and professionals.

Interpretation:

The social worker possesses knowledge about navigating the medical and social systems that frequently present barriers to clients. Social workers have expertise in communication, both within families and between clients/families and health care or interdisciplinary teams. Drawing on knowledge of family systems and interpersonal dynamics, the social worker is able to examine the family's experience in a unique way, to conduct a comprehensive assessment, and to assist the team to integrate biopsychosocial, spiritual factors into their deliberations, planning, and interactions.

Social work's view includes an appreciation of the socioeconomic, cultural, and spiritual dimensions of the family's life. As experts in helping individuals and families maximize coping in crisis—and at addressing the psychosocial domains of symptoms, suffering, grief, and loss—social workers are able to provide intensive counseling as well as practical services for those confronted by life-limiting illnesses and assist with complex problems.

Essential areas of knowledge and understanding about palliative and end of life care include:

- the multifaceted roles and functions of social worker clinicians

- the physical and multidimensional stages of the dying process
- the physical, psychological, and spiritual manifestations of pain
- the range of psychosocial interventions that can alleviate discomfort
- the biopsychosocial needs of clients and their family members;
- the impact of ethnic, religious, and cultural differences
- illness-related issues such as decision making, relationship with health care providers, dying and death
- the range of settings for palliative and end of life care, including home care, nursing homes, and hospice settings
- the available community resources and how to gain access to them
- the impact of financial resources on family decision making along the continuum of illness and at the end of life
- the development, use, support, and revision of advance directives throughout the progression of the illness
- disparities across cultures in gaining access to palliative and end of life care
- the accreditation and regulatory standards governing settings providing palliative and end of life care
- the needs faced by members of special populations and their families, such as children; those with physical, developmental, mental, or emotional disabilities; and those in institutionalized settings such as

nursing homes and nonmedical settings such as correctional facilities.

Standard 3. Assessment

Social workers shall assess clients and include comprehensive information to develop interventions and treatment planning.

Interpretation:

Assessment is the foundation of practice. Social workers plan interventions with their clients based on assessments and must be prepared to constantly reassess and revise treatment plans in response to newly identified needs and altered goals of care. Comprehensive and culturally competent social work assessment in the context of palliative and end of life care includes considering relevant biopsychosocial factors and the needs of the individual client and the family (as defined by the client).

Areas for consideration in the comprehensive assessment include:

- relevant past and current health situation (including the impact of problems such as pain, depression, anxiety, delirium, decreased mobility)
- family structure and roles
- patterns/style of communication and decision making in the family
- stage in the life cycle, relevant developmental issues
- spirituality/faith
- cultural values and beliefs

- client's/family's language prefer-ence and available translation serv-ices
- client's/family's goals in palliative and end of life treatment
- social supports, including support systems, informal and formal care-givers involved, resources avail-able, and barriers to access
- past experience with illness, dis-ability, death, and loss
- mental health functioning includ-ing history, coping style, crisis man-agement skills and risk of sui-cide/homicide
- unique needs and issues relevant to special populations such as refugees and immigrants, children, individuals with severe and persist-ent mental illness, and homeless people
- communicating the client's/fam-ily's psychosocial needs to the interdisciplinary team.

Standard 4. Intervention/ Treatment Planning

Social workers shall incorporate assessments in developing and imple-menting intervention plans that enhance the clients' abilities and deci-sions in palliative and end of life care.

Interpretation:

Social workers in all practice areas use various theoretical perspec-tives and skills in delivering interven-tions and developing treatment plans. Initial assessments and team input inform and guide plans of care. Social workers must be able to adapt techniques to work effectively with individuals from different age groups, ethnicities, cultures, religions, socioe-conomic and educational back-grounds, lifestyles, and differing states of mental health and disability, and in diverse nonmedical care settings.

Essential skills for effective palliative and end of life care include:

- the ability to recognize signs and symptoms of impending death and prepare family members in a man-ner that is guided by clinical assess-ment
- competence in facilitating commu-nication among clients, family mem-bers, and members of the care team
- competence in integrating grief theories into practice
- competence in determining appro-priate interventions based on the assessment
- competence in advocating for clients, family members, and care-givers for needed services, includ-ing pain management
- competence in navigating a com-plex network of resources and making appropriate linkages for clients and family members
- competence in supporting clients, families, and caregivers including anticipatory mourning, grief, bereavement, and follow-up serv-ices.

Interventions commonly provided in palliative and end of life care include:

- individual counseling and psychotherapy (including addressing the cognitive behavioral interventions)
- family counseling
- family-team conferencing
- crisis counseling
- information and education
- multidimensional interventions regarding symptom management
- support groups, bereavement groups
- case management and discharge planning
- decision making and the implications of various treatment alternatives
- resource counseling (including caregiving resources; alternate level of care options such as long term care or hospice care; financial and legal needs; advance directives; and permanency planning for dependents)
- client advocacy/navigation of systems.

Standard 5. Attitude/Self-Awareness

Social workers in palliative and end of life care shall demonstrate an attitude of compassion and sensitivity to clients, respecting clients' rights to self-determination and dignity. Social workers shall be aware of their own beliefs, values, and feelings and how their personal self may influence their practice.

Interpretation:

To practice effectively, social workers in palliative and end of life care must demonstrate empathy and sensitivity in responding to the pain, suffering, and distress of others. Specific social work attitudes and responses that encompass compassion and sensitivity in caring for clients shall include, but not necessarily be limited to, the following:

- flexibility and adaptability on a daily basis, to be able to confront human suffering
- consistent individualization of client/client system needs as the primary care unit
- facilitative interactions with clients/client systems
- ability to communicate and work collaboratively as an interdisciplinary team member to achieve care goals
- willingness to advocate for holding the focus in palliative and end of life care on client/client system choices, preferences, values, and beliefs
- awareness of compassion fatigue and the ethical responsibility to mitigate this condition
- confidence and competence in professional identify and in empowering the profession in its vital role in palliative and end of life care.

Standard 6. Empowerment and Advocacy

The social worker shall advocate for the needs, decisions, and rights of clients in palliative and end of life care. The social worker shall engage in social and political action that seeks to ensure that people have equal access to resources to meet their biopsychosocial needs in palliative and end of life care.

Interpretation:

In advocacy efforts, social work provides unique and essential skills and perspectives such as a rich understanding of the person-in-environment, communication skills, expertise in group process and systems, a social justice commitment, a strong background in values and ethics, and a broad psychosocial and spiritual knowledge base. Among the crucial components of effective empowerment and advocacy are identifying and defining needs from the client's perspective, including cultural and spiritual beliefs, and communicating the concerns and needs of the client to decision makers and providers of care. Advocacy and empowerment come into practice at both the micro and macro level.

Practice examples include linking clients with resources, identifying and supporting the family of choice, assisting individuals and families negotiate their goals of care, navigating through systems of care, monitoring pain and symptom management, addressing quality of life issues, team conferencing, consulting, and providing caregiver support. Broader examples of advocacy include advocacy with special populations, institutions, and communities, as well as the health care policy arenas where efforts need to integrate cultural and ethnic variation. It is essential to identify barriers to effective palliative and end of life care at the macro level by addressing issues of financial inequities, lack of culturally competent services, and other access issues and to address those barriers so that individuals experience the highest quality of life possible to the end of life.

Standard 7. Documentation

Social workers shall document all practice with clients in either the client record or in the medical chart. These may be written or electronic records.

Interpretation:

Ongoing documentation of social work service should reflect the assessment, issues addressed, treatment offered, and plan of care, and must assure continuity of care between all settings (for example, hospital to hospice, nursing home to hospital).

The transfer of medical records must be conducted in compliance with current federal and state law with an emphasis on confidentiality/privacy of medical information. Compliance with agency policy, particularly regarding the transfer of electronic records, is essential.

Standard 8. Interdisciplinary Teamwork

Social workers should be part of an interdisciplinary effort for the comprehensive delivery of palliative and end of life services. Social workers shall strive to collaborate with team members and advocate for clients' needs with objectivity and respect, to reinforce relationships with providers who have cared for the patient along the continuum of illness.

Interpretation:

Interdisciplinary teamwork is an essential component in palliative and end of life care. Social workers are integral members of a health care team. Social workers should advocate for the views and needs of individuals and families in palliative and end of life care within the team, and should encourage and assist clients in communicating with team members. Often, clients, families, and team members rely on the expertise of the social worker in problem solving concerns and conflict resolution.

Teamwork requires collaboration, and an ability to empower and advocate when necessary. The psychosocial expertise of the social worker assists the interdisciplinary team to enhance understanding, form interventions and decisions, and formulate treatment plans. In addition,

the social worker identifies resources, provides counseling, support services, and practical interventions.

Standard 9. Cultural Competence

Social workers shall have, and shall continue to develop, specialized knowledge and understanding about history, traditions, values, and family systems as they relate to palliative and end of life care within different groups. Social workers shall be knowledgeable about, and act in accordance with, the NASW Standards for Cultural Competence in Social Work Practice (NASW, 2001).

Interpretation:

Social workers respect and integrate knowledge about how individuals and families are influenced by their ethnicity, culture, values, religion- and health-related beliefs, and economic situations. Social workers should understand systems of oppression and how these systems affect client access to, and utilization of, palliative and end of life care. Many cultures maintain their own values and traditions in the areas of palliative and end of life care.

Culture influences individuals' and families' experience as well as the experience of the practitioner and institution. Social workers should consider culture in practice settings involving palliative and end of life care. Each cultural group has its own views about palliative and end of life practices and these need to be understood as they affect individuals' response to dying, death, illness, loss, and pain.

Social workers who understand how culture affects the illness and end of life experience of an individual and family will be better able to individualize care and intervene in the psychosocial impact of illness, pain, dying, and death. Therefore, social workers should be familiar with the practices and beliefs of the cultural groups with whom they practice to deliver culturally sensitive services.

STANDARDS FOR PROFESSIONAL PREPARATION AND DEVELOPMENT

Standard 10. Continuing Education

Social workers shall assume personal responsibility for their continued professional development in accordance with the NASW Standards for Continuing Professional Education (NASW, 2002) and state requirements.

Interpretation:

Social workers must continue to grow in their knowledge of theories and practices in palliative and end of life care to effectively work with individuals and families. Palliative and end of life care is a rapidly expanding

and changing field, which crosses all practice settings. In addition to clinical competence, social workers need to enhance their skills and understanding by keeping abreast of research, so their practice reflects the most current knowledge.

Numerous opportunities in professional development are available through NASW and other professional organizations, institutions, coalitions, and service agencies at local, state, and national levels. Social workers should participate in and contribute to professional conferences and training activities on a regular and consistent basis to provide the highest possible level of care. Social workers should also assist in identifying palliative and end of life professional development needs by participating in research and encouraging organizations and institutions to collaborate, advocate, and provide appropriate education for the field.

Standard 11. Supervision, Leadership, and Training

Social workers with expertise in palliative and end of life care should lead educational, supervisory, administrative, and research efforts with individuals, groups, and organizations.

Interpretation:

Social workers shall offer their expertise to individuals, groups, and organizations as well as offering training and mentoring opportunities to beginning social workers or those transitioning into palliative and end of life care. When able, skilled social workers shall work in conjunction with schools of social work to advocate for programs in palliative and end of life care and enhance and encourage interest in this specialization.

Social workers shall offer supervision to practicing social workers, interns, and students to provide a guiding expertise to clinicians in this area. Social workers shall contribute to research initiatives not only to demonstrate the efficacy of the social work profession and social work interventions, but also to advance the recognition among colleagues in other professions of the essential need to address psychosocial needs of individuals and their families.

INDEX